FINDING AMERICA
IN A MINOR LEAGUE
BALLPARK

FINDING AMERICA IN A MINOR LEAGUE BALLPARK

A SEASON HOSTING FOR THE DURHAM BULLS

HARRIS COOPER

Skyhorse Publishing

Copyright © 2024 by Harris Cooper

All Rights Reserved. No part of this book may be reproduced in any manner without the express written consent of the publisher, except in the case of brief excerpts in critical reviews or articles. All inquiries should be addressed to Skyhorse Publishing, 307 West 36th Street, 11th Floor, New York, NY 10018.

Skyhorse Publishing books may be purchased in bulk at special discounts for sales promotion, corporate gifts, fund-raising, or educational purposes. Special editions can also be created to specifications. For details, contact the Special Sales Department, Skyhorse Publishing, 307 West 36th Street, 11th Floor, New York, NY 10018 or info@skyhorsepublishing.com

Skyhorse® and Skyhorse Publishing® are registered trademarks of Skyhorse Publishing, Inc.®, a Delaware corporation.

Visit our website at www.skyhorsepublishing.com.
Please follow our publisher Tony Lyons on Instagram @tonylyonsisuncertain

10 9 8 7 6 5 4 3 2 1

Library of Congress Cataloging-in-Publication Data is available on file.

Hardcover ISBN: 978-1-5107-7860-3
eBook ISBN: 978-1-5107-7861-0

Cover design by Brian Peterson
Cover photo credit: Getty Images

Printed in China

To my grandchildren, Hudson and Blaise Cooper.
Thank you for playing spin baseball with me.

The Line Up

Chapter 1. Pregame Warm Up 1

Chapter 2. A Walk to the Ballpark 9

Chapter 3. Home Series 1: Opening Week 17
    Movie Profile: *A League of Their Own*

Chapter 4. Home Series 2: Kids and the K-Wall 27
    Movie Profile: *The Bad News Bears*

Chapter 5. Home Series 3: Happy Birthday Wool E. Bull 39
    Movie Profile: *The Sandlot*

Chapter 6. Home Series 4: Things Are Looking Up 51
    Movie Profile: *The Perfect Game*

Chapter 7. A Brief History of the Not-So-Minor Leagues 61

Chapter 8. Home Series 5: Memorial Day 75
    Movie Profile: *The Bingo Long Traveling All-Stars & Motor Kings*

Chapter 9. Home Series 6: Mid-Season Break 85

Chapter 10. Home Series 7: Happy Birthday, USA 93
    Movie Profile: *Sugar*

Chapter 11. Home Series 8: *Bull Durham* Night 105
    Movie Profile: *Bull Durham*

Chapter 12. Seasons Past: Club History 113

Chapter 13. Home Series 9: The Stakes Get Higher 121
    Movie Profile: *Million Dollar Arm*

Chapter 14. Home Series 10: Surf & Turf Series 131
    Movie Profile: *Trouble with the Curve*

Chapter 15. Home Series 11: A Playoff Preview? 141
    Movie Profile: *The Phenom*

Chapter 16. Who's On First? 149

Chapter 17. Home Series 12: Yankees Invade North Carolina 159
    Movie Profile: *Fear Strikes Out*

Chapter 18. Home Series 13: The Season Comes to an End 167
    Movie Profile: *Field of Dreams*

Chapter 19. Postseason Wrap Up 177

Acknowledgments 185
Book References 187
Image Credits 189
Index 195
About the Author 199

Chapter 1
Pregame Warm Up

Baseball is the hurrah game of the republic! That's beautiful: the hurrah game! well—it's our game: that's the chief fact in connection with it: America's game: has the snap, go, fling, of the American atmosphere—belongs as much to our institutions, fits into them as significantly, as our constitutions, laws: is just as important in the sum total of our historic life.
—Walt Whitman, poet, 1889[1]

The baseball mania has run its course. It has no future as a professional endeavor.
—Cincinnati Gazette *newspaper editorial*, 1879

All baseball fans have a warm spot in their heart for Annie Savoy. In the film *Bull Durham*, Annie keeps score while watching the Durham Bulls minor league baseball team play in the Carolina League. She is willing to give everything for her hometown club. Annie is a coach ("He's not bending his back on his follow through," "You're pulling your hips out too early."), general manager ("Bad trades are part of baseball—now who can forget Frank Robinson for Milt Pappas, for God's sake?"), therapist ("Physical exhaustion can be spiritually fabulous, what you need is a good game of catch."), and theologian ("I've tried all the major religions and most of the minor ones. . . . The only church that truly feeds the soul, day in and day out, is the Church of Baseball.").

Susan Sarandon embodies Annie Savoy in the movie. Wearing an off-the-shoulder sweatshirt draped down to her bicep, she uses her curves to warm up Crash Davis (Kevin Costner) and Nuke LaLoosh (Tim Robbins). Her payoff pitch: "These are the ground rules. I hook up with one guy a season. Usually takes me a couple weeks to pick the guy—kinda my own spring training."

Minor league baseball resides in the small cities and towns of America. While each city is unique—some are thriving, others starving—the city of Durham, North Carolina, where I live, is as good a choice as any to watch minor league baseball in action. In the 2020 census, Durham was the seventy-fifth most populous city in the United

---

[1] https://sites.temple.edu/historynews/2018/10/22/walt-whitman-and-baseball/

States, but its ball team is certainly the most recognizable minor league club in America, thanks to *Bull Durham*. When the movie came out in 1988, the Durham Bulls were a Level-A minor league ball club. In 1995 a shiny new stadium opened, and three years later the Bulls franchise moved up to Level-AAA, on the doorstep of the major leagues. In 2016, *Forbes* magazine valued the club at $39 million. There is nothing minor about the minor leagues. Not in the towns and cities with a team.

The house that served as Annie's home in the movie sits at 911 N. Mangum Street in downtown Durham. It was on sale for $1.15 million in 2021.[2] It is over one hundred years old but is clearly lovingly maintained. The Queen Anne home is on the historic preservation registry of the city—not only did Annie inhabit it, but it once was owned by James S. Manning, who served as a justice on North Carolina's Supreme Court and as the state's attorney general in the early 1900s. As I stand on the street admiring the home, it seems like the perfect time to think back on how I got to this place and came to write this book.

HOW I GOT HERE

I grew up in the shadow of Yankee Stadium during the Bronx Bombers' heyday of the late fifties and sixties.

A baseball ashram.

[2] https://bustedcoverage.com/2020/04/28/buy-annie-savoys-house-from-bull-durham/

My friends and I would hang around the stadium gates and wait for people to give us tickets they couldn't sell. Sometimes we'd miss an opening inning or two, but the price was right.

For the record, I didn't play much hardball as a youth. In the Bronx, punchball, stickball, and softball were favored over hardball because our fields were concrete with lots of cracks. Hardballs bounced too unpredictably. Broken and sprained fingers put us on the injured list. Little League was for kids who lived in the suburbs, where there was a lot more grass. We organized our own sports (no adults allowed) by waiting for enough kids to show up to field two teams, then the two best players would draft their team using a "best-two-of-three, odds-evens finger match." This went on every day, all day, until the sky grew too dark to see the ball. And the sport of choice was whatever professional leagues were in season.

My folks weren't baseball fans; in fact, for them living so close to the stadium was a real pain. They would often ask, "Is there a game tonight?" not for the possibility of a pleasant evening at the stadium, but for planning where the heck my dad would need to park the car when he came home from work. My folks had a friend named Rudy who worked the stadium concession stands. Rudy was a retired owner of a dry cleaning business. I used to drop by to say hi to him. Working at a ballpark seemed cool, and I was cool because I knew someone who did.

I once managed to talk my father, Sam, into taking me to a World Series game at the stadium. He worked as the manager of a hotel in Harlem and had "connections." It was 1962, I was eleven years old, and our seats were awful—last row in the left field stands. All I remember of the game was seeing Tom Tresh's number 15 when he took the field in front of us.

That's where my interest in baseball comes from.

When I left the Bronx for college, I majored in psychology and sociology, then received my doctorate in social psychology. Social psychologists study people's thoughts, feelings, and behavior. They look for the roots of who we are and what we do. They look within the person, their family and friends, the places they live, their country, and their culture.

That's where my interest in people and how they live comes from.

How'd my two interests come together? Well, they were always sorta entangled. Whenever I was asked to visit and speak at another university, I would agree on one condition: I'd come when the local baseball team was in town, and rather than a stuffy academic dinner, my hosts had to take me to a home game. For me, three hours at a ballpark is more of a vacation than three hours on a beach.

After retiring from my professorship at Duke University, within walking distance of the Bulls ballpark, the opportunity arose to work for the Bulls. This could bring my two loves together in a way I'd never thought before. What could be a better way to reflect on the American people and their culture than at a minor league ballpark? More than any other sport, minor league baseball draws the broadest array of Americans. Those fleeting moments spent talking baseball with the fan sitting next to you or with a ballpark employee provide too little time to discover the remarkable range of people who call themselves baseball fans. Let's take just a few moments to find out more about who these people are, where they're from, and why we share a love of this game. Maybe we'll learn something about ourselves as well.

You can find plenty of books on minor league baseball. Some are written by ballplayers, others by sports writers, radio announcers, folks who work the clubhouse, and even owners. You won't find another book like this one. You are holding the only book written from a social psychologist's point of view about the game of baseball, a baseball team's fans-in-the-stands, and the employees who work the concessions, sell tickets, and patrol the concourse and stands. I will relate to you not only my encounters with folks at the ballpark but also zoom out to look at the ballpark itself, the city of Durham, the Bulls' history, and the minor leagues writ large. All of this will provide the context we didn't know about that kid leaning over the outfield fence pleading with a relief pitcher in the bullpen to "Give me a ball!" I will also provide footnotes that contain books and websites to learn more about many of the topics I cover.

Finally, to understand how baseball fits into the lives of Americans, we need to go to the movies. Soon after I began writing this book, Major League Baseball (MLB) ran an online contest allowing fans to pick the best baseball movie ever. They "stole" an idea I had independently dreamed up. The movies MLB picked are very good, though some I would have left off, adding others. Anyway, I decided to change my approach by focusing only on films that largely featured the minor leagues, left-out professional leagues, or the little leagues, to fit more closely with the theme of this

MLB's Choices for the Most Valuable Baseball Movies of All Time
Let the Kids Play
Rookie of the Year
The Sandlot
The Bad News Bears
The Perfect Game
Hollywood Endings
The Natural
Field of Dreams
For the Love of the Game
Angels in the Outfield
Best Ensemble
Bull Durham
Trouble with the Curve
Moneyball
Major League
Based on a True Story
42
The Rookie
Eight Men Out
A League of Their Own

book. You will see a profile of one of these movies at the end of each of the twelve chapters. I will return to the movies at the end of the book and give my personal tournament results.

MY TRYOUT

Along with the Bulls, Durham Baseball Athletic Park (DBAP) plays host to the Duke University home baseball games. I attended the second game of the season against Virginia Military Academy. It draws a crowd of 835 in a stadium that holds ten thousand. It's hard to say what this means for a Duke team that aspires to be mediocre. I suspect that attendance number includes the players and the mascots; after all, the temperature is about fifty degrees at game time on February 18.

Walking the stadium concourse, I nearly bump into a woman with a big smile. She hands me a business card. She is hoofing the stadium in search of oddballs who love baseball enough to sit freezing in the stands while watching a college game, especially those who appear to be related to no one playing on the field.

"Interested in working at the ballpark?" she asks.[3]

"No, sorry," I say, but I thank her for asking and take her business card anyway.

Somehow, I can't throw the card out. It sits on my desk for ten days until I take the plunge. I email her. She tells me how to apply. Two weeks later I signal my interest on the Bulls' website. Next morning, while on my morning walk, I get a call and do a phone interview. I answer a few questions:

"What jobs are you interested in?" Seating Bowl Host.

"Can you stand up for four hours?" Yep, but not on one foot.

"Ever been arrested?" Nope.

"Are you willing to take a drug test?" Yep.

Two days later I'm at the ballpark for a face-to-face interview. I get the job on the spot, as did every other warm-bodied interviewee; it's a seller's market.

Three other new employees and I sit at a table facing laptops and complete the job's onboarding forms. Two of my tablemates are women who had applied for jobs as bartenders, a job paying over thirty dollars an hour. Those positions are filled; they take Concession Stand Attendant at twenty dollars, plus tips. That's twice my pay for being a Seating Bowl Host. But I'll be outside working in the stands. How much is fresh air and sunshine worth? Plus, I can watch the game. The fourth person at our table is a young man who stares at the laptop in front of him then thinks better of the whole thing. "I changed my mind," he says, stands up, and walks out.

Next comes the drug test. That very afternoon, I go to the storefront lab for a seven-panel urine test. What are the seven drugs? Amphetamines, barbiturates, benzodiazepines, cocaine, marijuana, opiates, and phencyclidine (PCP). I am the first one at the lab after lunch and would have zipped in and out (get it?) in five minutes, except I drop the full cup of urine into the toilet. I must drink sixteen ounces of water, wait thirty minutes, and try again. A sure-handed shortstop, I'm not.

I am surprised at the steady stream (get it, again?) of people who come to the lab. All sizes, ethnicities, sexes, and ages. I suspect most are there for job requirements, but others are coming under doctor orders.

SPRING TRAINING

The employee orientation is held at the ballpark's PNC Triangle Club, the posh, enclosed upper-level area directly behind home plate. Video screens and leather lounge chairs abound, and the walls have replicas of old-time advertisements related to baseball and *Bull Durham* tobacco.

The adventure starts in the elevator to the club room. The guy standing next to me, another gray-hair, offers, "I live up the street and was gonna get season tickets then thought, what the heck, let them

---

[3] My quotes throughout the book are not exact, just the best I can reconstruct from memory and brief notes on my smart phone. Also, I only use the names of employees and fans who have given me permission to do so.

PNC Triangle Club overlooking the ballfield.

pay me rather than me pay them." I hear this from more than one seating bowl host.

Two women recognize each another. After exchanging big smiles, they act out the "How many jobs you got?" routine from the old comedy television show *In Living Color*.

"I got three."

"I got five."

Are the jobs all part-time, I wonder? You got five jobs, but do you got health insurance?

There are about two hundred people in the club room, a bit less than half the seasonal staff employed by the Bulls. Most seasonals work in food and concessions, followed by operations (that's my group, with about ninety folks total). Only about a quarter of the attendees are rookies like me.[4] I take it as a good sign that so many folks return. The winner of the longest employee contests is a woman in her twenty-seventh season as a part-time Bulls employee.

The crowd is also diverse in terms of race, gender, and age. If there was a group that seems underrepresented it would be young white guys, age thirty to fifty.

After a feel-good raffle for swag bags, the meeting is turned over to Mike Birling, Operations Vice President, and Scott Strickland, Operations Assistant General Manager. Mike has been with the Bulls for twenty-five years and Scott for nineteen years. Mike's fun fact is that he is a part owner of the Green Bay Packers, an honor he shares with over three hundred thousand other fans (Green Bay is the only community-owned major sports franchise). Scott, in his forties I estimate, has a degree in turf management from North Carolina State University. He got interested in this less-than-lucrative green stuff while playing American Legion baseball in high school and started out with the Bulls mowing the grass. He also co-hosts the Bulls' podcast, *Hit Bull Win Steak*.

A few more back-of-the-card statistics. About half a million fans attend Bulls games each season and a third of those are coming to the ballpark for the first time. But only ten percent of these first timers return the next year. This seems to be a cause of concern for Scott, or perhaps he sees it as a statistic that can motivate us frontline folks to be as nice as possible to fans. I'm not sure I agree. Given that Durham has a brisk tourist market—visitors to the high-tech and bio-tech companies in the Research Triangle Park, and parents visiting their kids at Duke, the University of North Carolina at Chapel Hill, and North Carolina State University in Raleigh—maybe the Bulls shouldn't expect many first timers to return. You just want that ten percent of returnees not to decrease each season and tell other visitors it's a good time.

Anyway, we're told to feel "empowered to take care of our fans." We're also told we're entitled to free and reduced-price tickets, a discount at the team store, free parking, and a buffet dinner before each game.

---

4   The COVID pandemic has messed up my ability to get accurate numbers on how long the veterans have actually worked at the park. Some count their employment from their first seasons, some discard 2019 and 2020. But 2022 is the first year for rookies.

The presentation then turns to more serious matters. A slide comes on the video monitors that lists the club's top priorities for fan relations.

The number one priority is safety. We're asked what the safety concerns are during a ballgame.

"People get hurt. Foul balls." is shouted first. We're told this is taken very seriously and we should follow every foul ball and make certain no one is hurt. Emergency medical technicians do the same.

Someone from Food and Beverage offers, "People get sick from a hot dog." Laughter all around.

Let's get serious again, folks. The point is, if people don't feel safe, they aren't gonna enjoy themselves and won't come back.

Number two priority is courtesy. Help fans who look lost.

Someone shouts, "When a fan spills their popcorn bag can you get them another for free?"

The answer is yes, absolutely, just wave your staff badge at a concession stand.

"That fan has a better experience and is more likely to come back than if they didn't drop that popcorn."

"What about a drink or nacho cheese or ice cream spill?" Now we're back to safety.

This happens lots, we learn. We're told to stand over the spill (note to self: wear your hiking boots to work) and flag down someone with a radio or go to a concession stand where they have phones. They can call the clean-up crew. Or bring over one of the WET FLOOR signs strategically located around the concourse (the inside walkway that encircles about three-quarters of the ballpark). When all else fails, go to Guest Services. There will always be help there, including a police officer and emergency medical technician (EMT). Always.

Third priority: inclusion. This deals mostly with people who have restricted mobility, using a cane or wheelchair. When you see them, help them until they are in their seat. Guest Services will help them get out of the stadium safely.

Next priority is efficiency, but this is probably better described as awareness and initiative. "Look for service opportunities. Don't just be leaning up against the wall or don't just have your head down . . . You can rewrite the story for that customer's Durham Bulls experience by solving their problem, even if they haven't asked."

What about unruly fans? Back to safety. The neighbors of rude fans are reluctant to go to a host or police officer when a neighbor is "cursing all night." It's up to the host to approach a loudmouth. I suspect that cussing is associated with drinking and drinking with belligerence. (Can you guess which area of a stadium the ruffians are most likely to inhabit?)

"What's the evacuation plan?" someone shouts. Safety, yet again. Scott retells an episode that occurred on July 4, 2008. Kevin Costner and his band Modern West (country rock; Costner plays guitar and sings) were playing a concert out by second base when an extremely bad weather situation arose. All the power in the stadium went out. It was dark outside and this was before the stadium had emergency lights. The police department took over and evacuated the stadium, section by section. Know where the exits are so you can help.

Finally, the show. The big leagues are called "The Show," but it means something different in the minors. Unlike the bigs, for the Bulls, the time between innings is a time for on-field entertainment. Fans will sumo wrestle in oversized, blown-up costumes. Kids will race the mascot around the bases (the mascot always loses, even if it means he has to stop and yell at the umpire). T-shirts are launched into the crowd from air cannons. All experiences are guaranteed to bring a smile to your face.

POSITION PLAYERS

We break up into small groups to meet with our individual team supervisors. I head to the stands behind home plate with the others who signed on to be seating hosts.

There are about twenty hosts present, a majority of whom have done this before. What makes this crowd different from the general meeting is that there are only two Black men in the mix, a much smaller percentage than work for the club as a whole. Most hosts are just like me; old white guys, with a few white women sprinkled in. This didn't happen because people were told what job to take. I wasn't. I'm sure the difference in the size of a paycheck was the principal driver of people's job decisions. The stadium hosts are folks who are older and mostly retired, so they don't weigh the money as much in their decision-making. Instead, like me, they care about working outside, helping people, and watching baseball, not necessarily in that order. Still, the first thing that struck me was the de facto segregation created by the jobs and pay, near perfect as it was.

The meeting begins by handing out an operating manual. The manual describes eight positions, from custodian to K-Wall attendant—the person who hangs the Ks on the centerfield wall after a Bulls pitcher records a strike out.

The dress code for hosts requires a club-issued polo shirt tucked into khaki pants. The color of the shirts varies depending on your job, but the colors could all glow in the dark. Wearing a hat is okay, but it must be related to the team somehow and is preferably a Bulls cap. And the cap bill always must be facing forward, never backwards. We can carry a bottle of water, but it needs to be a product sold at the concessions, no competitors. Someone loudly whispers, "You can always bring your own and just remove the label."

We're told that Seating Bowl Hosts are the face of the Bulls to thousands of fans every game. Courtesy is always number one; give fans a friendly greeting, make sure your sections are clean and dry. But fans also must know you are the face of authority. Check tickets when you help people to their seats, especially if you are working premium seats. Stop kids from running and hanging out by the field trying to get the attention of players. Every other inning, walk down to the bottom of your section so fans know you are there. When the game is over, stand near the warning track to keep fans off the field (The need to do this has been greatly diminished since the netting that protects fans from balls that leave the field has been extended farther down the baselines). Baseball fans have seen hosts do this stuff many times. But seeing it and doing it are different things. I'm delighted to learn that rookies will be assigned sections next to old-timers until they get the hang of things.

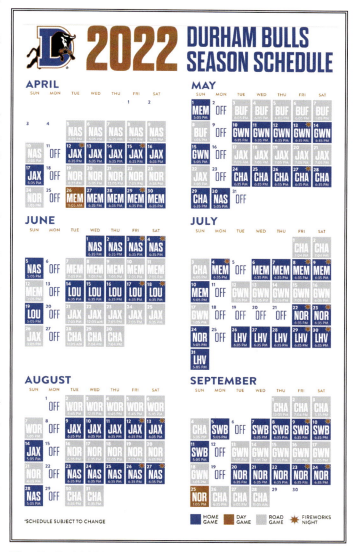

The Bulls' 2022 schedule.

The Bulls schedule reveals there will be twelve homestands, a total of seventy-five games. Typically, each homestand involves six games played against the same visiting team. It's one week at home then the next on the road. The only anomalies are a three-game set against the Norfolk Tide and two homestands played back-to-back. Most often, I will host four games for each six-game series.

I leave the stadium with a seating chart to study and figure out where all the different sections, boxes, and picnic areas are located. Here it is. You can use it to see where I was stationed for each game.

I'm a little apprehensive about my new job. All those safety issues! So much I'll have to learn on the fly! What's gonna pop up? I hope I don't strike out! But I'm also excited and feeling up to the challenge. After all, I've made it to the minors . . . sorta.

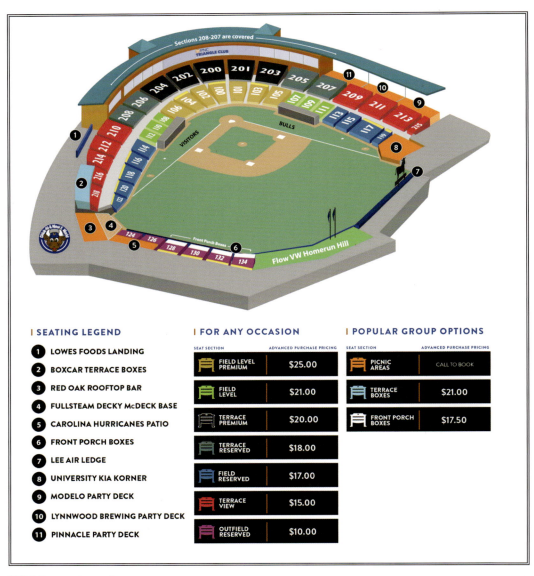

DBAP seating chart.

Chapter 2
A Walk to the Ballpark

Whoever wants to know the heart and mind of America had better learn baseball.

—Jacques Barzun, historian

Are you excited about the opening of the baseball season? Ah, the leather, the pine tar, the resin, the grass, the dirt. And that's just in the hot dogs.

—Colin O'Brien, comedian

It is three days before the Bulls' first homestand, which will be my first day at work. I decide to head to downtown Durham and meander along the streets leading to the Durham Bulls Athletic Park (DBAP).

A CITY BUILT ON SMOKE

After lunch at Brightleaf Square, a complex of shops and restaurants occupying former tobacco warehouses, I walk down Main Street on my way to the ballpark. Along the way I pass what is perhaps the best symbol for the history of Durham.

The Chesterfield Building was erected about seven blocks from the ballpark in the late 1940s by Liggett & Myers Tobacco Company. It was a plant for turning out Chesterfield cigarettes and remained in operation until 2000.[1]

Almost two decades later, after most of the downtown factories had been demolished or sat vacant, the Chesterfield building re-emerged when it was renovated to provide nearly three hundred thousand square

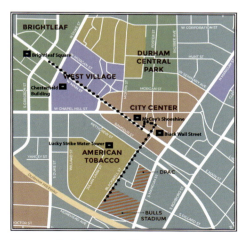

My walk to the ballpark.

---

1 https://www.bullcityrising.com/2010/10/durhams-chesterfield-from-the-inside.html

feet of office and lab space. The largest tenant now is Duke University, which is also the largest employer in a revitalized Durham (ahead of IBM, the city and its schools, and the drug company GlaxoSmithKline).[2] Today, when I walk through the entrance to the building, I am greeted by a directory that lists thirteen computer, biological sciences, and engineering groups that inhabit its confines.

Further down Main Street, I pass the sidewalk shoeshine chair of Pierce McCoy. McCoy is sixty-six and has been shining shoes in this location for years. When his chair started to get shabby, a patron took up his cause and raised, in a matter of hours, about $2,500. Now, McCoy has a refurbished sidewalk

Signs outside and inside the Chesterfield building, downtown Durham.

McCoy's chair.

---

2 https://en.wikipedia.org/wiki/Durham%2C_North_Carolina#Economy.

business establishment. A native, McCoy grew up in Durham's African American neighborhood known as Hayti. Hayti was a thriving, generally lower–middle class Black community that succumbed to urban renewal (referred to by those who experienced it as "urban removal") when an expressway was built through the neighborhood in 1958.

McCoy's chair sits around the corner from Parrish Street, the epicenter of Durham's Black Wall Street in the first half of the twentieth century. Back then, you could find Black-owned banks and insurance companies that created jobs for Durham's minority citizens and was the lifeline for the Hayti community. Yes, this middle-class enclave was largely separate and segregated from the white community. Yes, the civil rights movement of the 1960s ended segregation. It also sent Black Wall Street and Hayti into decline, as the end of segregation expanded opportunities for Black Durhamites to purchase goods and services from businesses outside the Hayti community.[3]

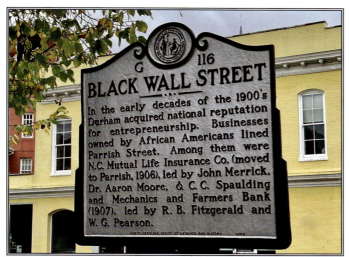

A commemorative plaque on Parrish Street.

I turn the corner to head down Blackwell Street, the street that runs past the ballpark. I pass the Self-Help Credit Union Building. Self-Help was founded as a nonprofit loan fund meant to help rural North Carolinians who had lost their jobs working in textile mills. The workers could form co-ops, get financing from Self-Help, and purchase the mills. Self-Help grew and grew, eventually becoming the largest financier of Durham's revitalization.[4]

On my left, I pass the Durham Performing Arts Center. This is a beautiful theater that hosts touring Broadway shows and musical concerts, among other live entertainment. It routinely ranks among the top ten theaters in America.[5] Not bad for a city of just over 280,000 residents.

A block closer to the park, I look up to see a smokestack looming overhead and water tower emblazoned with the logo of Lucky Strike cigarettes. I have arrived at the American Tobacco Campus, another repurposed tobacco manufacturing complex. These

---

WHY TOBACCO, YOU ASK?

In 1839, a teenage slave named Stephan fell asleep while tending a batch of tobacco curing over a fire at a plantation about forty miles northeast of Durham. When he woke, the fire was nearly out. He rushed to get more charcoal and tossed it onto the dying embers. A hot flame rose. By luck, Stephan had stumbled on a new curing technique, one that produced tobacco that was yellow in color rather than brown. It also was a tastier smoke. That curing technique and those bright leaves would become the industry standard. Bright leaf curing quadrupled the value of a pound of tobacco when it went to market. It would become the backbone of an industry and the city of Durham.*

* Wise, J. (2002). *Durham: A Bull City Story*. Charleston, SC: Arcadia Publishing. (p. 9)

---

3 Ibid.

4 Rice, E. S. & Anders, R. S. (2017). *Becoming Durham, Grit, Belief, and a City Transformed*. Raleigh, NC: Verdant Word Press

5 https://www.dpacnc.com/center-info/about-dpac

structures were originally built by the American Tobacco Company in the late 1800s. They were owned by J. B. Duke, who made his fortune selling tobacco and then electric power. The buildings now house offices and restaurants that surround a lawn used to host outdoor concerts and other events. It is across the street from the ballpark and is now owned by the same company as the Bulls, the Capitol Broadcasting Company. The ballpark and this campus are the stimulus of Durham's revitalization.

A symbol of the city.

BULL CITY

Durham prides itself on the way it has risen from the ashes (get it?) multiple times in its 150-year history. This image of the city goes back way before tobacco defined the city; in the eighteenth century, the Durham area was known as a live-and-let-live community of Native Americans, Blacks, and whites. Virginia's governor disparaged North Carolina, in general, as a place where "loose and disorderly people daily flock."[6] That was Durham.

So, the bull would be the perfect symbol for a city that prided itself on its fierce determination and strength. Dirty and ill-kempt yes, but confident and solid as a rock. I wish I could write that it was a match made in heaven but, more modestly, it may have been an early example of branding genius.

John Green was a tobacco producer in Durham who was looking for a way to set his brand apart from others. Lunching with his fellow tobacco producer John Whitted in Hillsborough, a jar of mustard sat on their table. Coleman's Mustard, one of the most popular brands in the US at the time, was made in Durham, England, and sported a picture of a bull on the label. Whitted suggested Green adopt the bull as his mascot on signs and advertisements. As the popularity of Durham tobacco grew, especially the brand *Bull Durham*, the city itself took on the moniker of the Bull City. So, maybe the line from the city's resilience and the bull branding isn't perfectly straight, but if it didn't fit it wouldn't have stuck.

OUTSIDE THE BALLPARK

I'm at the ballpark. I walk past the ticket windows and notice the sidewalk has concrete brick insets that give a shoutout to people, places, and events in Bulls' history. One inset lets people know about the Snorting Bull in left field: "Flashing eyes, smoking nostrils, and a wagging tail. It goes into action every time the Durham Bulls hit a home run." It also snorts and lights up after the Bulls win a home game. The current bull is the third iteration of the sign. Snorting Bull is now thirty feet wide and twenty feet high, larger than the original. The first bull resided at the old ballpark and was constructed for the *Bull Durham* movie. The bull entices Durham players to launch one; if a batter hits the bull, he gets a free steak. If he hits the grass the bull stands on, he gets a free salad. Makes sense. *Baseball Pilgrimages* calls Snorting Bull "one of the finest examples of local creativity you'll ever see in a ballpark."[7]

---

6 Ibid.

7 https://www.baseballpilgrimages.com/snorting-bull-durham.html

But there's more. One origin story for the term "bullpen" credits the Durham mascot. In the early days of the Durham Bulls, the original bull loomed over the enclosed area where pitchers warmed up. Another story claims Casey Stengel coined the term because the warm-up area was where pitchers sat and made polite conversation (okay, I cleaned that up a bit).[8]

The Snorting Bull.

Another inset on the street honors the Hot Stove League. Fans know the Hot Stove League as the off-season activity when they gather to talk baseball. The inset informs me that the name was also used for an annual banquet started in the 1950s to honor the best in North Carolina baseball.

Next comes a concrete brick for the Durham Black Sox/Eagles/Rams, a Negro Minor League team that played in Durham from the 1920s to 1965. The Negro Minor Leagues were semi-pro teams that fed the Negro League. There also appears to have been a Durham team called the Lucky Strikes.

The fans, broadcasters, and journalists also get insets on the sidewalk, as do the Atlanta Braves and Tampa Bay Rays, two of the Bulls' major league affiliates. Several players also get bricks. But let's save those for our dive into team history.

I arrive at the main entrance to DBAP on the corner of Blackwell Street and Jackie Robinson Drive. The main entrance is both grand and inviting. To the left, I see six plaques with jersey numbers on them. Five commemorate Bulls ballplayers and the sixth is Jackie Robinson's number 42.

Looming above the entryway are three pictures of a ballplayer in three different Bulls uniforms. The player's number is 29. Wonder why? Me too. When I ask, I discover there is nothing special about the number; the player who wore it was available on picture day.

When I arrive for my first day at work in about seventy-two hours, I will pass the main entrance by about one hundred yards and enter the service entrance on Jackie Robinson Drive.

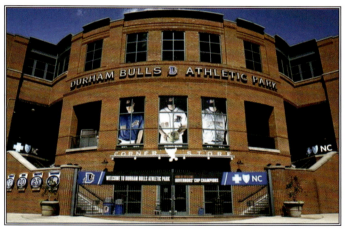

Welcome to the DBAP.

This beautiful structure almost never was. What was clear is that minor league baseball was catching on in Durham and the success of the movie in the late 1980s was bringing unprecedented attention to the Bulls franchise far beyond anything a minor league ball club had experienced previously. Durham Athletic Park, where the movie was filmed, was nearing its golden anniversary. It had never been renovated and was in disrepair. Something had to give.

---

8   https://www.mentalfloss.com/article/23013/6-theories-origin-bullpen

The city of Durham put building a new stadium to a vote of the people. The people said no. They had been burned before on proposals meant to renovate the downtown area and were feeling once bitten, twice shy. The Bulls owner at the time, Miles Wolff, put the team up for sale. Jim Goodmon, the owner of Capitol Broadcasting Company, had the idea that a sports complex located between Raleigh and Durham could unite the two cities. Goodmon bought the Bulls.

In Durham, the shock of potentially losing the Bulls set in. The typical political machinations ensued. Within weeks the Durham City Council voted unanimously to build a new stadium for the Bulls, right downtown. The city and Capitol Broadcasting worked hand in hand to make it happen.[9]

The design company HOK Sport, now called Populus, was hired to imagine the new stadium. HOK was the company that designed Camden Yards for Baltimore, Progressive Field for Cleveland, and Coors Field for Denver. These are all downtown "retro" parks that arose in reaction to those atrocious bowl stadiums serving multiple sports teams but serving fans poorly. The first pitch at DBAP was thrown on April 6, 1995. The seating capacity at the time was 9,033. DBAP has been renovated five times since then, with seats added three times. Now, its capacity is ten thousand seats, about one-quarter under a roof.

INSIDE THE BALLPARK

As I enter the main gate to the ballpark proper, I'm greeted first by the Corner Store, where I can load up on all sorts of Bulls swag. In addition to the seemingly endless variety of Bulls T-shirts, sweatshirts, and jerseys I can buy for the entire family, there are at least thirty different cap styles. I discover that a large variety of manufacturers turn out this stuff. My favorite is a company called *108 Stitches* (that's the number of stitches on a baseball). But, there's more! I can get bobblehead dolls, a stuffie of Wool E. Bull, the team mascot, and even Annie Savoy. I can get balls, bats, and six different kinds of can koozies. You get the message. A quick look at minor league team web pages suggests selling this stuff is a significant revenue source for all the teams.

Crash Davis doll.

Another big revenue generator, of course, is ballpark food. There's the typical fare but also a few local entries. I'm particularly interested in the pizza slices. They come from Pie Pushers, whose downtown Durham location is now my favorite spot to pick up a pie. There's also El Jefecito Tacos. This business started as a food truck and now has a permanent location in DBAP's left field. I'll definitely try those. The Bulls are also starting "Kids Eat Free Wednesdays," where kids get a hot dog, chips, and soda. On Thursdays, I can get all the traditional ballpark fare for reduced prices. Due to the COVID pandemic, DBAP went cashless, so a credit card is a must, though you can buy vouchers at Guest Services. There are no vendors in the stands,

Durham Bulls Athletic Park.

---

9 Rice, E.S. & Anders, R.S. (2017). *Becoming Durham: Grit, Belief, and a City Transformed*. Raleigh, NC: Verdant Word Press.

but there is a QR code on the back of seats that can be used to order food you can then pick up quickly.

Speaking of food, at orientation we were told the Bulls provide a buffet dinner for all the employees. Seating Bowl Hosts must show up for work at 5:00 p.m. The dinner line opens at 4:45 p.m. On Sundays, when games start ninety minutes earlier, I will arrive at 3:30 p.m., with dinner also being fifteen minutes before the team meeting. I'm expecting to eat dinner standing up most nights. I will find the spread is nice, but really not much different from what fans can eat. Some nights, I'll pass on the buffet and get a slice of the pizza or some tacos when I get a break during the game.

The most distinctive features of the stadium are in left field. The Blue Monster is a wall that looms thirty-two feet high and resembles Fenway Park's Green Monster. Like Fenway, it includes a manual scoreboard. Snorting Bull watches over the park from above the Blue Monster. As sturdy as Snorting Bull is, he had his head and forelegs ripped off in 2017 during a violent windstorm. Moving to the right while facing Snorting Bull, there are three office buildings, called Diamond View I, II, and III. These office buildings, housing mostly law and finance firms, were developed by the Capitol Broadcasting Company in partnership with regional architectural firms. The buildings match the brick color and style of the ballpark and offer around four hundred thousand square feet of office space. Nestled in Diamond View II is the restaurant Tobacco Road, a sports bar with an outdoor seating area that offers a view of the ballfield. More on the restaurant later.

From a hitter's viewpoint, there is nothing particularly inviting or intimidating about the field dimensions. You can hit a 303-foot home run down the left line, one to dead center field 395 feet away, and to right 339 feet. Fielders have a decent opportunity to catch a foul ball.[10]

It's a great ballpark for fans. Best of all, seats are a bit larger than you might expect at a ballpark. Once you are inside, you can circumnavigate the entire park on a walkway inside the stadium but in the fresh air. If you come with a group, you can reserve a box, private picnic area, or even a luxury, climate-controlled suite.

It's time for the DBAP's next renovation. The city has been told by major league baseball that the stadium needs $10 million in renovations to bring it up to current Triple-A standards. None of these renovations deal with the fan experience but rather relate to the quality of the players' experience; DBAP needs a new batting tunnel, player locker rooms, and renovated office space.[11] There's the usual handwringing about spending public money but the ramifications for the city if the Bulls move seem enormous.

RATING DBAP

Stadium Journey is a website that rates stadiums for five different sports, including major and minor league baseball.[12] They have rated more than 2,400 stadiums in thirty-one countries. On its website you can find information about the ballpark as well as food and lodging in the area. In 2021, James Hilchen rated DBAP using a scale of one to five on seven dimensions. Here's a summary of what he wrote, directly quoted:

> Food and Beverage: 5
> Among the areas that DBAP stands out, this is one of them. No matter what your taste, you can find something you will like to eat here . . . A neat feature of the ballpark is that it has its own brewery. Bull Durham Beer is brewed on the property and is highly recommended.

---

10 https://en.wikipedia.org/wiki/Durham_Bulls_Athletic_Park

11 https://www.athleticbusiness.com/facilities/stadium-arena/article/15290154/durham-must-pay-9m-in-upgrades-if-bulls-to-remain

12 https://www.stadiumjourney.com/stadiums/durham-bulls-athletic-park-s193

Atmosphere: 5
If I could go higher than 5 stars here, I would. DBAP is an absolutely fantastic spot to take in a ballgame and very aesthetically pleasing to the eye. . . . On the day I attended, it was hot and humid. The roof has industrial sized ceiling fans attached to the bottom and it makes a world of difference . . . there isn't a bad seat in the house wherever you choose to sit.

Neighborhood: 4
The ballpark is part of the American Tobacco Campus and is located in the middle of downtown Durham. This area has been part of a renovation effort and, as such, is home to many restaurants and bars within walking distance.

Fans: 4
The Bulls have quite a local following as well. Far more fans here seemed invested in the game, rather than being there for a social event. The reaction after a home-team home run is especially fun to see. The fans all look towards the bull sign to see the eyes light up and smoke come out of its nose.

Access: 4
The ballpark is located just off Durham Freeway and is very easy to get to. Public transportation is a good option . . . there are plenty of parking attendants that are around, and they are happy to point you in the right direction.

Return on Investment: 5
For the experience you get at DBAP, they could charge more for tickets and it would still be worth the cost.

Extras: 5
Again, if I could go higher than 5 here, I would.

Final Thoughts
The Bulls have a long and storied history in North Carolina. As someone who has seen my share of minor league ballparks over the years, Durham Bulls Athletic Park just might be my favorite. Great scenery, food for every taste, and fun reminders of an iconic movie makes this a ballpark that should be on every baseball fan's bucket list.

Hilchen's total score for DBAP was 4.57. Six fan ratings also equaled 4.57. In case you're wondering how DBAP's score compared to other ballparks, I averaged the Stadium Journey ratings of the nine other ballparks in the Eastern Division of the International League (see below). The average critic total score was 3.95 and the average fan total score was 3.90. Not even close; DBAP's total scores were highest in both ratings. (Coming in last was the Syracuse Mets' NBT Bank Stadium).

THE INTERNATIONAL LEAGUE

As a team in the International League (IL), the Bulls are one of thirty Level-AAA teams that exchange players directly to and from the major leagues. The Bulls are the affiliate of the Tampa Bay Rays. The IL has twenty teams, and the Pacific Coast League has the other ten clubs.

After their 150-game schedule, the winners of the Eastern and West Divisions will meet in a one-game playoff to determine the IL champ. The IL champ will then meet the Pacific Coast champ to crown the Triple-A champ.

Okay, let's get to work. It's game time!

Chapter 3
Home Series 1: Opening Week

Baseball is the only major sport that appears backward in a mirror.

—George Carlin, comedian

A ballplayer spends a good piece of his life gripping a baseball, and in the end, it turns out that it was the other way around all the time.

—Jim Bouton, pitcher

JACKSONVILLE

https://en.wikipedia.org/wiki/Jacksonville,_Florida
https://en.wikipedia.org/wiki/Jacksonville_Jumbo_Shrimp

Nickname: Jumbo Shrimp
MLB affiliate: Miami Marlins (2009–present)
Field: 121 Financial Ballpark; capacity, 11,000
Population (2020): 949,611
Economy: Banking and finance; rail, air, highway and shipping hub
Fun Fact: Jacksonville once hosted a team that relocated to the USA from Havana after the Cuban Revolution.

TUESDAY, APRIL 12

"The bird poop early in the season is a pain in the ass," advises a veteran host. "They hang out around the roof. Watch your head and examine your seats before the fans start arriving."

Not exactly what I wanted to hear as I arrive for my first day at work an hour early, hoping to meet some folks and get some on-the-job training from the veterans.

The Bulls began the season on the road and lost a series to the Nashville Sounds, winning only two of six games. Maybe things will look up at home.

It's time for the pregame meeting. Everyone's assigned section is read off. We are shown where to get rags to wipe off our seats. Then, we are handed confetti cannons which we are to explode right before the first pitch. Finally, we get a sandwich bag filled with plastic Durham Bulls wristbands that we'll toss out when we are given the signal.

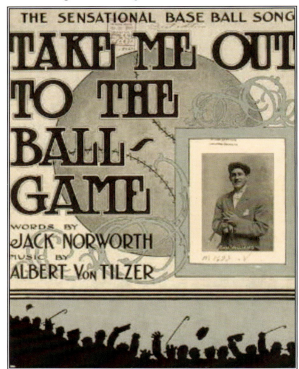

Baseball's anthem, first published in 1908.
(Written by two songsters who had never attended a baseball game.)

At my station, I learn about how to get the attention of the EMTs and folks with a radio. When a ball gets hit into the stands, I first have to check to see if anybody got hurt. If someone gets hit by the ball or pushed aside in the scuffle for it, I am to rotate my arms over my head to grab someone's attention. It's not like calling strikes and balls, nothing fancy.

Just before game time, the local television station's weather forecaster arrives to do a pre-game news segment down by the dugout (her channel is owned by the same company that owns the Bulls). Kat Campbell is a diminutive five feet three inches tall and "wanted to be a broadcast meteorologist as early as eight years old."[1] She was the president of the Future Meteorologists Club in college. People line up for autographs and pictures. I become a smart phone photographer. This is a role I will play numerous times every game. I learn to spot people taking photos and ask if they need my help so they can get everyone in the picture. I'm rarely turned down and always greeted with a smile. It becomes one of my favorite parts of the job.

The scoreboard announces that fans can visit a website and predict the speed of the first pitch. Get it correct and win a prize. In the stands, a young man zips past me collecting guesses from fellow employees. "Is this a betting pool?" I ask.

"Can't say," is his response, accompanied by a wry smile.

The opening pitch was 95 mph.

A fan asks me if the Jones jersey plaque on the wall outside the stadium is for Hall of Famer Chipper Jones. Yes, it is. Jones played seventy games for the Bulls in 1992, when the team was the Advanced-A affiliate of the Atlanta Braves. Want his Bulls baseball card? It'll cost you about two hundred dollars online.

The host for the seating sections to my right is angry. He's had a fan get in his face to complain about his wife waiting in line for half an hour to get a hot dog.

---

1 https://factsbuddy.com/kat-campbell/

"What the hell am I supposed to do?" he asks me rhetorically. "I said to him, 'come with me' and the guy says, 'I don't want to go nowhere.'"

We agree that the guy is a miscreant. Secretly, I'm reassured that if this incident agitated a veteran of seven seasons at the ballpark, it can't happen that frequently.

The wristband toss never materializes. Since I have a bag full of them, I take the initiative. Between innings there is a T-shirt toss conducted from atop the dugouts. Lots of kids jump up and down waving their arms. Few are rewarded for their efforts. Aha! The perfect use of my wristbands. I look for the kids who seem most disappointed and give them a wristband as a consolation prize. It works like magic turning their frowns around. I'll hold on to the rest of mine and dole them out when I see fit.

Kids congregate at the fence by the warning track and plead with the players to give them a ball. Sometimes the players do. They obstruct the view of the fans behind them. Plus, it's against the fire code to stand in the aisles.

Today, I would see two kids hit the jackpot. No matter how vigilant I am, kids come back to the railing waving their gloves in the air. Shooing them away makes me feel like a grinch. And I know my efforts will never succeed. The kids are on what behaviorists, think B. F. Skinner, call a variable ratio reinforcement schedule. That's a fancy sounding name for the kids thinking, "If I keep asking, eventually I'll get one. I don't know how many times I need to ask but eventually it will happen."

Skinner showed that reinforcing behavior on a variable ratio schedule creates persistence that is incredibly hard to extinguish. Pigeons will peck at a target hundreds of times to get a seed just once in a while, on a schedule they can't predict. The kids are doing the same thing (as are gamblers sitting at a slot machine). Knowing this, I also know my efforts at fire safety may hustle kids away temporarily, but I will be doing this over and over again.

The game itself is a bust for the hometown crowd. The Jacksonville starting pitcher needs just 40 pitches to complete four perfect innings. On the field, the Bulls botch a double play. Three players stand and watch a bloop fly ball fall between them. But there are good plays to go with the bad ones. The third baseman makes a great backhand stab and throws an on-target one-bouncer to first, expertly dug out of the dirt by his teammate. The centerfielder runs down a fly ball to dead center field and makes a catch with his glove over the wall, robbing the batter of a home run. Welcome to minor league baseball. The Jumbo Shrimp go on to win 7–0.

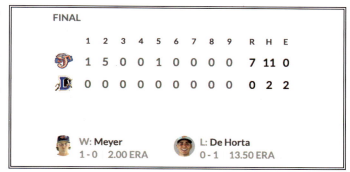

Attendance: 7,824.

WEDNESDAY, APRIL 13

We're told it is pollen season at the host's team meeting tonight. We're reminded again where the rags are, and that we should grab one. It's also "Bark in the Park" night. The website tells fans they are welcome to bring their dog to the game. But there are rules: All dogs require a Bark in the Park dog ticket, the owners are to keep their dogs on a leash, and they must stay in specific sections. Volunteers from a local pet shelter will be around to watch dogs should an owner need a break. The Park Bark appears to go off without a hitch.

Sure enough, the seats in my section are covered with pollen. John, a veteran host wearing a mask to protect him from COVID, sees me wiping down my seats.

He walks over and I see he has had a tracheotomy and uses a voice amplifier he touches to his neck. He tells me to walk fans to their seats, wipe the seat down again, and maybe I'll get a tip. I count 280 seats in the two sections that I cover. At game time about half of them are filled. No one offers a tip (not that I would take one).

Before the gates open, I visit the men's room. As I exit, I see a large plaque on the wall just inside the exit door with the image of the real Lawrence "Crash" Davis on it. The director of the movie *Bull Durham*, Ron Shelton, thought the name was perfect for Kevin Costner's character. According to the *Atlanta Journal-Constitution*, Shelton reached out to Davis to get permission:

> **Shelton**: Mr. Davis, we might have a problem if you don't want us to use your name.
> **Davis**: I have just one question, do I get the girl?
> **Shelton**: You sure do.
> **Davis**: Well, then, fine.

The real "Crash" Davis.

The real "Crash" Davis was born in Georgia in 1919 but was raised in Gastonia, North Carolina, and played middle infield for the Duke University baseball team.[2] He got the nickname "Crash" at the age of fourteen after an on-field collision with the left fielder. Davis recounted that he was also known as "Little" and "Squeaky."

Like many ballplayers in the mid-twentieth century, Davis played three seasons for the Philadelphia Athletics before enlisting in the navy to serve during World War II. More than five hundred major league ballplayers served in the war, including Hank Greenberg, Yogi Berra, Bob Feller, Warren Spahn, and Joe DiMaggio.[3]

War heroes.

When Crash returned from the war, he played for the Bulls in 1948, hit .317 with 10 homers, and led the Carolina League with 50 doubles. Davis quit baseball in 1952 and became a successful coach of high school and American Legion baseball. After the movie's release and its ensuing popularity, Davis crossed the country speaking about his life and career.

In the movie, Ebby Calvin "Nuke" Laloosh first thinks that maybe his nickname should be "Pokie." Imagine how Davis's life would have been different had he stuck with the moniker "Squeaky."

---

2   https://en.wikipedia.org/wiki/Crash_Davis
3   https://medium.com/@riley.poole/baseball-heroes-of-world-war-ii-9d07e0093b3f

HOME SERIES 1: OPENING WEEK

Not long before his death, Davis recounted a tale from his 1939 season in the Southern League: "Back in those days we didn't have all the trainers they have now. One of our players slid into second base and hurt his ankle. So, one of the guys picked up the medicine kit and rushed out to second base and opened the bag and all that was in there was a pint of whiskey!" Davis lived to be eighty-two years young.

Returning to my post, I meet the host in the section to the left of me. He works with students having academic difficulties at a middle school. Beside his duties for the Bulls, he is a member of the chain gang for Duke football games and plays host to the referees, picking them up at the airport and getting them to where they need to be. He also works at the pro shop at a local golf course.

I hear a story I will hear from several hosts about when Aaron Judge, the Yankees superstar and now the American League home run king, was rehabbing with the Scranton/Wilkes-Barre RailRiders and visited Durham. Both games were sold out. People watched from the windows of the surrounding buildings. When the RailRiders arrived on the team bus, Judge pulled up in a hired car.

My first fan issue: It seems that two seats have been assigned to more than one person, a couple and a party of ten. Sure enough, the paper and electronic tickets are for the same seats. The couple agrees to move to different seats. Phew!

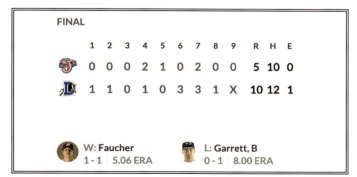

Attendance: 4,389.

FRIDAY, APRIL 15

At the seating bowl host meeting we learn that tonight is Jackie Robinson Night. Seventy-five years ago, on this day, Robinson made his first appearance in the majors with the Brooklyn Dodgers. It is celebrated throughout major and minor league baseball.

North Carolina had no teams in the Negro League but did contribute several players to the league's ranks. Negro League teams would come to North Carolina and play against semi-pro teams.[4] If the visiting team saw a player they liked, they'd take him home with them. Buck Leonard, elected to the Baseball Hall of Fame in 1972, along with Bob Gibson, hailed from Rocky Mount, North Carolina.

Dreaming of a future in baseball.

Another bathroom plaque at DBAP celebrates Wycliffe Nathaniel "Bubba" Morton, the first African American to play for the Bulls, though he shared the honor on opening day with pitcher Ted Richardson.

---

[4] https://www.wfae.org/sports/2020-09-04/negro-league-roots-found-deep-in-north-carolina-history

Morton spent the 1957 season with the Level-B Carolina League Durham Bulls. That season, Bubba led the Bulls in just about every offensive category. When the Bulls traveled, Morton had to stay in private homes because Blacks were not allowed to stay in hotels in the South. After a stellar minor league career, Morton made the Detroit Tigers opening day roster in 1961. He bounced around the majors and minors (briefly rooming with Hank Aaron in Milwaukee) until 1969.[5] Ted Richardson never made it to the majors.[6]

The hosts also learn at our meeting that in addition to our glorified titles as Seating Bowl Hosts (a.k.a. ushers), we refer to ourselves as "Seat Nazis." An unnamed host (but not me) gets called out for being overly thorough in checking tickets. A fan must have complained about undue vigilance.

Tonight, my assignment is in the bleachers—I mean, the Diamond View Seats, in right centerfield. There are 425 seats in my sections. Steve, the host to my right, tells me he makes a living as an enterprise architect. He works with companies that want assistance understanding how their management, planning, information flow, and computing systems fit with the organization's goals. Steve lost his second wife of over two decades to brain cancer. His girlfriend is at the game sitting in his section.

Steve asks me to cover his sections while he tries to find someone to help a fan. Seems the fan's six-month-old son dropped his dad's car keys in the space between the centerfield wall and the padding that protects players should they hit the wall hard. Fitting the keys in the narrow space is quite a feat in itself; never underestimate the ingenuity of a toddler. A couple of guys with radios show up, but MacGyver is nowhere to be found. Dad will have to wait until the game is over. But three-plus hours at the ballpark with a six-month-old ain't gonna shake it for this dad. He calls home for a ride and asks if he can pick up the keys at lost-and-found the next day. Arrangements are made.

"This reminds me of that Tom Hanks movie where he's stuck in an airport, except this guy's stuck at a ballpark," I comment to Steve. "What was the name of that movie?"

"*Terminal*," interjects an eavesdropping fan. He gets a wristband.

On my left is Leigh. She is one of the few woman hosts. She is both a freelance writer and graphic designer. Leigh is self-employed and works the ball games because she needs a crowd, loves baseball, and loves hospitality.

Attendance: 8,284.

SUNDAY, APRIL 17

Today, I decide to keep track of how much time I spend standing and walking during a game. On this five-hour shift, I stand for four hours and forty minutes. My smart watch tells me I walk three miles from the time I entered the ballpark until I leave.

I'm in the Diamond View Section again, with Steve on my right. On my left is Josh. Josh moved to North Carolina from Michigan to take a job promotion and get out of the cold winters of the Upper Midwest. His new job lasted a year. He now does marketing for small computer game companies. He tells Steve and me that he won't be around for the next homestand. He must travel

---

[5] https://sabr.org/bioproj/person/bubba-morton/
[6] https://www.milb.com/durham/news/morton-richardson-first-black-bulls-players

back to Michigan to attend his mother's memorial service. She died of COVID. His dad got vaccinated and his mom didn't. They both got sick. He survived, she didn't. Josh is a true baseball aficionado. He'll talk anything baseball and contribute impressive facts and figures. He tells us about a YouTube channel that collects bad calls by umpires and shows how often they go against each team.

A woman with two children in tow arrives and takes up residence in the Front Porch Boxes, right next to the outfield wall. I'm told to check her tickets.

"My daughter has them," she says, "she went to buy a hat."

Okay. When the daughter returns an inspection of the tickets reveals they should be up in the regular seats. Off they go. None of the boxes were sold and they all remain empty throughout the game. Feeling like a Seat Nazi, I give one of the kids who clearly has some physical challenges a wristband. It helps a bit.

In the tunnel to my section, I notice a public service poster: "Be a Superhero in the Opioid Battle." Important message, but it is a reminder of the grimmer world outside the ballpark.

This is the first game of the season in which the minors will enforce the pitch clock. The pitcher has 14 seconds to pitch if no one is on base and 19 seconds with runners on base. The experiment with the clock in the minors has sped up games by 21 minutes, on average.[7] I'm surprised when the first time the rule is invoked it results in a called strike on the batter. He was out of the batter's box talking to the first base coach. The second time the pitch clock rule is enforced it dings the pitcher.

The game lasts exactly three hours. This is not surprising given that the Jumbo Shrimp scored 8 runs on 15 hits. During the six-game homestand, Jacksonville scores 53 runs, averaging 8.8 runs a game. The Bulls scored 20 runs, or 3.3 a game. There's an easy explanation for this. The Tampa Bay Rays had some injuries to their pitchers. During the homestand they called up five Bulls pitchers. Count 'em, five. Two pitchers stayed in the majors one day, one four days, and two were still there at the end of the week. The Bulls got two pitchers to replace them from the Montgomery (Alabama) Biscuits, the Rays Level-AA team. Not the kind of trade Bulls fans like.

Steve, Josh, and I discuss other rule changes that baseball is considering. Should the shift that puts three infielders on one side of second base be banned? We agree that the ban is a bad idea. Steve thinks managers should be free to employ this strategic move. I agree but for a different reason: Why the heck can't a professional baseball player hit to the opposite field?

And how about robot umpires calling pitches? Josh likes it because the ump will still be behind home plate and can overrule the automated call. I'm less sanguine. I offer that I'm impressed with the number of calls umps actually get correct and think it adds a human element to the game.

An outside world intrudes.

---

[7] https://www.insidehook.com/daily_brief/sports/mlb-proposed-pitch-clock-timer-explained

> **HOW OFTEN DO UMPIRES MAKE THE CORRECT CALL ON BALLS AND STRIKES?**
>
> Most of the data I've seen suggest* umpires are quite accurate, on average, getting the call correct about ninety-three percent of the time. The best umps get 19 out of 20 pitches correct, the worst 9 out of 10. Assuming 100 pitches are thrown to each team in a game, that means umps miss between 10 and 20 pitch calls per game.
>
> * https://www.bu.edu/articles/2019/mlb-umpires-strike-zone-accuracy/

While I clean pollen off the seats before the game starts, I suffer my first injury. I smack my thumb into one of those hard steel armrests that separate the seats. Got a contusion. Not to worry. I'm a pro, I'll play through it.

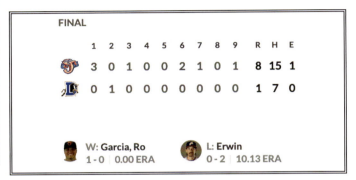

Attendance: 5,575.

Umps have different strike zones but use them consistently. Players need to know the idiosyncrasies of different umps. And watching a manager or ballplayer kick dirt at an umpire is always a fan treat. Of course, outright assaults on umps have been verboten since 1927 when commissioner Kennesaw Mountain Landis decreed that assaulting an umpire would lead to a ninety-day suspension without pay.[8] And dirt kicking is rare these days, though I'd love to see it gain favor again.

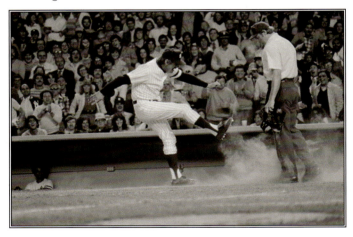

Billy Martin kicks dirt on an umpire.

---

8 Obojski, R. (1975). *Bush League: A Colorful Factual Account of Minor League Baseball from 1877 to the Present.* New York: Macmillan.

A LEAGUE OF THEIR OWN

Year of Release: 1992
Rating: PG
Director: Penny Marshall
Writer: The screenplay was written by Lowell Ganz and Babaloo Mandel based on a story by Kelly Candaele and Kim Wilson
Stars: Tom Hanks (manager), Geena Davis (catcher), Madonna (center field), Lori Petty (pitcher), Rosie O'Donnell (third base).

Plot Synopsis

From Wiki: https://en.wikipedia.org/wiki/A_League_of_Their_Own
A League of Their Own is a 1992 American sports comedy-drama film that tells a fictionalized account of the real-life All-American Girls Professional Baseball League (AAGPBL).
A League of Their Own was a critical and commercial success, grossing over $132.4 million worldwide and receiving praise for Madonna and O'Donnell's appearances. In 2012, the film was selected for preservation in the United States National Film Registry by the Library of Congress as being "culturally, historically, or aesthetically significant."
From IMDb: https://www.imdb.com/title/tt0104694/
Two sisters join the first female professional baseball league and struggle to help it succeed amidst their own growing rivalry.

Critic Ratings

Rotten Tomatoes: https://www.rottentomatoes.com/m/league_of_their_own
Tomatometer: 80 out of 100 (75 reviewers)
Audience Score: 84 out of 100 (250,000+ Ratings)
Critics consensus: Sentimental and light, but still thoroughly charming, A League of Their Own is buoyed by solid performances from a wonderful cast.
IMDb Rating: 7.3 out of 10 (105,000 raters)
Roger Ebert: https://www.rogerebert.com/reviews/a-league-of-their-own-1992, 3 out of 4 stars.
Ebert writes that the movie is about the changing roles of women during the mid-1940s. He says it has "a real bittersweet charm" driven by the personalities of the players, and how "women's liberation fit into the hidebound traditions of professional baseball."

Chapter 4
Home Series 2: Kids and the K-Wall

I have discovered, in twenty years of moving around ballparks, that the knowledge of the game is usually in inverse proportion to the price of the seats.
—Bill Veeck, baseball executive

Little League baseball is a very good thing because it keeps the parents off the streets.
—Yogi Berra, player, manager

MEMPHIS

https://en.wikipedia.org/wiki/Memphis,_Tennessee
https://en.wikipedia.org/wiki/Memphis_Redbirds

Nickname: Redbirds
MLB Affiliate: St. Louis Cardinals (1998–present)
Field: AutoZone Park; capacity 10,000
Population: (2020): 633,104
Economy: FedEx, International Paper, and AutoZone
Fun Fact: Memphis played with the nickname the Chickasaws, or Chicks, for sixty years. The Chickasaw are indigenous people of the southeastern US.

TUESDAY, APRIL 26

When the Bulls open their second homestand, their record is seven wins and eleven losses, safely ensconced in the bottom half of the International League standings. The open wound the Bulls call "pitching" is still in evidence.

We are told to arrive at the ballpark thirty minutes early because today is Education Day. It's one of only two day games during the season, starting at 11:00 a.m. That was all I thought was unique about it—little did I know. When the game begins, I estimate that about seven thousand of the eight thousand fans in attendance are between the ages of eight and fifteen. Kids and chaperones get in for five dollars ("And don't forget the bus driver!"). Box lunches are available for $6.50. Most of the season ticket seats are empty.

The Bulls offer the game as an alternative to the "boring" field trip. In addition to the game, kids can visit interactive stations (mostly science-related) on the walkway behind the Diamond View seats. Also, the Bulls website points educators to the website of the National Baseball Hall of Fame in Cooperstown. The Hall's site provides lesson plans for different grade levels covering all sorts of subjects. The math curriculum draws my attention. I recall that the first time calculating percentages meant anything to me was when I became interested in batting averages. Sure enough, that's the example on the Hall of Fame website.

Before the game starts the pitchers warm up in front of my section down the right field line. A coach reads off a bunch of motivational statistics, including that if the pitcher throws a first pitch strike, the batter's average is a measly .075. The pitchers listen politely. Isn't math fun?

The kids start filing in. First to arrive is Green Hope High School, a highly rated public school, from Apex, North Carolina.[1] The group in attendance is composed of kids with special needs, about forty total students and staff from the Physical Education and Personal Improvement program.

Next up is Spring Valley Elementary School from Durham.[2] Spring Valley is a school that serves enough underperforming students to qualify for special financial assistance.

In third is Silvan Elementary School from Snow Hill, North Carolina. The school has less than three hundred students (about forty are at the game) from a town of about 1,600 total residents. It's a ninety-minute bus ride to the ballpark (they leave to head home after the sixth inning). The town of Snow Hill was once the home of the Snow Hill Billies, who played in the Coastal Plain League, a Level-D league from 1934 to 1940. The Billies represented the smallest town ever to have a minor league baseball team.[3]

> **WHY CAN'T MATH BE FUN?**
>
> The Baseball Hall of Fame website* provides this example of how interest in baseball can be used to stimulate the learning of statistics and percentages:
>
> It's the final day of the 1941 season and Ted Williams' batting average is .39955. What will he do? Sit this one out and guarantee an historic .400 season or take a chance and aim for mathematic immortality? Find the answer to this and other exciting stories in a unit full of whole numbers, fractions and decimals, percentages, proportions and problem solving. This thematic unit teaches fundamental concepts that connect the calculator and the clubhouse while using and interpreting the statistics of famous ballplayers.
>
> * https://baseballhall.org/discover-more/education/batter-up

---

1 https://www.wcpss.net/greenhopehs

2 https://www.dpsnc.net/Spring-Valley

3 Holaday, J. C. (1998). *Professional baseball in North Carolina.* Jefferson, NC: McFarkand.

Next up is Falls Lake Academy, a public charter school from Creedmoor, North Carolina, population just over four thousand. The school emphasizes project-based learning: "students go through an extended process of inquiry in response to a complex question, problem, or challenge."[4]

Finally, fifty-four kids from Carolina Friends School in Durham show up. The Friends school is inspired by Quaker values; it follows no religious tradition but "believe[s] in the ability of each individual to become their best self, the power of community, and the importance of acting for the greater good."[5]

Two young ladies, maybe ten years old, walk up to me and ask where they go to exchange cash for vouchers. They are from the Durham Academy, a private school that boasts a six-to-one student-to-faculty ratio.[6] Tuition ranges between $22,000 and $31,000 a year.

Looking down on my sections, I'm taken by the diversity of the kids and their backgrounds. I am a little sad as well at how segmented American education has become. Growing up in the Bronx in the 1950s, I went to a six-story elementary school that occupied half a city block. At my school, all these kids would have spilled out onto a common schoolyard and played together, and fought, and made up, and learned that people are different, but they all have value—especially if they are good ballplayers. Today, these kids' teachers and parents all thought a day of baseball was in their best interest. Yes, I think, today is a perfect example of a shared national value. But the kids sit with their friends, and there is little interaction between kids from different schools.

I meet a father at the game with his eight-year-old son. He says it's his first trip to a ballgame in forty years. He's beaming from ear to ear. I learn that a man sitting in my handicapped section is at the game to celebrate his ninety-fourth birthday. He's at the game with his three sons, all in their sixties and seventies. That's an eighty-six-year age span between the youngest and oldest fan in my sections.

The Bulls lose the game, 10–0. The highlight for Bulls fans occurs when Tyler Zombro takes the mound. About eleven months earlier, Zombro was hit above his right ear by a line drive traveling at 104 mph. He fell unconscious, face first, to the mound while having

Tyler Zombro.

Attendance: 7,982.

a seizure. Surgeons used sixteen titanium plates and thirty-six screws to put his skull back together. The game was called. Zombro has no memory of what happened.[7] He returned to the mound on the road a few nights before today's Education Day game. He pitched

---

4   https://www.fallslakeacademy.com/
5   https://www.cfsnc.org/
6   https://www.da.org/

7   https://en.wikipedia.org/wiki/Tyler_Zombro

against the Norfolk Tide, which was the team the Bulls were playing when he was hit. The fans in Norfolk gave him a standing ovation. Both teams left their benches, walked onto the field, and did the same.

WEDNESDAY, APRIL 27

Today, I'm the K-Wall guy. While walking out to check my position, I pass a host who is on patrol in the Diamond View seats. He's hunting for balls that have left the park during the Bulls' batting practice.

"Memphis has some power hitters, so I may have to come back if they take batting practice," he tells me.

The K-Wall is a tradition in many ballparks. Each time the home team pitcher strikes out a batter, a large "K" is draped over a designated section of an outfield wall. In DBAP, it's left centerfield, just to the right of the Tobacco Road restaurant. I can't find the story of how the K-Wall came to be, but my vague memory suggests the tradition was started by hometown fans as a way to celebrate a pitcher who recorded lots of strike outs (was it Nolan Ryan?).

Hanging Ks.
(Eight strike outs, four swinging, four looking.)

In the operating manual, the world outside intrudes on the K-Wall attendants. It tells me to hold off on hanging the third K until I also have a fourth K to hang, to avoid "negative connotations." On my way to my position, I am reminded about this. I suspect all baseball operating manuals include the same instructions.

> **WHY A K FOR A STRIKE OUT?**
>
> The tradition is over 150 years old and was invented by Henry Chadwick, the guy who developed the box score. Chadwick had already used an S for a stolen base, so he chose the K because it was the last letter of "struck" and took three strokes to write. If a batter gets called out looking at a third strike, the scorekeeper records the K backward. Also, the K is hung backwards on the wall. The distinction may seem trivial, but when a batter watches a third strike it can mean the pitcher has some special stuff on the ball, or is very precise in location, or the batter's got a bad eye.* Or the umpire missed the call. These things matter to baseball nerds.
>
> * https://gethypedsports.com/what-does-a-backwards-k-mean-in-baseball/

The Ks are about two feet by three feet and hang from a steel bar above a clear barricade. John, the guy who uses the voice amplifier, tells me to watch out for the Ks flying off the hooks in the wind and landing on the field. I saw this happen yesterday. The centerfielder retrieved the K and handed it to the guy operating the manual scoreboard who was sticking his paw out the ninth inning hole.

There are three of us working the left centerfield wall. The K-Wall is clearly not where the action is. Next to me, the outside porch of the Tobacco Road restaurant has a gate that allows fans to move back and forth between the restaurant's outdoor patio and the ballpark. But you gotta have a game ticket to do this. The host next to me is serious about checking tickets. Also, fans can't pass through the gate with beverages. He's serious about not allowing this as well. He shows me two side entrances to the restaurant that are my responsibility to monitor.

The third host out here stands below the Snorting Bull. He patrols the entrance that is mainly used by fans with limited mobility. Mostly, he does crowd control when fans from the restaurant get rowdy as they leave the ballpark and restaurant.

As I get ready for the game to start, I realize I've got a problem—there is no scoreboard visible from where I stand. In fact, no one along the left center-field walkway, the pathway in the sunshine that encircles the entire park, can see a scoreboard that provides runs, hits, errors, balls, and strikes. Of course, there are no ballpark seating areas out here, so it's not a big issue for paying fans (though it is for restaurant diners who can sit outside and watch the game). But that is little consolation for me, as I'll have to follow pitch counts carefully. This is gonna require a lot of attention to the game on my part, at least when the Bulls are in the field and there is a strike out for me to record on the wall, including whether the third strike was swung at or not. I pull out my smart phone and check the minor league baseball app. It gives the score of the game, but no balls and strikes. Tough luck.

I meet an IBM software developer visiting from San Francisco. I've got ties to the area (one of my brothers and my daughter live in the Bay Area) and I spent many a day at the old Candlestick Park.

"What a dump that place was," the fan opines.

I add, "I remember the Giants gave out pins to fans who stayed until an extra inning night game was over. I remember the TV ads that told viewers about the badges by showing fans stumbling out of a stadium tunnel that bellowed fog." This is a fond memory.

For the first time, I meet someone I know. On the restaurant patio outdoor seating, I'm recognized by a fellow Duke social psychologist. After explaining myself, he tells me that he is at the game on business. He's hosting a conference dealing with how to ease the transition of military veterans to civilian life. There are three retired three-star generals at the conference. The group decided on a ballgame for their evening activity.

When the game is over, I've hung thirteen Ks, three facing backwards. The Bulls used five pitchers.

And, yes, I put up two Ks and waited until the fourth K to put up Ks number three and number four.

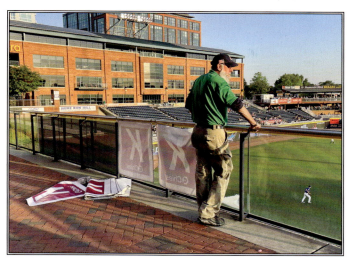

The author works the K wall.

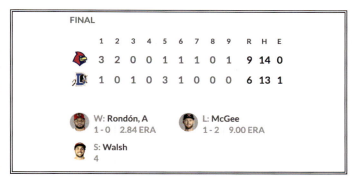

Attendance: 3,782.

FRIDAY, APRIL 29, 2022

At the hosts' dinner, I sit with two guys wearing black polo shirts, the only ones that don't glow in the dark. I ask what their jobs are. They tell me they work the picnic decks for the concessions company. There are about a half dozen of these picnic areas, reserved for large parties that rent them and get a buffet dinner.

One of my table mates offers, "Last night, I had two women try to pick me up."

Is this guy bragging? He's in his late sixties or early seventies. How old were the women? Did he misinterpret friendliness? I remain silent.

My other tablemate asks, "What did they look like?"

"One was wearing bellbottoms."

"Oh yeah, I remember her."

At an earlier game, another employee sidled up to me between innings. "I don't know if I want to watch the game or look at the pretty women," he says and wanders away. (This is one of only three instances I encounter during the entire season of comments that might suggest employees are attending to the wrong things during a game.)

While waiting for the team meeting to begin, I meet a host who is a retired physical therapist. He worked with people rehabbing their hands after surgery. John joins us, and upon realizing we are talking about our past lives, offers that he is a former criminal trial lawyer.

My station tonight is behind the Bulls' on-deck circle and is reserved for season ticket holders. A fan walks up to me with a big smile on his face and shakes my hand vigorously. Dave H. is retired from the construction business. He wants to get to know everyone. Sounds like a perfect candidate for a host job. He has the front row seat directly behind home plate.

My section has 64 seats in it, a far cry from the 425 I monitored in the Diamond View. I can tell from the behavior of another host, also a Dave H., a five-year veteran who is working Section 100 directly behind home plate, that providing vigilant service matters down here. He not only watches things very carefully but walks down to the bottom of his aisles every inning and scans the stands to let folks know he is there to help.

It was hard to engage Dave at first. Like most jobs, the veterans talk mostly to veterans and rookies to rookies. That's true in any work environment, but maybe a bit more so here. When a season starts, the old-timers back-slap and catch up. The rookies search to make connections with others. I bet the phenomenon is the same among the ballplayers. It takes time to make connections.

Another curiosity. I've probably met two dozen folks doing the same job as me or other jobs that keep them in the stands. No one has asked me what I do, or did, for a living, or how I spend my days. I'm clearly an outlier by broaching this subject with folks. Maybe the reticence is because most relationships here will be fleeting, though I do hear about two hosts who text one another when they are off duty. Maybe it's because this world of baseball is self-contained; its inhabitants (of which I am now one) come here to express a different segment of their self. No need to be who I am on the "outside."

I do get to talk to Dave in the late innings, and he's a really nice guy. He has worked in "warehousing" for twenty years, though exactly what aspect is unclear, and I don't probe. His most recent job was with a huge online retailer.

Dave offers, "I worked for them for four months and tried to get a day shift. The thing is all computerized and I couldn't get moved up on the list for the shift I wanted. So, when the Bulls' season started, I quit."

When I suggest these positions hosting behind home plate are cushy compared to the Diamond View

Not a bad place to watch a ballgame.

seats in right-center field, Dave confides that maybe cleaning every one of the seats in outfield sections is not necessary. I also ask whether, being a long-time veteran, he gets some preference for a section he wants. He says no.

Dave knows his baseball and watches the games as close as he watches his section.

"This guy is dipping his shoulder before he swings," he says. "He's in a terrible slump. Too many minor leaguers want to hit homers; they wait for fast balls."

"That's the way to get to the majors," I offer.

On one of my trips down my aisle, I notice that the ball player in the on-deck circle is making a cross in the dirt. Next time he gets up, he does it again.

Attendance: 8,081.

SATURDAY, APRIL 30

Tonight, is the "Copa de la Diversion'" or "Fun Cup," event at DBAP. It is "designed to embrace the culture and values that resonate most with participating teams' local Hispanic/Latino communities."[8] The night is celebrated in eighty-five minor league ballparks in thirty-three states. The Bulls event features "Cervezas de Durham," or the beers of Durham. You can buy hats and T-shirts with a special logo, or quaff a brew from the Bull Durham Beer Co., the only in-stadium brewery in minor league baseball (it disappears later in the season, why I don't know). Doors open thirty minutes early, mariachi music blares from the speakers, a live band plays on a party deck, and the flags of Central and South American countries decorate the seating bowl walkway.

Cervezas de Durham.

When I arrive at the stadium, I wander out to the Diamond View seats. Two guys are there with backpacks collecting the balls that were launched into the stands during batting practice. Last week, I talked with Tom C., a retired director of drug and alcohol rehabilitation facilities who comes to Durham after living previously in New Orleans and Seattle. We're on the walkway when we see someone rushing down the aisle to confront the host collecting balls. We can't hear the talk, but arms are waving, and a finger is pointed to the field. We see a ball retrieved earlier come out of the hosts backpack and get tossed back out on the field. Am I gonna follow his toss-back example and throw the balls I find back on the field? Probably not; I have started carrying a ball or two I come across to give to fans. Just the right fans at just the right moment. It's another "perk" of the job I come to love. Later, I discover that allowing fans to keep balls that go into the stands has a patron saint. Chicago Cubs owner Charles Weeghman, the man who built Wrigley Field in 1914, was the first owner to allow fans to keep balls that went into the stands. This auspicious day, which should be a national holiday, was April 29, 1916.[9]

Ninety minutes before the game starts, I'm sitting down cracking open some salted peanuts, looking out on the field. The fans haven't started filing in yet. Scott, the assistant general manager, sees me and calls me out for sitting and eating, maybe getting peanut shells on the walkway after the clean-up crew worked hard to make things spick-and-span. I'm using a bag

---

8   https://www.milb.com/fans/copa

9   https://www.wbur.org/hereandnow/2011/03/24/collect-baseballs

to catch the peanut refuse, but Scott is absolutely right—I'm on the clock and shouldn't be lounging. Rookie mistake, not gonna happen again.

Today, I have the section directly behind home plate. (While cleaning my seats, a bird poops on my hat. Maybe I'll keep track of how often this happens.) At the back of my section are eight seats for fans with limited mobility. Six are occupied, five by women. Not surprisingly, they know each other well. Their first conversation is about where you can watch or listen to Bulls games on TV or radio this season.

One woman keeps a scorebook. She's so busy talking to seatmates and passersby that when I ask her how many baserunners the Bulls have had she admits that her record is not complete, she'll fix it up watching the game replay when she gets home.

But the real star in my section sits next to her. She greets a constant stream of visitors, including cops who, for a moment, drop their stoic visage to smile and hug her. Seems she worked at the Duke Medical Center but also spent over thirty years working for the Bulls. She tells me she worked at the old ballpark and, yes, she was there when "the movie" was filmed.

Another attraction tonight is Ripken, the bat dog. Ripken is a black Labrador Retriever who runs out from the Bulls' dugout, grabs bats tossed by players, and carries them back to his handler. His web page (seems everyone has a webpage) informs me that Ripken is a Spokesdog in addition to being a Bat Dog. His hobbies are "Fetching Bats, Fetching Frisbees, Fetching Sticks, Fetching Balls, Fetching . . ." He likes "Frisbees, Hugs, Squeaky Toys, Cleaning up food from under the kitchen table. He dislikes squirrels."[10]

Seat scavengers are a big issue in the prime seating sections. I'm learning how to spot them. People with assigned seats act in a particular way. They say hello to the usher, ask for help, or go swiftly to their seats.

Scavengers act differently, at least the ones who get caught; they act tentatively. This leads me to offer some advice for successful seat scavenging. Here you go:

1. Wait until after the third inning. Most folks are seated by then and you're less likely to occupy a seat that the real occupants will show up for.
2. Don't stand at the top of the aisle and look for seats in the two adjacent sections. Stand a section or two away from where you want to land and look from there.
3. Pick out exactly the seats you're gonna head for.
4. Walk briskly to your chosen seats, don't look at the host if you don't have to.
5. If you get caught, be polite (please) and leave quickly. Head to the other side of the ballpark and try again.
6. If you strike out twice, give up. It's not your night.

It's the top of fifth and Steve, who's manning the section next to me, tells me he isn't feeling well and wants to go home. Can I cover for him? Sure. The next day,

The best fans of all.

---

10 https://www.milb.com/durham/fans/ripken

he texts me to say he went home and watched the end of the game. He saw me on TV. A text. Am I making a friend?

Lisa has the next section over, so I take the opportunity to visit with her. She works in the financial aid office at Duke and is training to be a freshman counselor. Working remotely is not meeting her need to be with people, which is what motivated her to take this job with the Bulls. She's a rookie too.

She offers, "I suggested that the Bulls stop wearing their white uniforms, they always seem to lose in them."

Tonight, to recognize Copa de la Diversion, the Bulls are wearing bright, neon green jerseys.

I counter, "That's superstitious behavior. I suggest they never wear these green jerseys again. They're just plain ugly."

This leads to a discussion of superstitious behavior. We agree that baseball players are the most superstitious athletes of all. The plot of movie *The Fan* involves a fan's obsession with the effect of a player's uniform number on the player's performance. In the real majors, Nomar Garciaparra made a name for himself because of the complex ritual he performed between pitches. Irate fans (not Boston Red Sox fans, for whom Nomar was an outstanding shortstop) complained that his ritual was responsible for slowing down the game.

Do you remember that "Nuke" Laloosh in *Bull Durham* wore a women's garter belt provided by Annie when he pitched (meant to keep his mind slightly off center, something needed by pitchers and artists)? One Bulls player in the movie blessed his bat and another had a glove that was supposedly haunted. Most importantly, a critical plot device involves Nuke abstaining from having sex with Annie until his winning streak ends.

Is this last one a superstition? Does having sexual relations affect athletic performance? The scientific evidence is scant and not of the highest quality. Still, a review of seven decent studies suggested that "having sex at least 10–12 hours before athletic events does not negatively influence physiological test results and possibly athletic performance. However, having sex immediately or a few hours before a competition has negative psychological or physiological effects on athletic performance."[11] Good thing Nuke, Annie, and Crash didn't know this. Who knows how differently their story might have ended.

ROGER MARIS, BALONEY AND EGGS

Perhaps the most famous superstition behavior was enacted by Roger Maris in 1961 as he pursued, and eventually broke, Babe Ruth's one-season home run record. David Halberstam relates:*

As the pressure closed in on him, [Maris] became more and more superstitious. Early in the season he had Julie Isaacson drive out to Queens to pick him up, and they went into Manhattan and ate a late breakfast at the Stage Deli, a famous New York Jewish deli in the theater district. Maris, who loved eggs and baloney, forced Big Julie to have eggs with chopped up baloney in it. "Roger, Jewish guys don't eat baloney and eggs," Isaacson protested, but Maris insisted that Isaacson eat his eggs in what he claimed was Fargo style. Isaacson, knowing how stubborn Maris could be, surrendered and ate his eggs and baloney. That day Maris hit two home runs. Clearly, the eggs and baloney were an omen, and so from then on, they had go to the Stage every day when the Yanks were home, and they had to have the same table, and the same waitress, and Big Julie had to eat his eggs and baloney.

* Halberstam, D. (1994). *October 1964*. New York, NY: Random House.

---

[11] http://aassjournal.com/browse.php?a_code=A-11-581-1&slc_lang=en&sid=1

A mom sitting in Steve's section has taken her daughters to get some snacks. She returns frantically.

She runs up to me. "One of my daughters is lost! Has she come back here?"

"No. I can watch out for her here. You need to go to Guest Services."

Lisa agrees to escort the mom to Guest Services while I watch her section.

Eventually, the girl is found. Turns out that as she walked back to her seat with her mom she was looking around and then accidentally followed the wrong people. Somehow, she made it to the service entrance of the ballpark and an employee took her to Guest Services. Lisa and I agree that this is every parent's worst nightmare. When children old enough to get lost are taken to large, crowded venues, they should know exactly what to do should they get lost. Many kids wear wristbands with vital information. We are relieved this episode ended safely.

I wait for the ballplayer who made a cross in the dirt by the warm-up circle last night to get up again. Sure enough, he performs his ritual again. I point this out to Lisa who walks down to see the marking. She returns with a smile and exclaims, "Superstitious behavior!"

The interesting thing about superstitions is that, by definition, they are based on a false belief in causality. Purely by chance, the superstitious behavior occurred before an event the person wants to happen again or thinks a bad event can be prevented if the superstitious behavior is carried out (like not stepping on a crack in the sidewalk). The word has been around since the thirteenth century and began with an association to magic. Clearly, superstitious behavior is a deeply rooted part of human psychology and is hard to extinguish.

"I agree that superstitious behavior won't improve the chances that an event will happen," I suggest to Lisa, "but will *not* performing the ritual *decrease* the chance it will happen? If you were managing the player drawing the cross, would you tell him to stop?" (In the *Bull Durham* movie, Crash does tell Nuke to stop wearing the women's garter belt.)

An EMT who works the stadium comes by. He laments the Bulls pitching: "If the Rays ever get their act together and some better pitchers come back here, things will get better."

"The hitting has stunk also," I say.

"Yes, but once the pitching gets better, I bet the hitting will improve also."

I'm not convinced. "Maybe that works in the majors, but these guys are so close to the big payday, I can't imagine they don't give 110 percent every time they get up."

My payday remark leads to discussion of baseball player salaries. The EMT talks about his young son, just learning about baseball and how he tries to explain to him the economics of the game. "It's a child's game," he says.

"But the money is there," I respond, "that's our fault. I'd rather see it in the pockets of the players than the owners." We agree to continue this conversation at a later date.

As I leave the ballpark, I pull out my phone to clock out. I realize I forgot to clock in. My timecard reads that I was at the park for a minute and made thirty cents. I get help straightening this out. Another rookie mistake.

Attendance: 8,033.

HOME SERIES 2: KIDS AND THE K-WALL

THE BAD NEWS BEARS

Year of Release: 1976
Rating: PG
Director: Michael Ritchie
Writer: Bill Lancaster
Stars: Walter Matthau (coach), Tatum O'Neal (pitcher), Vic Morrow

Plot Synopsis

From Wiki: https://en.wikipedia.org/wiki/The_Bad_News_Bears
The Bad News Bears is a 1976 American sports comedy film directed by Michael Ritchie and written by Bill Lancaster. It stars Walter Matthau as an alcoholic ex-baseball pitcher who becomes a coach for a youth baseball team known as the Bears. Alongside Matthau, the film's cast includes Tatum O'Neal, Vic Morrow, Joyce Van Patten, Ben Piazza, Jackie Earle Haley, and Alfred W. Lutter. Its score, composed by Jerry Fielding, adapts the principal themes of Bizet's opera Carmen.

Released by Paramount Pictures, *The Bad News Bears* received generally positive reviews. It was followed by two sequels, *The Bad News Bears in Breaking Training* in 1977 and *The Bad News Bears Go to Japan* in 1978, a short-lived 1979–80 CBS television series, and a 2005 remake.

From IMDb: https://www.imdb.com/title/tt0074174/?ref_=nv_sr_srsg_0
An aging, down-on-his-luck ex-minor leaguer coaches a team of misfits in an ultra-competitive California little league.

Critic Ratings

Rotten Tomatoes: https://www.rottentomatoes.com/m/1001567-bad_news_bears
Tomatometer: 97 out of 100 (33 reviewers)
Audience Score: 80 out of 100 (25,000+ Ratings)
Critics consensus: *The Bad News Bears* is rude, profane, and cynical, but shot through with honest, unforced humor, and held together by a deft, understated performance from Walter Matthau.
IMDb Rating: 7.3 out of 10 (23,000 raters)
Roger Ebert: https://www.rogerebert.com/reviews/the-bad-news-bears-1976, 3 out of 4 stars.
Ebert writes that *The Bad News Bears* is a "harrowing portrait of how we'd sometimes rather win than keep our self-respect." He is impressed at how director Michael Ritchie juxtaposes comedy with disturbing material.

Chapter 5
Home Series 3: Happy Birthday Wool E. Bull

Baseball isn't just a game. It's the smell of popcorn drifting in the air, the sight of bugs buzzing near the stadium lights, the roughness of the dirt beneath your cleats. It's the anticipation building in your chest as the anthem plays, the adrenaline rush when your bat cracks against the ball, and the surge of blood when the umpire shouts strike after you pitch. It's a team full of guys backing your every move, a bleacher full of people cheering you on. It's . . . life.
—Katie McGarry, author *Dare You To*

Why does everyone stand up and sing 'Take Me Out to the Ballgame' when they're already there?
—Louie Anderson, comedian

GWINNETT

https://en.wikipedia.org/wiki/Atlanta
https://en.wikipedia.org/wiki/Gwinnett_Stripers

Nickname: Stripers
MLB Affilate: Atlanta Braves (2009–present)
Field: Coolray Field, capacity 10,427
Population (2020): 498,715
Economy: transportation, aerospace, logistics, health care, news and media operations, film and television production, information technology, finance, and biomedical research and public policy.
Fun Fact: Since playing in Gwinnett, the team has retired no player numbers but did retire the number of a player and coach for the Richmond Braves, Tommie Aaron (no. 23), brother of Hank.

WEDNESDAY, MAY 11

Equipped with a new cleaning mitt that a buddy (my former boss at Duke, Peter Lange) bought for me to ease wiping off the seats, I head to my sections between the dugout and bullpen on the third base side. On the way, I see a guy sitting in the stands watching batting practice. He has an electronic pad and is taking notes.

I ask, "You a scout?"

"Yes, I am."

"Who do you work for?"

"Miami."

"Are you looking at anyone in particular, or is that classified information?"

"I don't really know anyone. Hopefully, I'll know these players by Sunday."

"Both teams?"

"Yes."

"How long have you been doing this?"

"About thirty-seven years. I was a ball player myself. Made it to Level-A ball."

"Cool. I'll let you do your job."

"Thanks."

He seems relieved that I'm gonna leave him alone.

The author and his nifty cleaning mitt.

I see someone who is checking two small, stationary cameras that are attached to the railing on the walkway that separates the sections closest to the field (the 100s) from those just above (the 200s). I ask whether these are the cameras that capture live action for the broadcast of the game.

"No," the gentleman says, "These record the game. The players use the video to maybe help them improve their swing. The live feed cameras are just outside the dugouts, above the stands at home, and in centerfield."

I can see the recording cameras are also behind home plate and above the two dugouts. There are two cameras at each station, so I assume one takes an image closer to the batter and one an image a little farther away.

Today, I find seven (count 'em, seven!) balls in the stands. I notice that five balls are inscribed with, "Official Major League Baseball" and are signed by the MLB commissioner, Robert D. Manfred Jr. I look him up when I get home. Seems he grew up near the Baseball Hall of Fame in Cooperstown, New York, and took over as commissioner in 2015. He graduated from Harvard Law School and his primary expertise is in labor relations. No surprise there. Bud Selig, the commissioner before him, hired Manfred and put him in charge of developing MLB's revenue sharing agreement, called the Competitive Balance Tax. Baseball owners claim the tax that wealthier teams pay when their payroll exceeds a threshold is meant to improve the league's competitive balance. Players say it's a salary cap. This is big business.

Though Manfred seems to be a lawyer through and through, he has worked in baseball since the late 1980s.[1] The 2022 season was in jeopardy when the owners locked the players out on December 2, 2021. Manfred was vilified in the press. Eventually, labor

---

[1] https://www.mlb.com/official-information/commissioners/manfred

peace was restored but not before the first two series of the season were cancelled and rescheduled so that a full 162-game season would be played (and players paid in full).

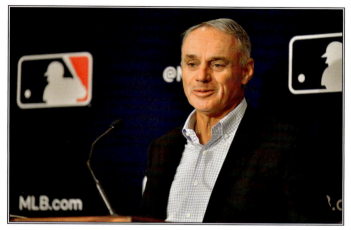

Robert D. Manfred Jr., MLB commissioner.

No more game action for these two.

Another one of the balls I find is tattooed with "Official Ball International League, Randy Mobley, president." Mobley's been IL president since 1990. That's a long time. Another ball is from the Florida State League, a Level-A circuit. The ball says Ken Carson is president. He retired following the 2019 season.[2] This one makes me wonder how the ball traveled here, kinda like the movie "Twenty Bucks" that followed a twenty-dollar bill as it made its way through the hands of a colorful cast of characters.[3]

There is a stand on the walkway near my sections that dispenses alcoholic beverages. The bartender, Greg, handles one of seven "bars" located throughout the park. He's been doing this at DBAP for eight years. He says the bartenders rotate but this is his permanent station.

"Somebody wrote a recommendation that said nice things about me."

For twenty-five years, Greg was the event coordinator for the United States Table Tennis Association. He traveled the world and loved it, but he says with a note of regret, "I didn't see much of my kids when they were growing up. Now, I'm living the dream."

He's the second DBAP employee who has used that phrase when describing their job. I ask if he mixes drinks and has any bartender training.

"I do rum and coke. Nothing fancy," he says.

Tonight, the national anthem is played by an electric guitarist. Pretty good, but unlike Jimi Hendrix's rendition at Woodstock, there are no bombs bursting in air.

Two fans ask me where they can get scorecards.

"You can pick one up at Guest Services," I respond.

There is a QR code on the back of every other seat that can be scanned for an electronic copy of the Bulls' "Playball" that has lots of information on the players and lets you order food for pickup, but you can't get a scorecard this way.

At Guest Services I'm told, "There are lots of apps that give downloadable scorecards. Most folks who keep score want a printed copy, though."

---

2 https://www.milb.com/press-release/florida-state-league-president-ken-carson-to-retire-following-2019-sea-301167000

3 https://en.wikipedia.org/wiki/Twenty_Bucks

A group of four fans sit right beside my station. They display noticeable exuberance when a particular player gets up to bat. Later, I learn they have a fantasy baseball team. Apparently, you can draft prospects who are still in the minors for your fantasy team. The player they are cheering for had a brief stint in the majors earlier in the season. I think they want to help him get back to the Rays.

I spot a mom in my section who is at the game with three boys, all under the age of six. She gets a baseball, after the boys promise to share.

Attendance: 5,343.

FRIDAY, MAY 13

I have dinner with Josh and another host who hails from northern Ohio, a five-year veteran of the hosting crew. Before retirement, he was a middle school teacher, worked in a machine shop, sold loading dock equipment, and taught in college.

I'm hosting the same section tonight as my previous game, between the visitor's dugout and bullpen. I see a television engineer adjusting the large camera that sits on a concrete pad just outside the dugout. I approach and ask him if this is a camera for the live feed. He says yes and offers that there are six such cameras around the stadium.

"Does the feed go to a central minor league headquarters where it is edited before broadcast?" I ask. I'm thinking of those shots of production facilities I've seen on TV and in the movies where the producer looks over several camera feeds and shouts out which one should be selected for broadcast.

"No," the engineer replies, "the feed comes from the press box right here."

Then he offers, "The Scouts do all the production tasks."

I learn that twenty-five years ago, the Bulls owner, Jim Goodmon, created the Explorer Post 50 program. The program gives adolescents aged fourteen to twenty the "invaluable opportunity to explore a career in television, gain hands-on experience, develop leadership skills, learning to work under pressure, teamwork, and much more."[4] The scouts get experience at nine different positions needed to produce

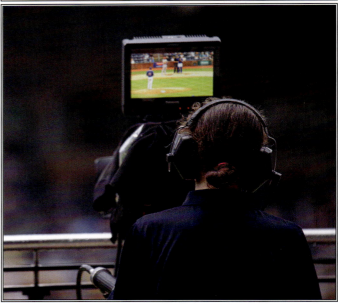

The scouts produce the Bulls' telecasts.

---

4 https://www.milb.com/durham/ballpark/explorer-post

a live TV program. This seems natural for the Bulls, given that their parent company also owns the local NBC affiliate, WRAL and the Fox affiliate (Channel 50). There are at least four ways you can watch the Bulls, over the air, on cable, and streaming.

The starting pitcher tonight is Josh Fleming. Except for one bad pitch that ends up over the centerfield wall, he has a strong first inning. Josh the host informs me that Fleming was just in the majors and "probably has a chip on his shoulder." Sure enough, Fleming had a 2–3 record with the Rays to start the season, an earned run average of 6.38 in 18.1 innings pitched. Not great, but tonight that homer would be the only hit he gives up in five innings, striking out five. I wish Fleming luck, but also hope the Rays pitchers stay healthy. The Bulls can use this guy.

It's the top of the second, no one on. The Gwinnett batter swings and launches a screaming line drive down the third base line. The only problem is he missed the ball and lost control of his bat. The bat is airborne until it hits the protective netting behind the bullpen, about six feet above the wall. I've never seen any bat travel so far at such velocity. I will never question the wisdom of extending the protective netting. The third base coach comes over, retrieves the bat, and scoots it under the netting to give it to a girl, maybe three years old, sitting in the first row where the bat hit the fence.

An EMT shows up and asks me if everyone is okay. I say yes. The paramedic tells me everyone calls him "Opie" because he used to have bright red hair and was skinny as a rail. He's been working for the Bulls since they were a Level-A team. When he's not working the ballpark, he is a flag man at auto racing tracks. Worked the Indy 500 once.

There's no school tomorrow and there are fireworks after the game (that happens every Friday and most Saturdays). I wasn't prepared for what that meant. Lots of kids have come to the game. By the fifth inning, some kids start to clog the walkway and the aisles leading down to the dugout and bullpen, about thirty in all, most with gloves, jumping, yelling, and generally annoying all the patrons in my sections. This will happen every time the Bulls are up. The kids want balls from the visiting team as they leave the field when the inning is over. Of course, the players occasionally launch a ball over the netting, sending the kids into a frenzy. I've got to shoo them away.

One boy I try to hustle away tells me, "A man said we could stand here."

"Which man?"

The kid runs away. I feel like a real heel knowing what a super part of growing up hawking baseballs can be. Then, a patron thanks me for my (fruitless) effort at improving their experience. It makes me feel a bit better.

I notice a dad with two young boys. One is well-behaved but the other goes on several crying jags. As they get up to leave, I hand the dad a ball. He breaks out in a wide grin and tells me it's his well-behaved son's sixth birthday and this is a great present (the kid is wearing an "I'm 6!" T-shirt). In the time he looked away to talk to me, the crying son has run off. Dad thanks me again and takes off after him.

The protective netting prevents an injury.

Attendance: 6,081.

SATURDAY, MAY 14

For my third game in a row, I host the same section between the visitor's dugout and bullpen. To my right, the host is a retired schoolteacher, principal, and two-year seating host veteran. He seems a bit older than most hosts, which by my estimation puts him in his mid-to-upper seventies. He grew up in Detroit and attended many Tigers games as a boy. He relates the story of helping the ushers at Tigers games by doing small tasks, wiping seats and so on.

With a broad smile he tells me, "The ushers would give us tips for helping." Now, he's the usher.

It rained before the game and there are still puddles under many of the seats. I notice a mess of soggy french fries and napkins under one of my seats and head out in search of someone with a broom and dustpan. No one in sight. A while later, I spy Scott sweeping water off the walkway. I mention my mess to him.

"Go get some napkins and we'll clean it up," he says. Of course, I remember "efficiency" from the orientation meeting.

Returning with the napkins, Scott sweeps the fries into a pile, and I scoop them up.

"Tag team," Scott says with a smile.

I point out to him there is water on the steps leading up to the second deck. He takes off and starts sweeping. I take off to dispose of the fries . . . and wash my hands.

I've seen Scott, the Operations Assistant General Manager, sweeping floors, riding various machines on the field, using a blower on the concourse, and manicuring the field, touching things up in general. A stuffed suit, he's not. But he's not alone; this is business as usual in baseball.

Scott and I pass each other in the tunnel.

"'preciate it," Scott says to me.

I feel some vindication after my rookie mistake a few nights earlier. I think I'm starting to get the message; treat this place like it was your own home, and the fans are your guests in it. That I can do.

About ninety minutes before the game starts, four adults and a young girl with a mouthful of braces, standing beside her father, are patiently waiting by the visitor's dugout with baseballs and books in hands. One woman, wearing a "Laloosh" T-shirt, holds a book filled with baseball cards.

"Collecting autographs?" I ask the group.

All agree.

"Anyone in particular you after?"

Delino Deshields Jr. is their prime target. He's the son of a former well-known major leaguer, now a coach with the Cincinnati Reds.

An older gentleman, Pete, with a gray ponytail and full beard informs me that Deshields, like so many other players, has a ritual during the game.

"He runs straight from the dugout to the foul line, then down the line until he's in the outfield." Superstition?

"I guess if you get a card signed by a future star, it might get valuable," I say.

Pete interjects, "The value of the card goes down. It's no longer clean and you can't verify that the autograph is real." I stand corrected.

Thirty minutes later there are nine fans at the gate. Deshields does stop and sign autographs. As the game begins, the autograph hounds disperse.

"How many you get?" I ask one hound.

"About eight, not bad but not great."

Early in the game, the host next to me approaches

a young girl in the stands. She has flaming red hair and he touches it. Not a great idea to touch a fan, but the girl and her folks seem undisturbed. He walks over to me and says the girl's hair reminds him of his mother's.

Turn Back the Clock night at DBAP, April 13, 2019.

"Were you a red head, too?" I ask.

The host doffs his cap. His hair is white, not gray, with a clear orange tint.

In the third inning I catch (on a bounce) my first foul ball during a game. I give it to a three-year-old girl sitting between her parents. Mom and dad both beam. I'm pleased that my strategy of giving balls to kids who are at the game with their parents is a good one. It makes multiple people happy, and after all, mom and dad buy the tickets.

"It's her first ballgame," the dad says.

Two guys in my section are wearing Durham Tobacconist jerseys. That was the nickname of the Durham team for a year in the early 1900s. The jerseys are an awesome shade of deep crimson. They were issued a few years back when the Bulls donned them for a turn-back-the-clock promotion.[5] I tell the guys their jerseys are really cool. They say they got the last two. Sure enough, there ain't none in the team shop and the team's online shopping link selling them is out of commission. Can't even find one on eBay. I'm disappointed.

The clothing people wear to the ballpark ranges from casual to slobbish. A small but noticeable plurality of T-shirts make some mention of the ball team. By category, I'd say patriotic T-shirts are also very popular, especially ones that give a shout-out to a branch of the military. Once a game, the PA announcer asks military veterans to stand for a round of applause.

Curiosity leads me to look up some stats. In mid-July 2021, North Carolina had thirty-six percent registered Democrats, thirty percent registered Republicans, and thirty-three percent unaffiliated voters. A blog titled "Hotline on Call" by Reid Wilson[6] used data from a survey of 218,000 interviewees in 2008–2009. It suggests football, auto racing, and golf fans tend to skew Republican. Baseball fans are pretty much down the center and minor league

---

5 https://www.milb.com/news/durham-bulls-turn-back-clock-as-tobacconists-306341854

6 https://web.archive.org/web/20100402234855/http://hotlineoncall.nationaljournal.com/archives/2010/03/sports_viewers.php

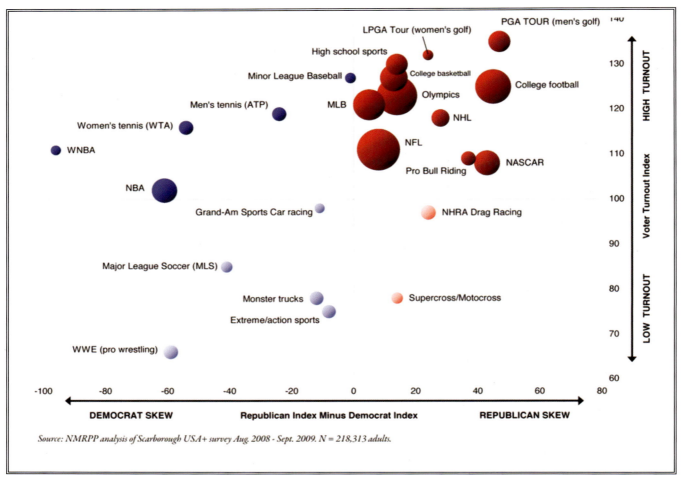

Political affiliations of sports fans.

fans are among the most likely to vote. About half of respondents attended an amateur or professional sports event. (More recent surveys have not included minor league baseball.)

The game outcome is decided early when Isaac Paredes hits a two-run homer for the Bulls in the bottom of the first. The Stripers would only get two hits all game. Paredes has just returned from a week in the majors. He went five for nineteen at the plate for the Rays. He's not a stranger to the bigs, accumulating nearly 200 at-bats over his seven-year career.

The Bulls' win brings their longest winning streak of the season to three. The game lasts only two hours and six minutes, an hour shorter than we've come to expect. My feet are thankful.

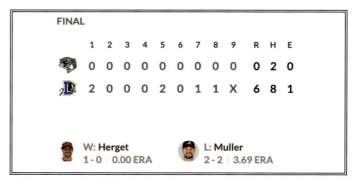

Attendance: 7,634.

HOME SERIES 3: HAPPY BIRTHDAY WOOL E. BULL

SUNDAY, MAY 15

Today I'm working the terrace boxes. Located just foul of right field and in front of the popular Jackie's Landing bar. Leigh has worked here a few times and tells me that the fans are fun. The boxes accommodate eight or twelve fans and adjacent boxes can be rented to hold even larger parties. Four attached seats are arranged around a half-moon table and there are movable chairs in each box. This arrangement makes the boxes attractive to fans who want to "upgrade" their seats during the game even though they should be sitting elsewhere. "It's easy to shoo people away if the boxes are sold out," Leigh says, "if not, you may be chasing people away."

It's the Bulls' mascot Wool E. Bull's birthday celebration. Mr. Bull is six foot six inches tall and weighs 409 pounds. His middle initial stands for "Education" selected from a pool of over five hundred suggested names. He was born in April 1992 but wasn't named until July. His favorite jewelry is rings, but he doesn't have one in his nose. His hobbies include gardening (that is, grazing in the outfield), collecting baseball cards, and polishing championship rings. He dislikes losing streaks and anything that is red. Mr. Bull is also a pretty good blues/rock drummer. Okay, a great drummer—I'm not one to anger a four-hundred-pound bull.

Wool E. is a full-time employee of the Bulls. You can host Mr. Bull at your party or event, for a fee of course, unless you are a nonprofit group. Kids can become a Wool E. Bull All-Star. You can contact him directly, but you can't interview Mr. Bull directly—he doesn't speak—however, you can query him through an interpreter.

In 2016, *Baseball America* named Wool E. the best minor league mascot. His website also says he's won the Daytona 500 Go-Kart race. Late in every game, he races his kart around the warning track and does a wheelie that always gets a cheer from the crowd. His website proclaims him the most accurate T-shirt

Wool E. Bull plays the drums.

shooter in the minor leagues. I await verification of this accolade.

To help Mr. Bull celebrate his birthday, about a dozen mascots from around the area have come to his party. They congregate for cake at Jackie's Landing before the game starts. Everyone in the park is invited to come have a piece of cake. The mascots are in attendance for party games and cake. None have cake. Not sure how they'd do that.

I am forced to wear a party hat. Outraged, I complain to my boss.

Wool E. Bull's birthday party.

"This is an affront to my dignity!"

"Hey, I'm wearing one too!" is the response.

The first arrivals sit right in front of me. Seems there's also a birthday boy at the Little School in Hillsboro, North Carolina, who has invited his friends to celebrate with him at the ballpark. I stop counting after about eighteen toddlers have arrived with about a dozen adults. Pizza and cupcakes for all. They are generally well-behaved until about the seventh inning, when wrestling matches break out, stairwell rails become climbing gyms, and keep-away games send multiple stuffed Wool E. Bull dolls into the air. Down a few rows is another toddler invasion. About a dozen are here with a church group for yet another birthday party. Best I can tell, absolutely no attention is paid to the ball game, not by the rug rats or their parents who, rather than monitor the kids closely, talk to one another. I doubt most of the toddlers even know they are at a ballgame.

The preschoolers are not the only field trippers occupying the terrace. A baker's dozen of employees from Monut's Donuts in Durham are also in attendance. I sense some are actually taking in the action on the field.

After the second inning, a party game on the field pits Wool E. against three other mascots from the Raleigh–Durham Triangle area in a race around the bases. The competitors are the Duke Blue Devil, the University of North Carolina's Ramses, and the Carolina Hurricanes' Stormy.

Mr. Bull takes off down the third base line. The other three head to first to run in the opposite direction. First to make it back to home plate wins. When Stormy reaches first, he inexplicably continues to run into right field. Blue Devil and Ramses round first and head for second. By the time they get to the base, they are engaged in a shoving match and are making no progress at all. The fierce rivalry between these two schools even affects their mascots! The two stall behind second base, seemingly too occupied with their tussle to continue the race. The birthday boy rounds second, then first, and heads home. He wins! This is perfect shtick for North Carolina Triangle fans. Long after the game, thinking of it still brings a smile to my face.

Today's game also provided my first medical emergencies. It seems someone spit up, and the mop man stops by to ask where he can find the seat. I take him to the aisle. I can't tell if the perpetrator was a toddler or a tippler. It's gone quickly. Later, a woman slips off a step and twists her ankle. Three EMTs arrive and spend a good deal of time ensuring she is all right. When they leave, she leaves as well. This is the only physical injury I will encounter.

After the game, the kids get to run the bases. All the toddlers head down to the field for a trip from home to third. Please stay on the dirt.

The game? Oh yeah, there is also a baseball game. The Bulls win for the fourth time in a row. They have risen to mediocrity (won 16, lost 20). Is this the beginning of something good?

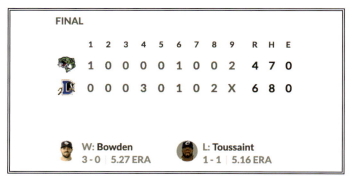

Attendance: 7,040.

THE SANDLOT

Year of Release: 1993
Rating: PG
Director: David Mickey Evans
Writers: David Mickey Evans, Robert Gunter
Stars: Tom Guiry (center fielder), Mike Vitar (right fielder), Arl LaFleur (The Babe), James Earl Jones (Mr. Mertle; retired baseball player)

Plot Synopsis

From Wiki: https://en.wikipedia.org/wiki/The_Sandlot
In the summer of 1962, brainy, shy fifth-grader Scott Smalls moves to a Los Angeles suburb, where his mother encourages him to make friends in the neighborhood . . . he is invited to join the team by their leader and best player, Benny Rodriguez, who teaches him the basic skills needed to play the game.

With [his father] away on business, Smalls borrows a baseball from his trophy room, which happens to be autographed by legendary player Babe Ruth, . . . and hits his first home run, sending (the ball) into the Beast's yard. The next day Benny goes over the fence and "pickles" the Beast to retrieve the ball . . . They meet Mr. Mertle. . . . He kindly trades them the chewed-up ball for one autographed by all of the 1927 New York Yankees, and asks them to visit every week to talk baseball with him. Smalls gives this ball to Bill, and their father-son relationship improves. . . . The boys continue to play baseball on the sandlot, with the Beast—whose real name is Hercules—as their mascot.

From IMDb: https://www.imdb.com/title/tt0108037/
In the summer of 1962, a new kid in town is taken under the wing of a young baseball prodigy and his rowdy team, resulting in many adventures.

Critic Ratings

Rotten Tomatoes: https://www.rottentomatoes.com/m/sandlot
Tomatometer: 64 out of 100 (59 reviewers)
Audience Score: 89 out of 100 (250,000+ Ratings)
Critics consensus: It may be shamelessly derivative and overly nostalgic, but *The Sandlot* is nevertheless a genuinely sweet and funny coming-of-age adventure.
IMDb Rating: 7 out of 10 (89,000 raters)
Roger Ebert: https://www.rogerebert.com/reviews/the-sandlot-1993, 3 out of 4 stars.
Ebert writes that "This is not your standard movie about kids and baseball." Rather than being about the outcome of a game, it's about maturing and confronting your fears. As the movie progresses Ebert thinks it gradually losses its realism and takes on the characteristics of childhood mythology.

Chapter 6
Home Series 4: Things are Looking Up

Baseball is a game where a curve is an illusion, a screwball can be a pitch or a person, stealing is legal, and you can spit anywhere except in the umpires' eye or on the ball.
—James Patrick Murray, journalist

A baseball game is simply a nervous breakdown divided into nine innings.
—Earl Wilson, columnist

CHARLOTTE

https://en.wikipedia.org/wiki/Charlotte,_North_Carolina
https://en.wikipedia.org/wiki/Charlotte_Knights

Nickname: Knights
MLB: Chicago White Sox (1999–present)
Field: Truist Field, capacity 10,200
Population (2020): 874,579
Economy: Banking and finance; motor sports
Fun Fact: For one season, 1900, Charlotte's ball team was nicknamed the Presbyterians.

WEDNESDAY, MAY 25

The Bulls returned home having won eight of their last ten games. Then they win the homestand opener. Things are looking up! I am back in the outfield Diamond View seats. This will be the most sparsely attended game I've worked. I overlook two sections with about nine hundred seats, about thirty of which are occupied. My assignment will be a relatively calm one, but also one with fewer interactions with fans.

Before the game begins and the national anthem is sung, the PA announcer asks for a moment of silence in recognition of a school shooting that happened in Texas the day before, killing nineteen children and two adults. The grim outside world intrudes again.

On my way to my station, I meet another of the few female seating bowl hosts. She's a three-year veteran.

When I ask what else she does to occupy her time, she responds, "I play golf and cards."

"Okay, so what did you do in a previous life?"

"I owned a retail business selling gifts and accessories. I was a schoolteacher but really liked retail."

The highlight of my evening is meeting two fellow employees, both thirty-one years old. But that's where the similarity ends. The first is pushing a cart with plastic bags filled with garbage. His job is to circulate around the walkway, collect full trash bags from the waste receptacles, and replace them with fresh bags. He is gregarious and sports a huge, infectious smile. I've seen him before and noticed that he always has earbuds in.

"What kind of music do you like listening to?"

"Heavy metal, rock, some hip hop."

"Who's playing now?"

"Man Must Die." Never heard of them. I look the band up when I get home and discover they hail from Scotland and play techno death metal music.

"What else do you listen to?"

"Lamb of God. I really like them. And Slipknot." Finally, a band I've heard of. The contrast between my new friend's big smile and his music taste confuses me.

"Not real happy music," I say. He smiles.

A few minutes earlier, the loudspeakers had blared Sly and the Family Stone doing their biggest hit "Everyday People."

"Do you like Sly Stone?"

"Who?"

"It was just on the loudspeakers." I cackle the chorus. "You know, the song they played at Woodstock."

"Woodstock? Is that a group?"

My friend, you're making me feel old.

The other thirty-one-year-old also patrols the walkway, but he carries a sign hoisted on a pole that reads "How May I Help You?" He is one of three floaters who assist fans. He is tall, muscular, and sports a neatly trimmed beard. He can stop to talk since there aren't many fans out here and everyone has settled into their seats.

Plenty of help.

HOME SERIES 4: THINGS ARE LOOKING UP

This new friend is also a DBAP rookie. His day job is as a general contractor. I ask him why he took the ballpark gig.

"To prevent boredom," he says, "If I wasn't here, I'd be home on my couch."

His blasé response is belied by his extensive knowledge of baseball. He hails from upstate New York and tells me of his numerous trips to see the Yankees. We also talk about the infield shift rule and, relatedly, the lost art of bunting.

"What's the most ridiculous question a fan has asked you?" I inquire.

He responds, "It amazes me how fans can ask where their seats are when they are standing right in front of them."

He also shares this exchange with a fan: "And then there's, 'What should I eat?' How the heck am I supposed to know what you should eat!? I tell them, 'The tacos are really good, they're over there.' Then they say, 'Nah, that's too far away. What else is there?' Gimme a break!"

Before he walks away, he hands me his business card.

A fan strolls by. I suspect he is heading back to his seats after catching a smoke out on the street. You can't smoke or vape in the stadium, but a pregame announcement tells fans they can leave the ballpark for a smoke and return. So far, I've only seen one fan sneaking puffs on a vape he had hidden under his jacket.

Mr. Smoker stops and says, "Hey, these seats are pretty good."

"There's not a bad seat in the house," I reply.

Mr. Smoker bemoans the fact that he and his wife are sitting behind the protective netting. He wanted to catch a ball for his grandson but it ain't gonna happen. I relate to him the story of the flying bat that hit the netting above a little girl a few nights before. I pull a ball from my pocket and tell him he can have it for his grandchild if he promises never to complain about the netting again. His eyes get wide, and he thanks me for the ball.

Two young female employees stop near my station and watch the game. I approach them and ask if they are interns. They smile.

"No, we're adults," they respond snidely. "We work year-round with companies that are Bulls' sponsors."

One young lady's job is to work as a "prospector." She seeks out new businesses that might want to advertise on the walls of the stadium or sponsor an event. The other is an "activator." She works with sponsors once they've signed up. Part of their job is to work an occasional ballgame.

Mr. Smoker strolls by again, on his way for another puff, I guess. He tells me that while he was away a ball came over the netting and was caught by a guy just a row in front of his seat. The guy who got the ball was from Lithuania and was attending his first baseball game. "Good for him," he says.

The Bulls win the game 1–0 on a solo home run. They have now reached .500 and are in the top half of the league standing.

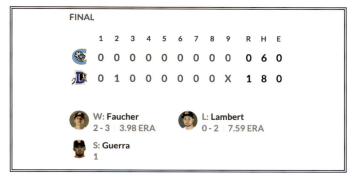

Attendance: 3,856.

FRIDAY, MAY 27

It is pouring rain and I didn't bring my raincoat. I sprint from my car to the stadium and arrive soaked and sweaty. On the field, there are blowers under a tarp protecting the infield. You don't see these if a rain delay occurs during the game, so this is new to me. I assume the blowers are there to puff up the tarp and get the water to the drains in the outfield. Good idea, but now the left field grass looks like a small lake. Not to worry, the drainage system works superbly. Ten minutes after the rain stops, about an hour before game time, the outfield grass looks dry as a bone.

I go to check the seats in my two sections, again in left field foul territory. My 238 seats are all dripping water. It takes me forty-five minutes to wipe them all down. "Pretend this is good exercise," I repeat to myself. Bend down, wipe two seats, stand up, wring the towel dry, shuffle over two seats, repeat 119 times. I aggravate my thumb injury again on the seat arms. I'll keep my (minimal) pain to myself. Don't wanna get benched. I'm a pro.

The host to the right of me is Wayne, a four-year veteran. He is a former kitchen manager for a county nursing home in upstate New York. Thanks to working for the government, he was able to retire at age fifty-five after twenty years of service. He and his wife (a schoolteacher who also retired early) moved to North Carolina to be near family.

In addition to working the Bulls games, Wayne works the luxury boxes at Duke football games and, get this, patrols the aisles at Duke basketball games. This means Wayne has season tickets to the most prized arena in college sports. Season tickets to Duke basketball cost thousands of dollars. He is courtside—and Duke pays him.

I'm getting a sense now that there is a subculture among the seating bowl hosts. These are people who have a passion for all sports, not just baseball, and want to be close to the action. Wayne wins the award for best gigs in town.

Each game, a child is chosen to come onto the field and yell "play ball." Today, a little girl in her dad's arms is supposed to do it. Ain't gonna happen. After some failed coaxing, Dad issues the call. Two innings later, it's time for Wool E. Bull's footrace around the bases. His competition is a three-year-old boy who is much more interested in seeing his image on the jumbo screen than running the bases. By the time he gets to third he appears exhausted and is practically running backward while looking out at the screen on the left field wall.

"I was worried we'd be here all night watching this kid run the bases," I say to Wayne.

"You'd think they'd know not to pick kids too young to understand what's going on," he responds.

A few innings later the Dizzy Bat Competition is held. Two fans must hold a bat upright, put their forehead on the top of the grip, spin around ten times, then run to a finish line, wobbling all the way. Tonight, the contestants are two young women in matching yoga pants and crop tops. I think all eyes are now on the jumbo screen, except maybe that three-year-old baserunner.

The starting Bulls pitcher, Easton McGee, pitches four perfect innings, striking out seven.

Wayne comes by to tell me about another no-hitter he was at that was broken up right after someone he was with mentioned it. This is a no-no among the baseball superstitious. McGee is taken out at the start of the fifth inning. The first batter is hit by a pitch, the next singles. Wayne comments, "I did it." More superstition.

Wayne and I talk about how we are supervised during games. I suggest, somewhat facetiously, "I suspect there's someone in the luxury boxes with binoculars, writing down demerits for us."

"No way," counters Wayne.

During games, full-time operations staff and interns circle the stadium and often check in with me, asking, "How's it going?"

A fan asks, "Do players really get a steak if they hit the Snorting Bull?"

"Yep, a hundred-dollar gift certificate to Angus Barn."

I have two boys trying desperately to get down to the field to ask for a ball from one of the pitchers sitting in the visiting Charlotte Knight bullpen. These two are a real pain; I scoot them away multiple times before they finally return to their seats in the second deck. But then, one returns with his mother. They stand respectfully on the walkway until the game is over. The boy then approaches a Knights staff member and asks for a ball. He gets it.

It's Friday night so there are fireworks after the game. The light show is delayed for some reason, so the crowd is led in a light show they create. The stadium lights are dimmed, and fans are asked to wave the flashlights on their phones and sing along while "Don't Stop Believin'" by Journey blares over the loudspeakers. I find this more entertaining than the fireworks.

My last task is to retrieve a wheelchair for a fan with limited mobility. Guest Services arrive, and then I'm on my way home to wash my clothes, still wet from the rain.

Attendance: 4,917.

SATURDAY, MAY 28

On the dinner line, I notice about a dozen young adults ahead of me all wearing the Explorer Post 50 polo shirts. Some shirts are black and some dark green, I ask if the different colors signify different jobs on the media production of the ball games.

"No, they just ask what color we what."

Half the group is female, so I tease one: "Are you in the Boy Scouts, don't they admit girls now?" I know that they do, having started to do so in 2017, to the objection of the Girl Scouts. I learn that the Explorer Post and Scouts have some connection, but it is tenuous. Many participants learn of the program from friends or express an interest in media to their school guidance counselors. Most are in high school, but some are freshmen in college. The young lady in front of me with curly, bright orange hair goes to the Durham School of the Arts where she plays in the orchestra.

When I go out to my station, I see another young lady wearing a black staff shirt sitting reading a book.

"What book you reading?" I ask.

She closes the book to show me the cover. The book is a novel titled *Pretending to Dance*, written by Diane Chamberlain.

"Are you a dancer?" I ask.

"I'm studying dance at the Barriskill Dance Theater in Durham."

"What kind of dance do you do?"

"I do them all. I like them all."

She works at Wool E. World, a playground for kids that offers inflatable play areas. I have met two aspiring artists this evening in Bulls polo shirts.

Just before game time, I run into Josh talking with a host I don't know on the walkway. Daryl works for a health-care non-profit that assists people with a rare lung condition, a form of genetic emphysema. He's got it. He works from home on the phone. Daryl mentions that he's a big fan of George Carlin, and there is an excellent Netflix special on his life. I agree that Carlin is a favorite of mine as well, especially his bit on the difference between baseball and football. Josh says he's never heard it. Josh is about twenty-five years younger than me and Daryl, but still I'm taken aback. I thought he knew everything about baseball, however tangential it might be. Dan and I start going through the bit. In case this one has passed you by, I'll save you from embarrassment:

Baseball is pastoral. Football is technological.
Baseball is played in a park. Football is played
  in a stadium.

Baseball . . . has no time limit. We don't know when it's gonna end. Football is rigidly timed. And it will end if we have to even go to sudden death.

Baseball has the bunt. Football has the punt.

Baseball's object is to go home . . . I'm going home! In football, we're down in enemy territory, reaching for the end zone.

In football we have the block, the clip, the kick, the blitz, the bomb, the offense, the defense. In baseball, we have the sacrifice.

And in baseball, you make an error. In football, you pay a penalty.

Woody Hayes wears a baseball hat during the football game. Can you imagine if Walter Allston wore a football helmet during a baseball game. They would truck him away, man. "Get him outta the dugout, man. Check his calendar."

George Carlin.

Josh promises to look up the bit on YouTube. I add Lenny Bruce's name to the conversation. Bruce, much like Carlin, was an advocate for free speech. Daryl brings up Carlin's bit "Seven Words You Can't Say on Television."

"Now you hear them all the time."

"I've heard that bit," says Josh, making a recovery.

I'm patrolling the terrace boxes tonight. In the box in front of me is a crowd of about thirty people ranging from a grandma to a two-year-old whose birthday party it is. The kids, about half the crowd, are generally well-behaved, but the birthday boy's dad says his two-year-old has had a nap and ice cream, so watch out. Dad sets up a barrier so his amped-up charge can't escape the box. Most of the women sit on one side of the birthday box and the men on the other. Two dads are there with three boys, all younger than the birthday boy. The dads and boys make a trip to Wool E. World. Upon return, Dad puts the honoree in his lap and turns cartoons on a tablet. The honoree sticks his thumb in his mouth and is content. I tell the fathers that they deserve a medal for how well they are handling these kids. The birthday boy's dad gets a baseball. "I'll save it until he's old enough to understand," he tells me.

"You deserve it," I say.

The Bulls get clobbered. The Knights' first batter hits a home run on the first pitch. It gets worse from there.

Attendance: 8,334.

SUNDAY, MAY 29

Today, kids get to play catch on the field after batting practice. Of course, the entrance to the field is at my station. Stay on the grass, kids. The game starts in an hour.

The first fan in my section is a young woman attending the game by herself. Throughout the game, no one comes to sit with her.

Catch on the Field Day.

Pete, the autograph hound, is back by the home team dugout this time with about a half dozen other autograph seekers.

An older couple with their grandchildren come and stand behind my station.

"It's still too sunny at our seats," Grandma says.

"Give it 15 minutes, you'll be fine."

Grandpa has a bag of peanuts. He begins shelling them and dropping the shells right in the middle of the walkway behind me.

"Do you have a bag for the shells?" I ask. "Didn't they give you a bag?" A woman walks by with a bag, and I point to her.

"Oh well," Grandpa says, "I only have two hands anyway."

"I'll go get a broom," I say with clear annoyance. Grandma picks up on my irritation. Not Grandpa.

There is no broom in sight for me to use. When I return, the group has moved two sections down and is now using a bag for the shells. Small victory, but I still have a pile of shells where I stand. I'm learning lessons about simple courtesy out here.

Two rows down from where I stand, a small child spits up. Dad doesn't say a word to me and moves quickly with his child to a bathroom. I notice there's still a small mess under the kid's seat. I look for a mop crew and go to inquire at Guest Services. One is sent my way.

Back at the seats, I ask Dad, "Everything okay here?"

"Thanks, we're fine."

Coming back from the restroom, Dad has bought his son a funnel cake. Egad, is this gonna be a long evening? (Thankfully, it's the boy's only incident.)

When the mop shows up, Dad says to forget the clean-up; he already did it. I do ask that the crew sweep up the peanut shells. My station is nice and clean again.

Two brothers who look to be in their sixties are in the seats for fans with mobility issues. One has his ankle in a cast, and he walks with a cane.

The brothers are full of questions about the team, the ballpark, and the city. I'm able to answer them all, which fills me with pride. Yes, I'm turning into a real Bulls nerd. And I love it.

The guy with the cane points to his cast, saying, "Completely new ankle to go with my new knees."

"Most people I know who have joint replacements wonder why it took them so long to get it done," I respond.

He then tells the story of sitting next a guy and his girlfriend at a Pittsburgh ball game who looked a lot like Franco Harris, the legendary Steelers running back and recipient of the "Immaculate Reception."

"I say to him, 'You look a lot like Franco Harris.' The guy replies, 'I get that a lot but I'm much better looking than him.' His girlfriend leans in and tell me, 'He's Franco.'"

Astoundingly, New Ankle Guy tells me he caught a foul ball at the game and Franco signed it for him.

Pete approaches me to snitch on a guy who is vaping a few sections over from me. I walk over to investigate. The guy is at least six feet, four inches tall and a muscular 260 pounds. I don't see him vaping, nor do I smell any smoke. Is Pete trying to get me killed?

Around the fifth inning, an entire little league

team from Virginia invades the walkway, jumping, tossing balls, and generally blocking patrons' views and passage. My attempts to shoo them away is fruitless, as always. I've decided that after cleaning seats, policing twelve-year-old boys is my least favorite part of this job. But I remind myself, their ubiquitous presence is one of the things that makes minor league ball games unique and special.

As the game ends, families line up for "Run the Bases Night." They will enter the field at my station. Please stay off the grass.

In the confusion, the young woman who showed up at five o'clock and sat alone the whole game with an empty seat beside her walks by. I decide to test a theory.

"What ball player are you related to?" I ask.

"No one," she says, "I just haven't been to a ball game since I was twelve."

Good for her.

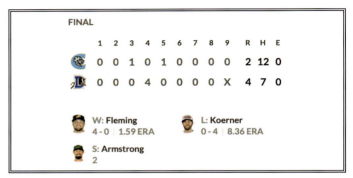

Attendance: 7,316.

THE PERFECT GAME

Year of Release: 2009
Rating: PG
Director: William Dear
Writer: W. William Winokur (book)
Stars: Clifton Collins Jr. (coach), Cheech Marin (Padre)

Plot Synopsis

From Wiki: https://en.wikipedia.org/wiki/The_Perfect_Game
The Perfect Game is a 2009 American drama film directed by William Dear, based on the 2008 book of the same name written by W. William Winokur. The film is based on the events leading to the 1957 Little League World Series, which was won by the first team from outside the United States, the Industrial Little League of Monterrey, Mexico, who defeated the heavily favored US team. Mexican pitcher Ángel Macías threw the first, and so far only, perfect game in championship game history.
From IMDb: https://www.imdb.com/title/tt0473102/?ref_=tt_sims_tt_i_1
Based on a true story, a group of boys from Monterrey, Mexico who became the first non-US team to win the Little League World Series.

Critic Ratings

Rotten Tomatoes: https://www.rottentomatoes.com/m/1197992-perfect_game
Tomatometer: 57 out of 100 (44 reviewers)
Audience Score: 70 out of 100 (10,000+ Ratings)
Critics consensus: Its bogged down with an unfocused script and countless sports movie cliches, but *The Perfect Game* still manages to charm with its unabashed sweetness and a stirring final act.
IMDb Rating: 6.8 out of 10 (3700 raters)
Roger Ebert: https://www.rogerebert.com/reviews/the-perfect-game-2010, 3 out of 4 stars.
Ebert writes that the movie could have been just another flick where the underdog wins. But he thinks it is more, stating the movie "so expertly uses the charisma and personalities of the actors, especially the young ones, that it's thrilling anyway."

Chapter 7
A Brief History of the Not-So-Minor Leagues

In Kansas City, I had a phone in my bathroom. In the Minors, I stayed at a hotel where the fire escape was a rope.
—Tony Torchia, Boston Red Sox coach

I managed a team that was so bad we considered a 2–0 count on the batter a rally.
—Rich Donnelly, Pittsburgh Pirates coach

SOME EXISTENTIAL QUESTIONS

Can you have minor leagues if there is no major league?

Which league is minor and which major? The one that has had teams in 49 of the 50 states of the union[1] or the one with teams in less than half the states? The one that has had teams in 1,400 different cities at one time or another, and currently has 120 to over 200 teams (depending on how you count) or the one with teams in 27 cities, (though, admittedly those cities contain a larger part of the population)? The one that has fielded over 150,000 players or the other for which about 20,075 have taken the field? [2]

Okay, I'm being facetious here, to make a point. Yes, more people attend major league baseball games

---

[1] The Hawaiian Islanders were a Triple-A Pacific coast league team from 1961 to 1987; the Alaska Goldpanners are an amateur team with an impressive roster of players that went on to major league careers, including Barry Bonds, Tom Seaver, and Dave Winfield; https://goldpanners.pointstreaksites.com/view/goldpanners/early-team-history

[2] https://www.ballparksofbaseball.com/2010s-ballpark-attendance/

each year (over 68 million in 2019[3], pre-pandemic, with a high of about 80 million in 2007) than minor league baseball (depending on how you count, about 41 million in 2019;[4] the Bulls ranked 11th out of 160 teams).[5] And, by definition, the majors win on talent.

But baseball teams that traveled to meet other teams have been around a lot longer than what we call major league baseball. And some early amateur ballplayers were even compensated for it, including being on payrolls for nonexistent jobs. Some teams formed leagues to play against one another before the Civil War. For a good part of baseball's history, the "minors" were the only game in town. And in many, many towns, they still are.

RIPPED FROM THE HEADLINES

So, let's take a look at the nearly two-hundred-year history of the minors. Let's rip from the headlines some major milestones written by an overzealous sportswriter (me). Unless otherwise noted, the factual material is taken from seven histories of baseball and the minor leagues.[6] Unless indicated, the news accounts and quotes, of course, are the products of my imagination.

It's Not Cricket. It's Not Rounders. What Is It?

June 20, 1846, Hoboken, New Jersey—A bat and ball game was played yesterday between the New York Knickerbockers and New York Nine. The players guffawed when I asked them if this was the first game of New York rules baseball ever played. They pointed out that inter-club games were frequent in parks of New York City, Brooklyn, and Northern New Jersey for maybe two decades. An inter-club game between New York City and Brooklyn had been played a year earlier.

The ball players are fine, upstanding gentlemen and citizens. Their clubs are formed around the workplace, involving butchers, firemen, market traders, militias, and shipwrights to name a few. Generally, they are members of that new social class that is emerging from America's urban centers.

Base Ball Clubs Form a Governing Body!

1857—Sixteen baseball clubs in the New York City area met and developed standards for the rules of the game, for championships, and for ensuring the integrity of the contests. Until this time, clubs have been deciding on the rules at each game.

10,000 Soldiers and Prisoners Attend Base Ball Game!

Christmas, 1862, Hilton Head, South Carolina—Thousands of Union soldiers and Confederate prisoners attended a baseball game today in the midst of the Civil War. The players were drawn from infantry regiments hailing from New York City. The 165th New York Volunteer Infantry wore some colorful

---

3 https://www.baseball-reference.com/register/league.cgi?year=2021
4 https://www.milb.com/news/taking-a-deeper-look-at-minor-league-attendance-312876304
5 https://ballparkdigest.com/2019/09/09/2019-affiliated-attendance-by-total/
6 Blake, M. (1991). *The Minor Leagues: A Celebration of the Little Show.*
Chadwick, B. (1994). *Baseball's Hometown Teams: The Story of Minor League Baseball.* New York, NY: Abbeville Press.
Gilbert, T.W. (2020). *How Baseball Happened.* Boston, MA: Godine.
Hogan, L.D. ((2006). *Shades of Gray: The Negro Leagues and the History of African-American Baseball.* Washington, DC: National Geographic.
Irvine, A. ((2018). *The Comic Book Story of Baseball.* New York, NY: Ten Speed Press.
Obojski, R. (1975). *Bush Leagues: A Colorful, Factual Account of Minor League Baseball from 1877 to the Present.* New York, NY: Macmillan.
Pietrusza, D. (1995). *Minor Miracles: The Legend and Lore of Minor League Baseball.* South Bend, IN: Diamond Communications.
Zoss, J. & Bowman, J. (1996). *Diamonds in the Rough: The Untold History of Baseball.* Chicago, IL: Contemporary Books.

A BRIEF HISTORY OF THE NOT-SO-MINOR LEAGUES

uniforms—red balloon pants, ornamental cloth jackets, white spats, and fezzes with blue tassels.[7]

"This game of baseball looks interesting," commented one spectator, "I think I'll organize a club when I return home." Confederate prisoners were also intrigued.

Questionable Celebrity Called on to Ump a Game!

February 28, 1864—Two semipro Kansas City teams, the Antelopes and the Pomeroys, known for engaging in fisticuffs on the field and for having fans that drank and fought in the stands, resorted to drastic measures to calm things down. They enlisted the assistance of gunslinger Wild Bill Hickok to serve as umpire. Hickok, a baseball fan, kept his six-shooter at his side throughout the game. A fine and tranquil time was had by all. The Antelopes won the game, 48–28.

First Professional Team Finally Loses a Game!

June 14, 1870—The Cincinnati Red Stockings, the first professional baseball team, completed the 1869 baseball season with a perfect record of 65 wins. However, today they lost their first game in 82 outings when the Red Stockings lost to the Brooklyn Athletics, 8–7.

Cincinnati Red Stockings, 1868.

---

7   https://blogs.fangraphs.com/the-civil-warchristmas-day-game-hilton-head-1862/

George Zettlein was hit by a pitch in the bottom of the eleventh inning and forced in the winning run.[8] "He stepped into the pitch!" cried a Red Stockings fan.

Baseball Minor League Formed!

February 20, 1877, Pittsburgh, Pennsylvania—Following the establishment of the National League last year as the first major circuit for baseball teams, the International League was formalized today when seven teams, including two from Canada, signed an operating agreement. After years of barnstorming, the traveling nines agreed to play one another and keep standings of game outcomes. Games will be played on weekends, as all the players have full-time jobs.

Candy Cummings, a pitcher who has developed a new pitch called a "curve ball" (which some claim is an optical illusion), was named league president.

Upstart American Association Spooks the Senior Circuit!

1883—Want to attend a baseball game for twenty-five cents rather than fifty cents? Want to go on Sunday? Want to buy a beer or spirits at the ballpark? These innovations by the American Association, formed last year, have the National League looking over its shoulder. So much so that the senior circuit is stealing players from the American Association and trying to ruin the AA's reputation by labelling it "The Beer and Liquor Circuit." "Will this moniker hinder or help the junior league?" remarked an astute fan.

Peace Comes Between the National League and American Association!

February 17, 1883—The National Agreement of Professional Base Ball Clubs was ratified by the presidents of the National League, American Association, and signed onto by the Northwestern League. The agreement marks the beginning of professional

---

8   https://en.wikipedia.org/wiki/Cincinnati_Red_Stockings

baseball as a truly organized sport. The "Tripartite Agreement" protects the territories of teams, and all three leagues agree that all player contracts would be considered valid. This prohibits teams from raiding other teams for players or players signing contracts with more than one team. The agreement allows teams to reserve up to eleven players and sets a minimum salary of $1,000. The agreement also establishes an Arbitration Committee to settle any disputes between clubs that are part of the agreement.[9]

Concern was raised by editor of *Sporting Life* Francis Richter that leagues not part of the agreement—now the minor leagues—could still be raided for players by the signees and that this would put upward pressure on salaries. Richter wrote [real quote], ". . . players can get as much salary in a minor league, under less severe discipline and without reservation, as they can in a big league . . ." Richter called for a reserve clause for the minors to be an amendment to the Tripartite Agreement, a suggestion that was looked upon favorably.

Women Invade the Boys Bastion of Baseball!

August 1, 1885—[Real account of a baseball game played at the Polo Grounds in New York City]: The ladies are regular and numerous attendants at the grounds. The hundreds of them who stood on the seats and screamed and waved their handkerchiefs and brandished their fans in ecstasies of applause yesterday know enough to come early and avoid the crush. How much they knew of the game, though none of them ever played, was to be seen by the way they behaved. As they took their seats in the grandstand, they brought out their score cards and pencils, argued of the merits of the coming players, and consulted little diaries, in which they had entered records of the past League games. The rough and blackened finger tips of some of them showed them to be working girls; others, by unmistakable signs, even when they had not their children with them, showed that they were housewives and mothers; others still by their costly dresses and the carriages they came in were seen to be well-to-do women and young girls; and a few were the class of gamblers and sporting women that has grown so considerably in this city of late.

Minor League Baseball Agrees to a Color Line!

July 14, 1887—The International League entered into a "gentlemen's agreement" to ban a Black catcher, Moses Fleetwood Walker, from playing baseball in the league. The agreement follows an incident that happened three years earlier when the Chicago White Stockings refused to play the Toledo Blue Stockings if Moses took the field. Prior to the ban, it is estimated that as many as sixty Black players played on integrated teams.

American League Recognized as a Major League!

Chicago, January 28, 1901—After the National League was reduced to eight teams from twelve, the American League has formed to compete directly with the senior circuit. Bancroft "Ban" Johnson, the commissioner of the new league, announced that the former Western League, rechristened the American League in 1899, would have eight teams playing 140 game schedules with rosters of 14 players.

The National Leaguers were not happy and not looking forward to the competition. Johnson was defiant [real quote], "The National League is forcing this war on us. All we ask is a chance for good, healthy rivalry and competition, but if the National League insists on fighting, we shall be able to take care of ourselves."[10]

The American League teams are in Baltimore (Orioles), Boston (Americans), Chicago (White Stockings), Cleveland (Blues), Detroit (Tigers), Milwaukee (Brewers), Philadelphia (Athletics) and

---

9 https://sabr.org/journal/article/1882-winter-meetings-reconciliation-and-cooperation/

10 https://www.history.com/this-day-in-history/american-league-founding-mlb

Washington (Senators). They join the National League teams in Philadelphia (Phillies), Pittsburg (Pirates), Brooklyn (Superbas), St. Louis (Cardinals), Boston (Beaneaters), Chicago (Orphans), New York (Giants) and Cincinnati (Reds).

"Hey, wait a minute!" shouted a minor league baseball fan. "They're killing us off by taking the best players and locations. Our leagues are gonna die!" The fan was never heard from again.

Minor Leagues Get Graded!

September 5, 1901—A new National Agreement has established a grading system for the minor leagues. Level-A leagues are given protection for their contracts and cannot be raided by the majors, but Level-A teams can raid teams at lower minor league levels. Level-B teams can be plundered by the majors, but the majors need to secure the player's agreement and must compensate the looted team. Level-C contracts are protected but their players are up for grabs. Level-D teams' ballplayers have their contracts protected but they can be raided by high-graded minor league teams, with compensation.

National and American League Make Peace!

1902—As part of a more general reduction in hostilities, the National and American Leagues decided it was in their best interest to control the minor leagues. The National Association of Professional Baseball Leagues, an association of seven minor leagues, was formed and would be the vehicle the major leagues will use to assert their dominance of the sport.

Cartwright Sues Doubleday for Intellectual Theft! Wheaton Sues Cartwright for the Same!

1905—"Bad call!" shouted the ghost of Alexander Cartwright upon reading that the Mills Commission[11] had proclaimed Abner Doubleday the inventor of baseball in the year 1839. "The claim is based on one unsubstantiated account by a seventy-one-year-old Colorado mining engineer, named Abner Graves," Cartwright shouted. "He claimed to have seen Doubleday lay down the rules of baseball in Cooperstown, New York, in 1893. But Graves was five years old at the time, and Doubleday was at West Point!"

Major General Doubleday may have been a favored contender for this honor because of his service in the Civil War; he fired the first shot in defense of Fort Sumter and fought at the battle of Gettysburg.[12] "I developed the rules of baseball in 1845, not Doubleday," proclaimed Cartwright, "I did it for the New York Knickerbockers Base Ball Club!"

Not so fast. We're not finished yet. The ghost of William R. Wheaton is suing both Cartwright and Doubleday. He claims he drew up the first rules of baseball for the Gotham Baseball Club in 1837. Wheaton asserted, "I was on the committee that drafted the Knickerbocker rules, and also tossed out the rule that said a runner could be made out by hitting him with a thrown ball!"

The New York Knickerbockers Baseball Club, circa 1847. Cartwright is allegedly top middle.

---

11 https://en.wikipedia.org/wiki/Abraham_G._Mills#The_Mills_Commission

12 https://en.wikipedia.org/wiki/Abner_Doubleday

Wheaton based his rules on those of a game played on the streets of England called "rounders." The Mills Commission's dismissal of the notion that baseball had its origin in rounders was driven by patriotic zeal; baseball was an American invention, and the commission didn't want the Brits to have any claim to it. In fact, Mills served as host at a dinner several years earlier celebrating baseball as America's ambassador to the world. The dinner, with three hundred attendees including Mark Twain and Theodore Roosevelt, burst out in a chant of "No rounders!"

The suits were dismissed when none of the deceased complainants showed up in court.

Renowned Umpire Assaulted with Face Mask!

1917—Flamboyant umpire "Steamboat" Johnson was whacked in the face today by a catcher's mask after a disputed call at home plate. As a result, Johnson ejected five players and finished the game holding a handkerchief to his eye.[13]

This was not Johnson's first violent dispute with fans and players. It is claimed that he has had thousands of bottles thrown at him and has seventeen scars on his scalp as mementos of those that found their mark. Most disturbingly, Johnson had a gun fired at him by a disgruntled fan after a home team loss. Johnson was in the shower at the time and claimed [real quote], "The bullet missed me because I was bending down washing my feet."

War Threatens Existence of Minor Leagues!

1918—Because of World War I, only one minor league circuit, the International League, completed its season this year. Eight leagues that began the season never made it to their final game. Forty leagues were flourishing in 1914, but that number dropped to twenty in 1917.

"Who cares?" queried one former baseball fan, "I got tickets to a Charlie Chaplin movie!"

Negro League Formed!

February 14, 1920—Last night, at a YMCA in Kansas City, the Negro National League was formed. Composed of eight teams (Chicago American Giants, Kansas City Monarchs, Chicago Giants, Indianapolis ABCs, Cuban Stars, Dayton Marcos, Detroit Stars, and St. Louis Giants), the league will be led by Rube Foster, who owns the Chicago American Giants, coaches, and plays for them. All but one of the teams has a Black owner. It is thought the league will bring economic stability to the teams, though they will still barnstorm the country, playing up to 150 games against local teams not part of the league.

Baseball Ruled Exempt from Anti-Trust Laws!

May 29, 1922—Chief Justice of the Supreme Court Oliver Wendell Holmes Jr. has ruled that the two major leagues are not in violation of the Sherman Anti-Trust Act, meant to prevent restraint of trade, because they are not engaged in interstate commerce.

"What?!" responded a fan who was never heard from again.

Baseball Game Played at Night!

May 1, 1930—Championed by Judge William Bramham, the proclaimed first professional baseball game was played last night under the lights in Independence, Kansas. But, like so much of baseball lore, the counterclaims are numerous.[14] As early as 1880, a night game was played between teams representing two department stores near Boston under temporary lights. The game was described as "error-filled" and ended in a 16–16

---

13 https://tht.fangraphs.com/the-most-entertaining-umpire-in-minor-league-history/

14 https://www.sportingnews.com/us/mlb/news/first-night-game-baseball-history-hull-lynn-fort-wayne-grand-rapids-independence-des-moines-wilmington/a8n0x2c4xvth19cepmnwom3b4

tie. A night game played on July 4, 1896, involving the Paterson Silk Weavers in Wilmington, Delaware, led the local newspaper to report [real quote], "The ball became lost so many times and so many runs were made that they were not counted." The first night game between two minor league teams may have happened in Grand Rapids, Michigan, on July 7, 1909. The lighting was so bad, the players asked the scorer to count all dropped balls as hits.

Judge Bramham was unavailable for comment.

Buffalo Bisons Win First Baseball Playoffs!

1933—The first playoffs in baseball history were played this year. The brainchild of Frank "Shag" Shaughnessy, the International League conducted a playoff series involving the top four finishers in the eight-team league. As intended, the prospect that more teams had a chance to be champions meant the playoffs had a noticeable impact on game attendance and fan interest.

The Buffalo Bisons, who finished fourth during the regular season with a .494 winning percentage, won the playoffs and the championship.

"We was robbed!" cried a representative of the Newark Bears, who finished the regular season in first place with a .622 winning percentage.

Lady Pitcher Strikes Out Babe Ruth and Lou Gehrig!

April 2, 1931—Jackie Mitchell, a seventeen-year-old female pitcher for the Chattanooga Lookouts, accomplished an amazing feat today. In an exhibition game against the New York Yankees, Mitchell struck out Babe Ruth and Lou Gehrig back-to-back. Mitchell then walked Tony Lazzeri and was removed from the game. This wasn't the first appearance of a woman in organized baseball. In 1898, Lizzie Arlington was brought into a game and pitched the last inning. Edward Barrow, the brain behind the maneuver wrote, [real quote] "I used every device I could think of . . . to bring out the fans . . ."

A plaque commemorating Jackie Mitchell's feat hangs at DBAP.

Negro League Stars Abandon League for Dominican Baseball!

1937—A group of eight Negro League ballplayers agreed to a thirty-thousand-dollar contract to play six weeks for Los Dragones de Ciudad Trujillo in Dominican Republic. While it is not unusual for ballplayers to switch teams in search of more lucrative deals, this move is noteworthy because they will play outside the US and have among them some real stars. The pitcher Satchel Paige, who instigated the move, is perhaps the best-known Black ballplayer. He recruited Cool Papa Bell (the fastest baserunner in the league) and Josh Gibson (known as the league's Babe Ruth).

Branch Rickey Owns 32 Minor League Teams! Relations Between the Minors and Majors Transformed Forever!

1940—The St. Louis Cardinals organization now owns thirty-two minor league ball clubs and has agreements with eight others, thanks to the efforts of general manager, Branch Rickey. With about six hundred players at his disposal, Rickey is using the minors to test and evaluate talent for eventual promotion to the Cardinals. The corralled minor league clubs favor the relationship because the cash they receive for players is important to their economic health.

"Hey, we're going to do this, too!" said George Weiss, of the New York Yankees.

Scandal Rocks the Minor Leagues!
1946—With over five hundred major league baseball players off fighting in World War II, the minor leagues saw their rosters severely depleted. As their best players were promoted to the big leagues, the minor league teams were filled with the young and infirm. However, the return of the players at war's end is being clouded by concerns regarding the ownership of some minor league clubs. Teams out west are owned by gamblers, and one league, the Arizona Mining League, has teams owned by brothels. Also, Judge Bramham determined that players on the Houma Indians and Abbeville Athletics, both in Louisiana, conspired with gamblers to fix the outcomes of three playoff games. The judge tossed the players out of the league.

Color Line Erased in Minor League Baseball!
April 20, 1946—Jackie Robinson broke the race barrier in minor league baseball when he took the field for the Montreal Royals. The Royals won the game, 14–1; Robinson had four hits, including a home run. Other Black players are slated to make appearances for minor league teams, including John Wright with the Royals, and Roy Campanella and Don Newcome with Nashua of the New England League.

Pitcher Strikes Out 25 Batters in a 15-inning Performance!
May 31, 1948—Pitching for the Schenectady Blue Jays, lefty Tommy Lasorda, struck out twenty-five Amsterdam Rugmakers in a fifteen-inning

Jackie Robinson and Branch Rickey.

performance. "I love this game," said Lasorda, "I think I'll hang around a while."

Negro Leagues Hit Hard Times!
1950s—The integration of major league baseball has sounded the death knell for the Negro Leagues. Over the protests of owners, ballplayers are disregarding their contracts with Negro League teams and signing with the major leagues. Negro league ballplayers who migrated to major league teams include Roy Campanella, Willie Mays, Henry Aaron, Ernie Banks, Monte Irvin, Larry Doby, Minnie Minoso, and Satchel Paige. Attendance is dropping as fans follow their favorite players to the major league teams, many in the same cities.

Women's Professional Baseball League Folds!
1954—The All-American Girls Professional Baseball League shut down operation after 12 years of existence. Formed in 1943, the league once had 10 teams. In 1948, it drew over one million fans. The teams were scattered throughout medium-sized cities in the Midwest that were home to war-related industries. The league was the brainchild of Philip K. Wrigley, owner of the Chicago Cubs.

A BRIEF HISTORY OF THE NOT-SO-MINOR LEAGUES

Dodgers and Giants Say "Goodbye" to New York! Pacific Coast League Cries "Foul!"

1958—In the latest major league relocations, the Brooklyn Dodgers and New York Giants moved to the California, following a growing number of Americans moving west. "Foul!" cried a representative of the Pacific Coast League, "These carpetbaggers just stole our two top markets!"

This was not the first time the minors bemoaned major league team relocations. Earlier this decade, the Braves moved from Boston to Milwaukee, the Browns left St. Louis for Baltimore, the Athletics left Philadelphia for Kansas City. The blow to the departed cities was tempered due to the presence of professional minor league baseball clubs. Residents of the new locations welcomed their promotion to the majors. Like the Pacific Coast League, the minor leagues fumed and worried about their future as their most lucrative markets were gobbled up.

Stay Team Stay!

Grade Inflation Comes to the Minor Leagues!

1962—Concerned that the minor leagues were in a state of atrophy, the baseball bigwigs decided that seven classifications for the talent on minor league teams is too many. The seven classifications were reduced to four, combining the B, C, and D leagues into one A league.

"Grade inflation!" cried a baseball fan, who was also a schoolteacher, "The talent ain't any better but the grades are higher!" The fan was never heard from again.

The number of minor league ball teams will be reduced from the current 130, creating much anxiety among many team owners and townspeople. To assuage these fears, it was agreed that the number of minor league teams would not drop below 100. Also, the major leagues will pay a portion of the players' salaries on their farm teams.

Longest Baseball Game Ever Finally is Over!

June 23, 1981—It took eight hours and twenty-five minutes played over two days in April and one day in June, but the game between our Pawtucket Paw Sox and the Rochester Red Wings finally ended today. After being suspended by International League President Harold Cooper at 4:09 a.m. on April 18, the Paw Sox took a hard-earned victory by scoring a run in the bottom of the thirty-third inning over two months later. The Red Wings third baseman, Cal Ripken, played all thirty-three innings and made fifteen plate appearances. "That kid's an ironman!" remarked one Red Wings fan.

Majors and Minors Agree to Player Development Contract!

1997—Minor league and major league baseball agreed to a ten-year player development contract. Under the contract, the major league club is responsible for all the players and coaches' contracts and can move players around among minor league affiliates and the "parent" club as they wish. The minor league team owners are responsible for maintaining a front office and staff that oversees all the club's business, including providing a ballpark, selling tickets, promotions, advertising, and radio and television for broadcasting games.

Minor League Baseball Season Cancelled!

April 2020—Due to the COVID pandemic, the 2020 minor league baseball season has been cancelled. The Durham Bulls issued a commemorative T-shirt reading, "This is some bullshirt."

Minor Leagues to Play Ball in 2021! No, They Won't! Wait, Yes, They Will!

Depending What Day You Ask, 2021—The 2021 minor league season was on, off, then back on again. Teams' finances took a serious hit due to refunds for the missed 2020 season. Front offices were depleted and could not be fully restaffed due to the uncertainty surrounding the season. To stabilize the minors, the majors take over governance of the minors and eliminate 40 teams. "Is there a game tonight?" queried a confused fan, "Wait, do we still have a team?"

Minors Take the Field for First Full Season Since the COVID Pandemic Began!

April 5, 2022—After two seasons shortened by the COVID pandemic, minor league ballplayers took the field on opening day hoping for a much-desired return to normalcy.

With another nod to normalcy and tradition, the minors were rechristened with the old names they went by for decades, replacing letter and number designations. The four levels of minor league play are divided into eleven leagues:

- AAA
  - International League
  - Pacific Coast League
- AA
  - Eastern League
  - Southern League
  - Texas League
- High-A
  - Midwest League
  - Northwest League
  - South Atlantic League
- Low-A
  - California League
  - Carolina League
  - Florida State League

Each major league team starts the 2022 season with four affiliated minor league clubs:

The minor league affiliates are distributed around the United States with density mirroring the population of the country:

In addition to the minors, teams can maintain rookie league teams that play a short season at their spring training complex. Rookie league players are mostly players selected in recent drafts who are not ready for a higher classification of play. Every club has at least two rookie teams, some as many as four. There are also over 60 teams in five independent leagues, but they cannot be called minor leagues.[15] Minor League Baseball is an official name adopted in the 1990s to distinguish teams affiliated with major league clubs from teams in independent, unaffiliated leagues.

Minors Lead the Way (Again) Experimenting with Baseball Rule Changes!

April 2022—During the upcoming season, as it has done so many times before, minor league baseball will serve as a proving ground for changes meant to speed up games and make them more exciting and fair.[16]

The pitch clock that was started in the Triple-A and Double-A ball in 2018 will now be used throughout the minors. All minor league pitchers have 14 seconds to release the ball when no runner is on base and 19 seconds when a runner is on.

Pitchers can only make three pick off moves per at-bat; if the last one fails to catch the runner off base, the runner will advance a base.

All leagues below Triple-A will not be allowed to position more than two players on either side of second base and all infielders must stand on the dirt.

Triple-A ball will begin experimenting with a

---

15 https://www.baseball-reference.com/register/league.cgi?id=e42854f1
16 Baseball America (April 2022). Minor League Preview: 4. New Playing Rules.

A BRIEF HISTORY OF THE NOT-SO-MINOR LEAGUES

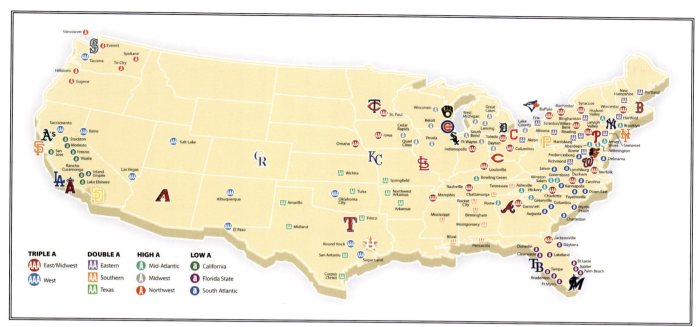

Minor league baseball map.

Division	Team	Founded	MLB Affiliation	Affiliated Since	City	Stadium	Capacity
East	Buffalo Bisons	1979	Toronto Blue Jays	2013	Buffalo, New York	Sahlen Field	16,600
	Charlotte Knights	1976	Chicago White Sox	1999	Charlotte, North Carolina	Truist Field	10,200
	Durham Bulls	1980	Tampa Bay Rays	1998	Durham, North Carolina	Durham Bulls Athletic Park	10,000
	Jacksonville Jumbo Shrimp	1962	Miami Marlins	2021	Jacksonville, Florida	121 Financial Ballpark	11,000
	Lehigh Valley IronPigs	2008	Philadelphia Phillies	2007	Allentown, Pennsylvania	Coca-Cola Park	10,100
	Norfolk Tides	1961	Baltimore Orioles	2007	Norfolk, Virginia	Harbor Park	11,856
	Rochester Red Wings	1899	Washington Nationals	2021	Rochester, New York	Frontier Field	10,840
	Scranton/Wilkes-Barre RailRiders	1989	New York Yankees	2007	Moosic, Pennsylvania	PNC Field	10,000
	Syracuse Mets	1934	New York Mets	2019	Syracuse, New York	NBT Bank Stadium	10,815
	Worcester Red Sox	2021	Boston Red Sox	2021	Worcester, Massachusetts	Polar Park	9,508
West	Columbus Clippers	1977	Cleveland Guardians	2009	Columbus, Ohio	Huntington Park	10,100
	Gwinnett Stripers	2009	Atlanta Braves	2009	Lawrenceville, Georgia	Coolray Field	10,427
	Indianapolis Indians	1902	Pittsburgh Pirates	2005	Indianapolis, Indiana	Victory Field	13,750
	Iowa Cubs	1969	Chicago Cubs	1981	Des Moines, Iowa	Principal Park	11,500
	Louisville Bats	1982	Cincinnati Reds	2000	Louisville, Kentucky	Louisville Slugger Field	13,131
	Memphis Redbirds	1998	St. Louis Cardinals	1998	Memphis, Tennessee	AutoZone Park	10,000
	Nashville Sounds	1978	Milwaukee Brewers	2021	Nashville, Tennessee	First Horizon Park	10,000
	Omaha Storm Chasers	1969	Kansas City Royals	1969	Papillion, Nebraska	Werner Park	9,023
	St. Paul Saints	1993	Minnesota Twins	2021	Saint Paul, Minnesota	CHS Field	7,210
	Toledo Mud Hens	1965	Detroit Tigers	1987	Toledo, Ohio	Fifth Third Field	10,300

Major League Team Affiliate	Minor League Level				# Rookie Teams
	AAA	AA	Adv A	A	
International League East					
Baltimore Orioles	Norfolk	Bowie	Aberdeen	Delmarva	3
Boston Red Sox	Worcester	Portland	Greenville	Salem	3
Chicago White Sox	Charlotte	Birmingham	Winston-Salem	Kannapolis	2
Miami Marlins	Jacksonville	Pensacola	Beloit	Jupiter	3
New York Mets	Syracuse	Binghamton	Brooklyn	St. Lucie	3
New York Yankees	Scranton/Wilkes-Barre	Somerset	Hudson Valley	Tampa	3
Philadelphia Phillies	Lehigh Valley	Reading	Jersey Shore	Clearwater	3
Washington Nationals	Rochester	Harrisburg	Wilmington	Fredericksburg	2
Tampa Bay Rays	Durham	Montgomery	Bowling Green	Charleston	3
Toronto Blue Jays	Buffalo	New Hampshire	Vancouver	Dunedin	2
International League West					
Atlanta Braves	Gwinnett	Mississippi	Rome	Augusta	2
Chicago Cubs	Iowa	Tennessee	South Bend	Myrtle Beach	3
Cincinnati Reds	Louisville	Chattanooga	Dayton	Daytona	2
Cleveland Guardians	Columbus	Akron	Lake County	Lynchburg	3
Detroit Tigers	Toledo	Erie	West Michigan	Lakeland	3
Kansas City Royals	Omaha	Northwest Arkansas	Quad Cities	Columbia	3
Milwaukee Brewers	Nashville	Biloxi	Wisconsin	Carolina	4
Minnesota Twins	St. Paul	Wichita	Cedar Rapids	Fort Myers	2
Pittsburgh Pirates	Indianapolis	Altoona	Greensboro	Bradenton	3
St. Louis Cardinals	Memphis	Springfield	Peoria	Palm Beach	2
Pacific Coast League					
Arizona Diamondbacks	Reno	Amarillo	Hillsboro	Visalia	4
Colorado Rockies	Albuquerque	Hartford	Spokane	Fresno	3
Houston Astros	Sugar Land	Corpus Christi	Asheville	Fayetteville	4
Los Angeles Angels	Salt Lake	Rocket City	Tri-City	Inland Empire	2
Los Angeles Dodgers	Oklahoma City	Tulsa	Great Lakes	Rancho Cucamonga	3
Oakland Athletics	Las Vegas	Midland	Lansing	Stockton	2
San Diego Padres	El Paso	San Antonio	Fort Wayne	Lake Elsinore	2
San Francisco Giants	Sacramento	Richmond	Eugene	San Jose	4
Seattle Mariners	Tacoma	Arkansas	Everett	Modesto	2
Texas Rangers	Round Rock	Frisco	Hickory	Down East	3

Minor League Team Affiliations.

larger base (growing from a fifteen-inch to eighteen-inch square). The larger base is meant to make stealing a bit easier and to prevent collisions.

And, in the most controversial new rule, in the Triple-A Pacific League and Charlotte of the International League, teams will be allowed to challenge three calls by umpires. An automated-ball-strike (ABS) system will be the arbiter. Multiple cameras will be used to track the ball in three dimensions. A successful challenge won't count as a used challenge.

THE LESSONS OF HISTORY

Labor relations, scandal, feats of daring-do, reactions to broader events in the country and the world. If you know how these things have affected major league baseball, now you know they all affected the minor leagues as well. Innovations that dramatically changed the nature of the game—night baseball, playoffs—were first developed and adopted by the minors. While the majors and minors work hand-in-hand on player development and experiments with game rules, you will see the stars of tomorrow and new baseball rules and strategies in the minors first. And, the ticket will be cheaper, the parking closer, the fans more friendly, and downtime between innings more entertaining in the minors.

It should be clear; the minors have always led the way.

Chapter 8
Home Series 5: Memorial Day

[Baseball is] not a sport, and it's not a game, it is in fact a kind of crucible, an X-ray for the totality of the human experience. It speaks to all of the decisions we all have to make, everywhere in our lives, over and over again, even inside every game, and it's filled with ethics and quandaries and opportunities and failures.
—Thom Mount (former president of Universal Pictures)

After Jackie Robinson, the most important Black in baseball history is Reggie Jackson.
—Reggie Jackson, ballplayer

NASHVILLE

https://en.wikipedia.org/wiki/Nashville,_Tennessee
https://en.wikipedia.org/wiki/Nashville_Sounds

Nickname: Sounds
MLB: Milwaukee Brewers (2021–present)
Field: First Horizon Park, capacity 10,000
Population: 689,447 at the 2020 US census
Economy: Country music industry, automotive industry, church headquarters
Fun fact: In 44 years, the Nashville team has been the farm club for eight different major league teams.

MONDAY, MAY 30

Today is Memorial Day and is designated Military Appreciation Day at the ballpark. I sit for dinner with Wayne and Tom F., a host I haven't met before. Wayne does the introductions. Tom had worked at Duke for thirty-eight years before retiring. He was a tech guy. Wayne points to a huge ring on Tom's finger.

"I worked tech for Duke's football team, the coach's headsets," says Tom. "They gave me a ring when they won the Independence Bowl."

Wayne asks if I served in the military.

"No," I respond. "How about you?" He shakes his head no.

"How about you?" I ask Tom.

"Six years in the navy and twenty in the National Guard."

I notice Tom has a tattoo on his forearm that reads, "Death Before Dishonor."

"Thanks for your service," I say.

"Thank you," responds Tom.

I gripe about my last game when the kids were such a handful. Wayne offers that he doesn't work Sundays for that reason, when the kids can run the bases after the game. I didn't know you could ask not to work on a certain day of the week, but I suppose it makes sense, since no one works every game of a homestand unless they ask to. Wayne has this thing wired. Live and learn.

On the concourse, I notice Leigh. She's wearing a Bulls T-shirt, not her host polo shirt.

"What are you doing here? Busman's holiday?"

"I'm here with my nephew. Last time I took him to a game he was too young to remember."

"Understood. Sometimes you just want to sit and watch the game. And have a cold beer."

"I'll have one for you," Leigh smiles.

Pete is beside the visitor's dugout tonight gathering autographs. How does he decide which dugout to work each game? I suppose he targets particular players on the visiting team. When no one interests him, he works either dugout.

I'm working the section behind home plate. A woman arrives in a wheelchair with two helpers. The chair seems like a rolling hospital room. It has a breathing device, attached to her neck, and three computer screens, one clearly monitoring her vitals.

Instead of the usual acknowledgement of the military that happens around the fifth inning, each branch of the service gets its own shout out. Military members and past members are asked to stand and receive a round of applause. The man helping the woman in the wheelchair stands behind her when one branch is recognized and raises her arm for her. I'm humbled by her fortitude and by the dedication of the people who brought her to the game. I suspect her disabilities are from combat-related injuries. "Thank you for your service" seems like such a trivial way to acknowledge my gratitude and respect right now. When I get home, I make a contribution to the Wounded Warriors Project.[1] Still not enough.

Today, I pick up a sheet titled "Durham Bulls Media Relations Department Game Day Information." This is a photocopied handout that fans can get at the Guest Services counter. It's four pages filled with facts and figures and information about the game, prepared fresh every day.

The second page gives an in-depth analysis of the history and record of the Bulls starting pitcher. Today, the pitcher, Shane Baz, can smell the big leagues, having spent two starts at Tampa in 2021, notching a 2–0 record and a 2.01 ERA in 13.1 innings pitched. Arthroscopic surgery to remove bone spurs from his right elbow has kept him quiet this year. He's rehabbing in Durham now. Tonight, he will pitch four innings, giving up one hit, one walk, and striking out four.

The third page of the information sheet fills you

---

[1] https://www.woundedwarriorproject.org/donate

DURHAM BULLS MEDIA RELATIONS DEPARTMENT
GAME INFORMATION

LEAGUE CHAMPIONS: 2002, 2003, 2009, 2013, 2017, 2018, 2021
DURHAM BULLS ATHLETIC PARK — 409 BLACKWELL ST, DURHAM, NC 27701
AGREEN@DURHAMBULLS.COM — 919.687.6574 | JWRIGHT@DURHAMBULLS.COM — 919.687.6516

GAMES #49, HOME GAME #25, MONDAY, MAY 30TH— DURHAM BULLS ATHLETIC PARK, DURHAM, NC
DURHAM BULLS (25-23) VS NASHVILLE SOUNDS (32-15)
RHP SHANE BAZ (0-0, 1.93) VS RHP DYLAN FILE (2-1, 3.99)

TODAY'S GAME
After Durham posted their best record so far this season in a six-game series, going 5-1 against Charlotte, the Bulls homestand continues on Monday for the six-game series opener against the Nashville Sounds. Monday's series opener will mark the second six-game series between the teams this season as Nashville won the first series 4-2 April 5th-10th. RHP **Shane Baz** (0-0, 1.93) is expected to start for Durham on MLB Rehab Assignment and RHP **Dylan File** (2-1, 3.99) is expected to start for Nashville.

LAST TIME OUT
After dropping their lone contest of the series in game five, Durham bounced back in game six against Charlotte, picking up a 4-2 win to close out the series. In the contest, the Bulls were outhit by Charlotte 12-7, but made key defensive plays to secure the win. The Bulls used a big fourth inning, scoring four runs, starting with a **Tristan Gray** double, and the team capitalized off of three pitching errors by Cahrlotte to move around the bases, getting two scores from **Rene Pinto** and Gray.

BULLS VS SOUNDS
Durham & Nashville face off at the DBAP for the 1st time in their respective club histories after squaring off in a 6-game set to begin their seasons in Nashville between 4/5-10. The Sounds topped the Bulls in 4 of 6 contests in that series, though Durham outscored Nashville 24-21 in that 6-game set. C **Ford Proctor** hit .462 (6-13) in 4 games versus the Sounds, adding 1 double, 3 RBI & 4 walks for a 1.126 OPS, while INF **Jim Haley** batted .316 (6-19) with 3 runs, 2 homers & 4 RBI in his 5 games versus the Sounds.

BULL-ET POINTS
- OF **Cal Stevenson** owns a .351 mark (20-57) in his 18 home tilts this year, while INF/OF **Miles Mastrobuoni** has hit .321 (25-78) in his 21 matchups at the DBAP.
- Mastrobuoni has also posted a .400 average (12-30) with the Bulls when batting with runners in scoring position.
- C **Joe Hudson** has homered in each of his last 2 games after going deep just once in his 1st 10 games with the Bulls.
- OF **Luke Raley** has also gone deep in each of his last 2 games, totaling 3 hits, after recording just 1 hit in his previous 6 games (16 at-bats).
- INF **Tristan Gray** has recorded hits in 12 of his last 14 games after tallying a hit in 9 his his 1st 25 contests of 2022.
- The Bulls' 13-3 record since 5/12 ranks as tied for the 2nd-best mark among MiLB teams in that period with Myrtle Beach (A+), trailing only Fort Myers' (A) 14-3 mark.
- Durham is averaging 5.4 runs scored & 3.3 runs allowed per game over their last 16 contests after averaging 4.6 runs scored & 5.5 runs allowed per game through their 1st 32 tilts.
- The Bulls have allowed 1 or more runs in the 1st inning in 20 of their 48 games this year, including 13 of their 24 home tilts.
- Durham has won each of their last 4 series after failing to win each of their 1st 4 series.
- The Bulls dropped 3 of their 1st 4 series of the season, splitting the other between 4/19-24 at Norfolk.
- Durham enters play today tied for 3rd place in the IL East after entering play on 5/5 in 10th place out of 10 teams.

HOT STREAK
Durham enters play today having won 13 of their last 16 contests dating back to 5/12. During that stretch, the Bulls have outscored their opponents 86-53. That run includes a 6-game win streak between 5/12-18, the club's longest win streak of the year. In the month of May, Durham has compiled a 17-8 record after tallying an 8-15 clip in the month of April.

HOME SWEET HOME
The Bulls have also won 9 of their last 10 home games at the DBAP dating back to 5/12. In those contests, Durham has outscored their opponents 57-32, including a 50-25 run since being down 7-0 to Gwinnett in the middle of the 4th inning on 5/12 in an 8-7 victory. Prior to this stretch, the Bulls had won just 3 of their 1st 14 games at home.

YARD WORK
Bulls batters have homered in 22 of their 25 games this month, totaling 38 roundtrippers. Durham's 38 big flies in Mayrank them 2nd-most among International League teams behind only Charlotte (39). 11 different Bulls batters have gone yard this month after Durham totaled 19 homers in 23 April matchups, with 9 different Bulls batters homering that month.

MY KINDA PLACE
OF **Josh Lowe** in 8 games played at the DBAP this year has hit .419 (13-31) & has reached base via a hit or walk in 16 of 35 plate appearances in those tilts. In 61 career games at the DBAP, Lowe has posted a .304 average (65-214), adding 44 runs, 20 doubles, 2 triples, 18 homers & 58 RBI, along with 17 steals in as many attempts, in addition to a .399 OBP.

LEAGUE RANKINGS
INF **Jonathan Aranda** enters play today ranked 2nd in the International League in hits (56), in addition to 5th in batting average (.327) & 6th in on-base percentage (.402). Aranda also leads all Rays MiLB players in hits, batting average & RBI (29), in addition to 3rd in OPB (.911) & 6th in SLG (.509). INF **Tristan Gray** also ranks T-5th in the circuit in home runs (11), which also paces all Rays MiLB players, while INF **Jim Haley**'s 7 longballs rank him T-2nd in that category alongside OF **Jordan Qsar**.

HEY, YOU LOOK FAMILIAR…
The Milwaukee Brewers announced today that INF **Willy Adames** has joined the Sounds as part of his MLB Rehab Assignment. Adames played in 194 games with Durham between the 2017-18 seasons, compiling a .280 average (210-751), adding 110 runs, 39 doubles, 10 triples, 14 homers & 96 RBI. He was a member of 2 Governors' Cup Championship teams with the Bulls, which included winning the 2017 Triple-A National Championship over Memphis. One of his more memorable home runs with Durham was hitting a grand slam off of the Hit Bull Win Steak Snorting Bull sign on 4/22/18 versus Lehigh Valley. In 98 career games at the DBAP he has hit .277 (102-368) with 55 runs, 15 doubles, 7 triples, 6 homers & 44 RBI.

'22 BY THE NUMBERS

Place in Division	T-3rd
Games Behind (Division)	-6.0
Current Streak	+1
Home	12-12
Road	13-11
vs. RHP (starter)	20-17
vs. LHP (starter)	5-6
vs. East Division	18-12
vs. West Division	7-11
Day	6-3
Night (5:05+)	19-20
Extra Innings	0-0
Shutouts	2-4
One-Run Games	2-7
Three or fewer	2-9
Four or more	19-12
Scoring First	14-4
Opponent Scores First	9-19
Leading after 6	24-3
Trailing after 6	0-20
Tied after 6	1-0
Series Openers	3-5
Series Finales	5-3
Rubber Matches	0-0
Doubleheader Games	2-2
Sweep/Swept/Split	0/0/2
6-Game Series	4-3-1
Sweep/Swept	0/0
Monday	0-0
Tuesday	2-5
Wednesday	5-4
Thursday	7-1
Friday	3-5
Saturday	3-4
Sunday	5-4
April	8-15
May	17-8
June	0-0
July	0-0
August	0-0
September	0-0

2022 BULLS vs. SOUNDS
Overall	2-4
DBAP	0-0
First Horizon Park	2-4
2021 Head-to-Head	0-0

BULLS ALL-TIME RECORD
Overall	6,730-6,339
International League	1,710-1,476

UPCOMING SCHEDULE AND PROBABLE STARTERS

DATE	OPPONENT	DURHAM STARTER	OPPONENT STARTER	TIME (ET)
Tuesday, May 31st	OFF			
Wednesday, June 1st	vs Nashville	RHP Kevin Herget (3-0, 0.56)	RHP Tyler Herb (0-1, 8.10)	6:35 PM
Thursday, June 2nd	vs Nashville	RHP Easton McGee (2-3, 5.79)	RHP Josh Lindblom (1-2, 2.89)	6:35 PM
Friday, June 3rd	vs Nashville	RHP Tommy Romero (2-3, 5.12)	RHP Caleb Boushley (5-2, 3.66)	6:35 PM

Tonight's game will be broadcast on Buzz Sports Radio: 96.5 FM in Durham, 99.3 FM in Raleigh.

Game information sheet for fans (and hosts).

in on the rest of the Bulls roster. You learn the biometrics of over forty players, their hometown, 2021 baseball record, and more, even how to pronounce their names. You can learn which players are on the Tampa Bay forty-man roster and are next in line to go to the majors. There are ten Bulls listed who have their foot in the door. The fourth page does the same for the visiting team.

I've left the first page for last. It's where you find a narrative rendition of the team's news. Catchy headlines tell you about hitting streaks, and other team trivia that provide good context for watching the game. Definitely worth the cost (it's free) for fans who don't follow the team closely. I've come to pick up a copy just about every game since I found out about their existence. Before the game starts, I try to stand behind one of those immaculate seats I've cleaned and look it over. I've found that the content helps me answer a lot of fan questions.

Attendance: 4,298.

THURSDAY, JUNE 2

After dinner, I sit and watch the players go through fielding drills. Some play catch in the outfield. The catcher crouches behind home plate, a batter takes light swings at pitches with no intent to hit the ball. The catcher bullets the ball down to second base where the baseman swipes it in front of the base, as if to tag a runner sliding in. A few players go through stretching exercises, some with the help of a trainer. Two players sit on their knees about six feet apart and toss speedy one-hoppers at each other's crotch. Each player attempts to grab the ball with a bare hand before it hits them.

Another host stops by and tells a story about his son playing a hockey game on a rink at the United States Naval Academy. The rink was about to be used for practice by the Pittsburgh Penguins. The dad and his son stayed to watch the pros.

"It's the same thing," he says. "They practice the fundamentals. No matter how good you are, you practice the fundamentals."

I'm stationed at the gate that separates the Tobacco Road restaurant from the ballfield walkway. I must check tickets if people want to pass through (and they can't carry drinks). Thankfully, the gate has a push-button lock that slows people down who want to get into the game when I am occupied elsewhere. Throughout the course of the game, I scan about a hundred tickets and stop about ten folks without tickets. I tell these folks this device is a scanner but also a taser. All smile and understand I'm kidding. No problems. The scanner works pretty well, but occasionally loses the screen and I have to press several buttons to get the scanning screen to appear. The screen says the person using the scanner is named "Alfred." That's not me. Hope this works.

The host who oversees the K-Wall to my left has some mobility issues, but this doesn't stop him from leaving his post when the Bulls are up (and he doesn't have to hang Ks) and socializing with friends standing under the Snorting Bull. It wouldn't be a problem, except there is an unlocked side door leading from the restaurant to the field. He's supposed to monitor this entrance, but for half the game he's nowhere in sight. Just my luck, there are about fifteen kids with their folks at a party in the restaurant. The kids have discovered the door and try multiple times to sneak on the field through the side entrance. This requires me to run back and forth between the two entrances.

Finally, I tell the boys, next time they can take me to their parents, and I'll check tickets. That's the last I see them.

A gentleman approaches the gate. He tells me he is from Israel attending a wedding. This is his first baseball game. "There is no baseball in Israel," he says.

Clearly. I have to explain what an inning is, what outs are, and when a batter is safe.

His girlfriend from Manhattan arrives. She is equally clueless.

The visiting pitcher from Nashville gives up three home runs in a row. The pitching coach goes out for a visit.

"I suspect the coach has a bus ticket to Double-A ball in his hand," I muse to five guys watching from the walkway.

"We know that coach," says one of the men.

These guys are four coaches and a teaching assistant from the University of Illinois at Springfield. Their team is in the Division II College World Series

---

NCAA DIVISION II BASEBALL

The three hundred–plus colleges and universities that make up the NCAA's Division II are mostly schools with fewer than 2,500 students. Division II schools can provide athletes with scholarships (nine for baseball) but are typically much less well-funded than Division I schools.* Athletes must take specified courses in English, math, science, and social science and maintain a minimum grade point average. Division III schools do not provide scholarships to athletes.

About 187,000 students compete in NCAA Division I sports. About 124,000 compete in Divisions II and III.** The NCAA writes of Division II***:

- If you want a more balanced approach to college, consider a D2 program. Being a Division 2 athlete also requires a lot of training and practice, but less than D1.
- There are still the demands all student-athletes face, but it is not as intense and rigorous as the year-round total commitment of a D1 athlete.
- Additionally, you're more likely to be rewarded with aid. Sixty percent of D2 athletes receive athletic aid.

There are 256 Division II schools competing in 24 conferences.

The NCAA conducts a Division II World Series in early June. The tournament is double elimination. In 2022, the eight teams that competed in the World Series were:

Southern Arkansas
Point Loma Southern
Illinois Springfield (the guys I met at DBAP)
North Greenville

Rollins
New Hampshire
Angelo State
West Chester

North Greenville University was the national champion. NGU is a private Baptist university in Tigerville, South Carolina, population 2,025—less than the school's enrollment. Congratulations Crusaders!

* https://en.wikipedia.org/wiki/NCAA_Division_II
** https://www.ncsasports.org/recruiting/how-to-get-recruited/college-divisions
*** https://www.ncsasports.org/recruiting/how-to-get-recruited/college-divisions

being played in Cary, North Carolina. The University ranked fifth in the Midwest Division during the season and are bracketed seventh in the championship playoffs.

"The Nashville pitching coach was our coach when we played in college."

The coaches pass into the restaurant, surround a table, and begin to order beers. Eventually, they are joined by a few of their players, all of whom consume ice cream only.

"Good luck!" I offer them when they leave.

Pete walks by and I finally get to exchange pleasantries with him.

"Get any autographs today?"

"None today."

"Are you a season ticket holder?"

"Yep." He talks with a slight lisp. "Since this ballpark opened, and I did volunteer work at the old ballpark."

"How many games you come to a season?"

Pete thinks for a minute, "About sixty," he says, "but I go to other ballparks also. I've been to over three hundred different major league, minor league, independent, and collegiate ball parks."

By the seventh inning, many of the folks hanging over the railing on the restaurant side have clearly had a few drinks.

"Whooz puh-lay-in'?" asks one.

"Can we shmoke?" asks another.

I see a woman sitting among four men, all of whom appear to have had a beer or two. I toss her a ball.

"Hey, how come you didn't give me a ball?" slurs the gentleman sitting next to her.

"You tell me, friend. She deserves it."

"You know, my grandfather was a Yankee. He played with Babe Ruth."

"What was his name?"

"Benjamin Cowan Shields," he says with pride.

"Cool," I reply.

"I'll sign the ball for her," he decides.

At home, I look Shields up. Sure enough, Benjamin Cowan Shields was a pitcher for the Yankees who played alongside Babe Ruth and Lou Gehrig in 1925. He holds the record for having the most major league career wins (four) without a loss. He also had a career earned-run average of 8.27.[2] Shields had great hitting backing him up.

Damn, I shoulda got his autograph. Coulda given it to Pete.

Attendance: 4,976.

SUNDAY, JUNE 5

Tonight is "Pirate and Princess" night. Dads and sons are dressed as pirates, daughters are dressed as princesses (I didn't see any princess moms). During the first few innings, girls are lined up in the walkway to have their picture taken with five Disney princesses. I query a pirate dad in line with two princess daughters.

"What's a pirate's favorite letter?"

He thinks. Then, "Arrr!"

"Well done, Pop!"

I've lucked into Section 102, just to the right of home plate. Hopefully, this means it will be an evening without drama, except on the field. Josh is to the left of me, so I'll learn a lot about baseball. He starts my lessons right away by telling me about a YouTube channel where the voiceover points out flaws in pitchers' deliveries that tip their next pitch. The voiceover

---

2 https://en.wikipedia.org/wiki/Ben_Shields

Ariel, Elsa, Anna, Cinderella, and Belle take batting practice.

also lip reads arguments between umpires, players, and managers.³

Josh is looking for a new job. His day gig with a video game company seems to be going south. He's preparing his resume to send to a local soccer club. "I'll have to clean up my Twitter account," he tells me, "I've said some not-so-nice things about them."

Now for the rules I didn't know about. Josh tells me that pitchers on a rehab assignment from the majors don't need to adhere to a pitch clock; they can take as long as they like between pitches. I also learn that second base, which has been expanded to eighteen inches from fifteen inches in the minors this season, will soon be moved on the field. The perpendicular line that runs through the back end of first and third base out to second base now runs through the middle of the base. That's gonna change and the lines will meet right behind second," Josh tells me.

I think, now that I know this, I can really impress my friends.

We talk a bit about baseball movies. I'm shocked, truly shocked, that Josh has never seen *Cobb*, starring Tommy Lee Jones, nor *Fear Strikes Out: The Jimmie Piersall Story*, starring Anthony Perkins (Norman Bates from *Psycho*). It feels good to have something to share with Josh.

I meet a part-time Bulls operations trainee who also works operations for a non-profit organization. She's a college graduate with a major in marketing. She rolls her eyes and says, "Don't do much marketing."

The marketing major and I have a brief discussion with another host about how to treat people who have switched genders but still want to play organized sports. We all agree that people ought to be the people they want to be. The host says he knows some people who have transitioned. But the impact of switching genders on sports participation is a tough issue. My friends beg off answering the question.

I offer, "What if athletes born or transitioning to male are allowed to play in men's sports?"

"That would prohibit the advantage men who transition to women might have in women's sports," adds the host.

But the conversation ends there, with no resolution. I think I made my friends uncomfortable by bringing up this topic. Remember, I tell myself, when you're at the ballpark you're in the baseball bubble.

Purely by chance, I meet a dad of one of the University of Illinois Springfield ball players I met a few nights earlier. He is sad to report the team lost their first game and have an elimination contest the next day. I wish him luck. After work, I look up the elimination game results. No luck.

The visiting Nashville Sounds mess up a run down between first and second base leading to a score by the Bulls. The visitors coach comes out to argue. That's his appeal; a face full of umpire. There are no video replays in the minors.

During a fan activity between the seventh and eighth innings, a preschool girl stands on the visitor's dugout and must choose between a prize and the opportunity to hit her dad in the face with a pie. The crowd weighs in and, no surprise, pie-in-the-face wins. The daughter agrees. Dad gets pied, shown on

---

3   https://www.youtube.com/results?search_query=jomboy+media

the jumbo screen, and the fans go wild. His daughter gets the prize anyway.

I learn that there are new rules for kids running the bases after the Sunday games. The baserunners will be split into under and over six-year-olds groups, and they will enter the field through different gates. Hopefully, this will prevent the chaos that happened in the aisles and on the walkway last week. Because of my location, I'm asked to check that there are only six-and-unders in my line. Chase the bigger kids away, make them get on the other line.

"Sure," I say, and I shake a fist with an angry face.

"Don't do that!" is the response I get, and we both have a laugh.

The new system works very well.

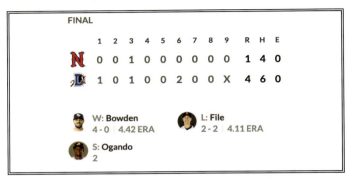

Attendance: 7,587.

HOME SERIES 5: MEMORIAL DAY

THE BINGO LONG TRAVELING ALL-STARS & MOTOR KINGS

Year of Release: 1976
Rating: PG
Director: John Badham
Writers: Hal Barwood and Matthew Robbins; based on novel by William Brashler
Stars: Billy Dee Williams (pitcher), James Earl Jones (catcher), Richard Pryor (right fielder)

Plot Synopsis

From Wiki: https://en.wikipedia.org/wiki/The_Bingo_Long_Traveling_All-Stars_%26_Motor_Kings

The Bingo Long Traveling All-Stars & Motor Kings is a 1976 American sports comedy film about a team of enterprising ex–Negro League baseball players in the era of racial segregation. Loosely based upon William Brashler's 1973 novel of the same name, it starred Billy Dee Williams, James Earl Jones and Richard Pryor. Directed by John Badham, the movie was produced by Berry Gordy for Motown Productions and Rob Cohen for Universal Pictures, and released by Universal on July 16, 1976.

The film was a box office success, grossing $33 million on a $9 million budget.

From IMDb: https://www.imdb.com/title/tt0074207/?ref_=fn_al_tt_1

Tired of the slave-like treatment of his team's owner, charismatic star Negro League pitcher Bingo Long takes to the road with his band of barnstormers through the small towns of the Midwest in the 1930s.

Critic Ratings

Rotten Tomatoes: https://www.rottentomatoes.com/m/the_bingo_long_traveling_all_stars_and_motor_kings
Tomatometer: 89 out of 100 (18 reviewers)
Audience Score: 68 out of 100 (250+ Ratings)
Critics consensus: None provided.
IMDb Rating: 6.8 out of 10 (1,900 raters)
Roger Ebert: https://www.rogerebert.com/reviews/the-bingo-long-traveling-all-stars-and-motor-kings-1976 , 2.5 out of 4 stars
Ebert has issues with the direction of the movie. Still, he feels Bingo Long is fun, it's pleasant to watch, but it "cakewalks too much on its way to the box office."

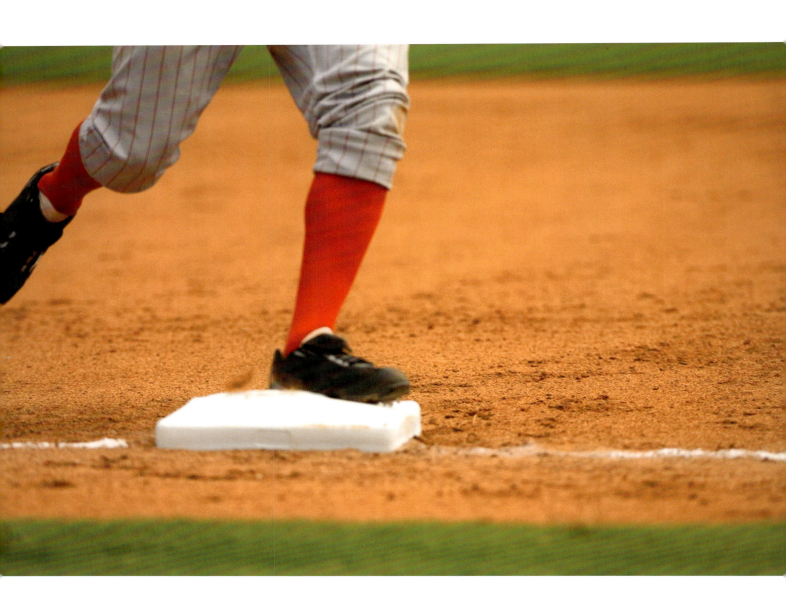

Chapter 9
Home Series 6: Mid-Season Break

Baseball fans love numbers. They love to swirl them around their mouths like Bordeaux wine.
—Pat Conroy, author

Ninety percent of this game is half mental.
—Yogi Berra, ballplayer, manager, philosopher

The Bulls were on the road for all but one homestand from June 6 until July 4. This was the perfect time for me to take a road trip of my own and only miss a few days of work. But that doesn't mean things weren't happening. The break also gave me an opportunity to indulge my passion for statistics.

The team we played at home when I was away was the Louisville Bats.

LOUISVILLE

https://www.milb.com/louisville/
https://en.wikipedia.org/wiki/Louisville%2C_Kentucky

Nickname: Bats
MLB: Cincinnati Reds (2000–present)
Field: Louisville Slugger Field, capacity 13,131
Population (2020): 782,969
Economy: Shipping and cargo industries, auto and appliance manufacturing, whiskey.
Fun fact: The first Louisville Slugger bat was made by seventeen-year-old Bud Hillerich in 1884. The bat was made for Pete Browning, a star for the Louisville Eclipse, a team which played in the American Association.

STADIUM RENOVATIONS

We learned earlier that Major League Baseball had informed the city of Durham and the Bulls organization that DBAP needed about $10 million in renovations.[1] The cost of those improvements had doubled since before the COVID pandemic began. No surprise there. The work needed to be complete by April 2025. If not, the team could not play at DBAP anymore.

Starting in March, the city council began performing its due diligence, requesting an assessment of the economic impact of the stadium and the Bulls on the economy of Durham. One or two council members wrung their hands at the cost, ninety percent of which would fall on the city, the rest on the team owners. But for most council members the intangibles already outweighed the economics. "That heartfelt tie for a lot of Durhamites, including myself, you can't monetize that," said the mayor, Elaine O'Neal. "That's a part of who we are, it's a part of what makes Durham great." For the record, the best estimate suggested the total economic impact of the Bulls on Durham in 2019 was just short of $50 million, with $1.4 million paid in local taxes, and twenty-three thousand jobs directly related to the team.[2]

We also learned earlier that, from the fan-experience point of view, DBAP was the highest-rated ballpark in the International League Eastern Division.[3] What gives? What improvements are so important? The MLB-required improvements are behind the scenes, out of sight of the fans. There will be a new batting tunnel, more batting cages, and improvements to the offices and locker rooms, including a women's locker room.

On April 4, the city council voted 5–0 to foot the full amount of its share of the bill. The renovations will begin in August on the offices and need to be completed before next season begins or some home games might be in jeopardy. The city could lose $300,000 for each lost home game.

Always community minded, on May 14, the Bulls organization (along with Coastal Credit Union) initiated a Ballpark Project meant to help local organizations renovate other baseball and softball facilities around the city. Four projects would be funded at $10,000 apiece.[4]

Ten grand seems like a pittance compared to the cost of the stadium renovations. Still, it will mean lots to the fields that get spruced up. But, there's more. The Miracle League of the Triangle has the mission "To create positive life experiences for children and adults with special needs and for their families through baseball." Their motto: "Everyone deserves a chance to play baseball." Can't disagree with that. There are 250 Miracle League organizations in United States, Puerto Rico, Canada, and Australia. The league serves more than two hundred thousand children and adults with disabilities worldwide.[5]

In 2017, the Bulls and their parent company, Capitol Broadcasting, took the lead in building the Miracle League's third field in the local community. Capitol Broadcasting gave money, led the fundraising drive, the planning, and construction. This Durham Bulls Miracle League Field will sit in the shadow of DBAP, just steps from the main entrance. In February 2021, construction began on the field. Last week, when I stuck my head in the construction curtain, the green outfield was in place and the bricks, matching DBAP's, were piled high. The entrance will include a tower that is a replica of the tower at the entrance

---

1 https://www.athleticbusiness.com/facilities/stadium-arena/article/15290154/durham-must-pay-9m-in-upgrades-if-bulls-to-remain
2 https://www.newsobserver.com/article260122985.html
3 https://www.stadiumjourney.com/stadiums/durham-bulls-athletic-park-s193
4 https://www.milb.com/durham/news/durham-bulls-ballpark-project-to-renovate-four-facilities-276687724
5 https://www.mltriangle.com/

HOME SERIES 6: MID-SEASON BREAK

Renderings of the Durham Bulls Miracle League Field.

to the old Durham ballpark. It'll also have its own Snorting Bull.

THE CAROLINA MUDCATS

A steamy Sunday afternoon road trip takes me to Five County Stadium in Zebulon, North Carolina. I'm here to watch a game between the Carolina Mudcats (a Milwaukee Brewers affiliate) and the Down East Wood Ducks (a Texas Rangers affiliate, from Kinston, North Carolina, population 19,140). These are two Low-A level ball clubs in the Carolina League. Zebulon has a population of about seven thousand but is also considered to be part of the North Carolina Research Triangle. Still, the road to the stadium is a two lane. The stadium can hold 6,500 fans, but today there are only 1,822 tickets sold and maybe a thousand fans in attendance.

The fan base looks remarkably like that of DBAP. Mostly white, lots of families with small children. If there is a noticeable difference in clientele, it is in the deeper Carolina accents I hear when talking to fans and employees. To my New York City ears, this is like singing. A pure Carolina accent is beautiful to hear.

As might be expected, there is more personal attention paid to fans here; three preteens get their images on the video screen and the entire crowd is asked to sing happy birthday. We do. Although most food stands are closed today, there is clearly no exotic fare—though several local microbreweries serve up a variety of beers.

The caliber of play seems lower than that in Durham, but my sample size of plays is just one game. The left fielder misplays two flies in the first three innings, circling one for what seems like twenty minutes before it hits the ground untouched. His subsequent catch brings a cheer from the crowd. The pitcher and catcher collide going for a popped-up bunt. Later, the catcher would get hit in the chin by

Five County Stadium, Zebulon, North Carolina.

a foul tip. After a spell in the dugout, he can be seen walking out of the park down the third base foul line with a towel pressed to his face.

I notice a Down Easter makes a cross in the dirt just outside the batter's box before he steps in. He goes one for five, three strike outs but also a solo dinger. The Down Easters win 5–3.

THE BATTING CAGE

A septuagenarian knows better than to try to pitch a baseball with any velocity. My creaky old rotator cuff ain't gonna withstand that kind of abuse. A soft catch at forty feet, maybe. But sixty feet, six inches with any velocity? Forget it.

Swing a bat? Anybody can do that, right? So, off to the batting cage I go. I get to choose from four cages that pitch balls at you at four different speeds. Fifteen balls for a token, tossed at about ten second intervals. I buy six tokens. That's enough for ninety pitches. There are two other folks at the cages with me, a young couple from Olathe, Kansas. They have a one- and three-year-old at home being babysat by the grandparents. As you can imagine, they are having a wonderful time.

I start at the medium speed cage and foul a few pitches off, not many. I move to the slow cage thinking I'll really cream these, but I miss every pitch. Back to medium velocity and a bit more success. The contact brings back the vague memory of the sting when an aluminum bat connects with a hard ball. The Kansas mom cringes each time she makes contact. The dad is most successful, suggesting he's had practice.

Now, my forearm starts to ache. One more token, then another. This ache is getting serious. I hand my last two tokens to the couple, we fist bump, and I head for my car.

In a couple hours, my bicep and forearm are so large that Mark Maguire would be impressed. But he probably wouldn't be too keen about the purplish-green color that's running eight inches above and below my elbow. I expected a bit of soreness, but this? Was I swinging too hard, trying to dazzle those folks from Kansas? How bad was my swing? I know I was bailing out so bad my ass was in the next county. Am I gonna need Tommy John surgery?

Not to worry. My recovery only took a few days, and I got to wear a cool elbow brace that perfectly complemented my short sleeve shirts. At least I thought it was cool. Strangers probably felt sorry for an old man with a deteriorating body. My friends had a great time teasing me about how stupid a former college professor could be. Lesson learned: swinging a bat is no less physically challenging than throwing a ball. I'm not saying old folks can't remind themselves of their baseball days gone by. I would say to just be careful and start slow. Very slow.

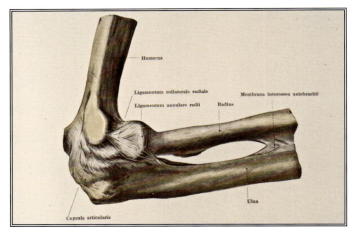

Elbow anatomy.
From a 1923 anatomy book

HOW'RE THE BULLS DOING?

Quite well, thank you. On June 30, the Bulls played their seventy-fifth game, half the season.

After a horrendous start, losing 16 of its first 24 games (.333), the Bulls have really turned it around, winning 33 of their next 51 games, a .647 clip. They sit in second place in the International League East, just a half game off the pace. (One day later, after the seventy-sixth game, the Bulls would be in first place by half a game.)

THE MINOR LEAGUE'S LIMIT ON EXCELLENCE

One thing I learned about minor league baseball—no great revelation—is that success breeds failure. The better a ballplayer plays, the more likely he will get called up to the majors and replaced by a player not doing so well in the bigs, or a guy from Level-AA. Injured players on the parent club will come to the minors to rehab and play Level-AAA ball when they may not be one hundred percent healthy. This should reduce the chance that a minor league club will play really, really, well and win lots of games. We must remember, from the point of view of the major league organization, the primary purpose of the minors is player development. Winning comes in a distant second. If this is correct, we should see a "compression" effect on the winning percentages of the minor league teams in any given year, compared to their major league parent clubs. Let's look at a few recent seasons.

In 2018, there were 14 teams in the International League. The team with the best record, the Lehigh Valley IronPigs, played .600 ball, finishing the season with 84 wins and 56 losses. The team with the worst record was the Buffalo Bisons; with 61 wins and 77 losses, they played .442 ball. That's a winning percentage range of .158. The standard deviation (a measure of variability in a set of scores) of the winning percentages for the 14 teams was 0.048.[6]

How about the majors? For the parent clubs of the 14 International League teams, the team with the best record in 2018 was the Boston Red Sox, who played .667 ball (103–59). The team with the worst record was the Baltimore Orioles, at .290 (55–107), a range of .377. The standard deviation of the winning percentages for the 14 parent teams was 0.10, twice that of their IL affiliates. So as expected, there was more variation in the MLB standings. Of course, the minor league teams in the calculation only played against one another, but the MLB records include games against 16 other teams, adding a caution to how we interpret these stats (though the average winning percentage for the 14 parent clubs was very close to .500).

The 2019 season was pretty much the same. The Columbus Clippers had the best record among the 14 IL teams (.579, 81–59) while the Pawtucket (now Worcester) Red Sox and Louisville Bats shared the worst record (.421, 59–81), a winning percentage range of .158. The standard deviation for the 14 clubs was 0.054. In the majors, the Yankees had the best record (.636, 103–59) with the Tigers bringing up the rear (.292, 47–114), a range of .344. The standard deviation for the 14 parent teams was .107, again showing twice as much variation.[7]

The 2021 season, now with 20 International League teams, broke the rule. The Durham Bulls had a phenomenal season (.662, 86–44) as did the Buffalo Bisons (.627, 79–47). Not so the Charlotte Knights (.367, 47–81). The IL range of winning percentages ballooned to .295. The standard deviation for the league, 0.090. In the majors, the Rays finished on top with a .617 record (100–62) while the Orioles brought up the rear (.321, 52–100), just edging out the IL range at .296. The parent club standard deviation was 0.079, just a bit less variable than their farm teams.[8]

At mid-season in 2022, the leagues were back to form. The IL East had six teams bunched at the top of the division within 1.5 games of one another. Buffalo sat on top with a .554 winning percentage (41–33). The IL's standard deviation was .063. In contrast, the parent club's winning percentage standard deviation was .098. The Yankees were having a historic first half

---

6 https://www.baseball-reference.com/register/league.cgi?id=1f477608

7 https://www.baseball-reference.com/register/league.cgi?id=1f477608

8 https://www.baseball-reference.com/register/league.cgi?id=d615ccef

compiling a .727 winning percentage. If I exclude them from the standard deviation calculation it drops to .085, still much higher than the IL teams.

So, the numbers—that is, the winning percentages' range and standard deviation—support the notion that, in general, there will be less variation in IL team winning percentages than those of their parent clubs. Putting a positive spin on this, since the parent clubs prune the best talent from IL teams, the competition among the teams is tighter in the minor leagues.

HOW ARE THE PLAYERS DOING?

At the halfway mark of the season, the Bulls as a team were hitting just over .250 with an OPS just over .760 (on base percentage plus slugging percentage, a statistic that comes closer than batting average to predicting how many runs a team will score). Both those numbers were around the middle of the IL teams.

The Bulls started the season with 14 position players. After 75 games, three of these players were on the Rays' roster. They had been replaced by four players. All four were promoted from the Double-A Montgomery Biscuits.

How did players who played for both the Bulls and the Rays do on each team? This is fun to look at because it holds the individual players skills constant and gauges how well they play against the two different levels of competition. You'd expect the answer to the question to be "Better in the minors than the majors." Let's see.

During the first half of the season, there were seven position players who came to bat for both the Bulls (767 at-bats) and the Rays (573 at-bats). As Bulls, these players had a collective batting average of .293 and an OPS of .902. As Rays, they didn't do nearly as well, averaging .215 and .635 respectively.

The standout player was Isaac Paredes. This infielder averaged .243 for Tampa Bay, after hitting .263 for Durham. His OPS for the Rays was a whopping .903, compared to .838 for the Bulls. Both are great numbers. He hit 11 homers for the Rays. Three of these home runs came in one game against the Yankees. Paredes hit his dingers in the first, third, and fifth inning. In the seventh inning, he was hit by a pitch. I don't think I'll be seeing much of Paredes in Durham during the second half of the season.

How about pitching? The Bulls started the season with 23 pitchers on their roster. At half season, 15 of them were on the Bulls roster and 6 were pitching for the Rays. One pitcher, Adrian De Horta, was released outright. In his nine minor league seasons, De Horta pitched for a dozen different teams and never made it to the majors. Jack Labosky, who pitched for Duke University down the street from DBAP, pitched in the minors for three seasons before he retired at the ripe old age of twenty-five.

The Bulls had 37 different pitchers toss at least an inning for them in the first half of the season and 18 of them also tossed for the Rays. As Bulls, these pitchers tossed 306.1 innings and had a collective ERA of 3.50. The number of walks plus hits they gave up each inning (WHIP) averaged 1.25. As Rays, they pitched 209.1 innings with a collective ERA of 5.06 (ouch!) and a WHIP of 1.55. So, the pitchers were also more successful in the minors than the majors.

Of the pitchers who started the season on the Bulls roster, the most successful in the majors was Colin Poche. Poche had pitched in 26 games for the Rays in relief. He had two wins and no losses and had converted five of six save opportunities. His ERA was 2.25 and he had a WHIP under 1 (0.92). Poche had pitched only six innings for the Bulls in six appearances, with one save, before his promotion on April 22. In those six innings, he gave up one hit and two walks but struck out eleven.

HEADING BACK TO WORK

So, what did I learn during my month away from DBAP? First, I learned the Bulls are staying in Durham for a good long time. The guts of DBAP will get an upgrade and I suspect another long-term lease will be signed shortly thereafter. Fans won't see these improvements, but complaints about the fan experience at the ballpark are few and far between anyway.

Second, I gained a new, first-hand appreciation for the skills exhibited by professional baseball players. I've argued in the past that hitting a baseball that is

> a sphere formed by yarn wound around a small sphere of cork, rubber, or similar materials covered with two strips of white horsehide or cowhide, tightly stitched together . . . [and weighing] not less than 5 nor more than 5¼ ounces avoirdupois and measure no less than nine nor more than 9¼ inches in circumference[9]

thrown at you between 80 and 100 miles an hour with a movement meant to deceive you while you try to hit it using

> a smooth, rounded stick not more than 2.61 inches in diameter at the thickest part and not more than 42 inches in length[10]

is the most difficult challenge in all of sports. Can you think of another athletic activity where being successful once in four attempts is acceptable?

Third, I learned that a few obscure statistics can be generated that confirm what we sense about minor league baseball. Cream rises to the top and in this case is skimmed off. Life as a minor league baseball fan is filled with conflicting emotions, wishing the best for players but knowing that if they do succeed, they will be gone. The Bulls listed 101 comings and goings—promotions, demotions, injuries, releases, retirements—from opening day until the end of June. That's more than one a day. If you're hoping your team will run away with a championship, you'll likely be disappointed.

Fourth, I learned I'm excited about getting back to work.

---

[9] Official Baseball Rules, 2019, Section 3.1, https://img.mlbstatic.com/mlb-images/image/upload/mlb/wqn5ah4c3qtivwx3jatm.pdf

[10] Official Baseball Rules, 2019, Section 3.2(a), https://img.mlbstatic.com/mlb-images/image/upload/mlb/wqn5ah4c3qtivwx3jatm.pdf

Chapter 10
Home Series 7: Happy Birthday, USA

A man once told me to walk with the Lord. I'd rather walk with the bases loaded.

—Ken Singleton, ballplayer

Three more saves and he ties John the Baptist.

—Hank Greenwald, ballplayer

MEMPHIS (AGAIN)

https://en.wikipedia.org/wiki/Memphis,_Tennessee
https://en.wikipedia.org/wiki/Memphis_Redbirds

Nickname: Redbirds
MLB Affiliate: St. Louis Cardinals (1998–present)

MONDAY, JULY 4

They warned me about today. It's the Fourth of July. It's ninety-five degrees on the street outside the ballpark when I arrive. For the fireworks display after the game, all ten thousand seats will be filled, standing room only tickets will be sold out, and after the seventh inning the gates will be open for everyone who wants to come in and watch.

My assignment tonight is behind the visitor's dugout. It is already shady there when I arrive at four-thirty in the afternoon and the roof fans are providing a gentle breeze. Dinner for the hosts is as American as apple pie, but with no apple pie—hot dogs, mac and cheese, baked beans, and watermelon. While eating standing up before the host's meeting begins, Josh excitedly tells me he got to work the tunnel the night before at a non-Bulls game. He had a radio and an opportunity to use it when a woman had a violent stomach episode. Bon appétit.

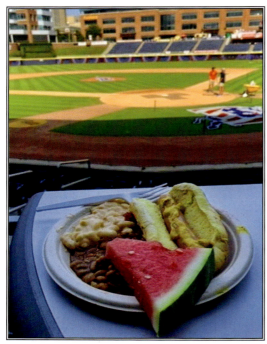

The Fourth of July employees' dinner at the ballpark.

After wiping down my seats, I approach two guys occupying seats well before the gates are open for fans.

"You're here early. You work here?"

I learn one is a scout. My effort at making baseball talk is shooed away. "We got to talk shop," says one. Minutes later, I hear the clank of metal cleats against concrete and see a player on the visiting Memphis Redbirds making his way up the aisle from the dugout. Jacob Bosiokovic is a pitcher from Ohio who knows the scout. They greet each other warmly and have a ten-minute conversation.

"Things are gonna get weird tonight," host John tells me. "At least we get paid time and a half." This I didn't know. It appears the uniqueness of this night has been institutionalized for staff.

The fans start to pile in. Before the game begins, I can sense there are lots of folks here who don't visit the ballpark very often. Two women with mobility issues climb twenty steps to get to their seats, which are less than ten yards from an elevator they could have used. I assist them and show them where the lift is. A woman walks by me while she casually breastfeeds her infant child. A man walks by sporting a six-inch goatee dyed purple.

Then there is the attire. A burly young gentleman passes me wearing a backwards ball cap, camo shorts, and a T-shirt that reads "Rebel Scum." A young woman wears goth-style makeup, a heavy black dress, and black suede boots up to her thighs. In this heat? The price we pay for fashion! An older gentleman walks by wearing a T-shirt with an outline portrait of a man and the name "Chomsky" underneath it. Noam Chomsky is an influential American linguist, philosopher, and leftist political activist. I hope he's not sitting next to Rebel Scum guy. Or maybe they should talk. A "Father Sithmas" T-shirt strolls by with a picture of Darth Vader as Santa Claus. There's a Star Wars night coming up. Maybe this guy will return.

I stop to talk to a woman wearing a Savannah Bananas jersey. This brings a smile to my face. The Bananas are making a play to become the Harlem Globetrotters of baseball. The players dance to pop music (for example, Britney Spears, Michael Jackson, Toby Keith) before, after, and even during games. Reportedly, the Bananas' first base coach is an exceptional dancer. Home runs send the ball players into the stands for high-fives. The rules of the game are a bit different too. Bunting and visits to the mound are not allowed. Most impressive, if a fan catches a foul ball on the fly, the batter is out. But unlike the Globetrotters, the Bananas don't travel with a "opponent." Rather, they play "real" games against local teams.

The game has begun. A Hispanic gentleman standing next to me yells in Spanish to a Memphis Redbirds player. The player turns, waves, and smiles warmly.

"You know him?" I asked.

"I'm his agent," he tells me. "I have been for six years. I signed him out of Puerto Rico."

Sure enough, Delvin Perez is a ballplayer who resides in San Juan, Puerto Rico. He plays infield. The Cardinals picked him 23rd in the first round of the 2016 draft, despite the fact that he was accused of using performance enhancing drugs, a charge vehemently denied by his agent.[1]

While all the seats are sold, there are seats still empty through the first six innings. People not terribly interested in the Bulls buy tickets to have a seat for the fireworks. In a typical game, most fans will be settled in by the end of the third inning. Tonight, assistance with finding seats lasts all night, as does hustling people from seats they have not purchased. By the top of the seventh inning, the stands are almost full. By the eighth, the place is packed, and the walkway is filled with standing room only folks.

A dad with his grown daughter asks, "Which direction do the fireworks go off?"

"Straight up," I respond. The daughter smiles and rolls her eyes.

"I mean, where do they set them off?"

"Behind second base. And I promise you they are not aimed at the stands."

We all smile.

A ninth inning rally fizzles for the Bulls and they lose the game. While the fireworks are set up, on to the field come the mayor pro tem of Durham, Mark-Anthony Middleton, and several other city officials. The fireworks are sponsored by the Durham Department of Parks and Recreation.

Middleton begins his remarks by asking for a moment of silence to express Durham's solidarity with Highland Park, Illinois, where six people were killed and thirty injured in an act of gun violence at a Fourth of July celebration. I hold my breath for the interlude. The moment of silence is followed by a few remarks about how we are all Americans and will soon all be looking up to the sky together. A video about the city's parks and how they are meant for everyone plays on the big screen.

The fireworks last about fifteen minutes. When the show is over, the PA announcer suggests folks sit for a few minutes, so the concourse and roads don't get too congested. This sets off a deluge of people wanting to take pictures while standing on the dugout. This is a no-no for safety reasons. Most picture takers are adults and quickly take the shot, then head off. One group is composed of three adults and six preschoolers, not including the infant in his dad's baby carrier on his chest. The kids clamor onto the dugout, push against the protective netting while jumping around. This must stop. The adults ignore my admonitions, busy talking to one another. I address the kids directly and finally get one's attention. I help him down from the dugout then realize I may have done something wrong. Should I ever touch a fan, especially a child? What if the boy stumbled and hurt himself while I was holding his hand? Note to self: don't do that again. I am told by an employee on the field to get the kids off the dugout. I think, "Easier said than done."

There is a young girl with wet eyes sitting next to her mom in the front row. She has a cork-like ash from the fireworks in her hand that landed on her thigh, causing a small red mark. The girl is clearly unharmed, and mom is spinning this to her as a great souvenir from the Fourth of July celebration at the ballpark. I wish a had a baseball to give her, but I'm clean out.

---

1 https://en.wikipedia.org/wiki/Delvin_P%C3%A9rez

All in all, the weirdness I was led to expect this night did not materialize. Yes, the work was a bit harder and longer. Yes, the diverse crowds that typically fill the stadium for ball games got a bit more diverse. I think that's a good thing. Maybe some of the folks who came because it was a special evening will return when it isn't a holiday occasion.

As I walk to my car, I can't help but construct in my mind how I might moderate a conversation between Mr. Rebel Scum and Mr. Chomsky T-shirts. Would my first question be, "When did you first discover you enjoyed baseball?"

Attendance: 10,757.

THURSDAY, JULY 7

Another blistering day; the 95 degrees feels like 107. There's warnings of severe thunderstorms (that never materialize) and excessive heat (that does). I'm patrolling the outfield Diamond View seats tonight. No shade.

In a rare event, a group of six hosts congregate on the walkway after the gates have opened. The ballpark is quieter and more relaxed than most nights, maybe because we're expecting a sparce crowd.

The conversation among the hosts turns to the USA collegiate team that completed its training camp last week at DBAP.[2] Fifty collegiate ballplayers who are not eligible for the major league draft play at the camp and twenty-six are named to a team that will represent the USA a week later in the Netherlands. A few hosts took on the extra work and hosted at the games.

Dave H. was one host who worked the training camp. He says he was surprised at the lack of intensity exhibited by the players. He also thinks the ball that's used in collegiate play is "deader" than that used in the majors and minors: "Foul balls that hit on the roof didn't make the same bang, more of a thud. I've got one in my bag. I'm gonna have to examine it closely."

The NCAA Baseball Rule Book specifications for balls are exactly the same as those used in the majors. However, the rule says the core of the ball can be "rubber, cork, or a combination of both." This potential variation may explain the difference Dave senses. Interestingly, major league and minor league balls are manufactured in different countries (Costa Rica and China, respectively) with a different kind of leather. Tests show the balls perform similarly but major league pitchers can request major league balls when they are on a rehab assignment in the minors. When pitchers are asked to describe the difference in the balls, they mention that major league balls have tighter seams and are slicker. The pitchers also say that college balls have raised seams.[3]

The conversation turns to a new sign above a party deck in right field. The banner now reads "Decky McDeck Base."

"Who the hell came up with that?" someone exclaims. "I guess sponsors gets what they want, as long as they pay up."

All agree the name is pretty silly. But it's memorable, I think, and will elicit smiles when it's the answer to a fan's question about where they are supposed to find their seats.

As the game begins, I meet a college student serving as an intern. The internship is his last requirement

---

[2] https://www.usabaseball.com/team-usa/collegiate-national-team

[3] https://blogs.fangraphs.com/four-perspectives-how-do-mlb-and-milb-balls-differ/

HOME SERIES 7: HAPPY BIRTHDAY, USA

before getting his degree in recreation operations. It's not his first summer at DBAP, though. In high school he worked as a host when his father worked here as well. He grew up in Connecticut but moved here when he was nine years old. He loves the area but hates the heat of summer. Amen. About halfway through the game, he disappears. An inning or two later, another intern comes looking for him. I have no idea where he is.

There are about two dozen people sitting in the nine hundred or so seats I'm surveilling. Still, a couple chooses to show me their tickets before they take their seats. "Sit wherever you want," I tell them. After chasing so many people from the more expensive seats, it feels really good to say this. Later, I see the guy carrying his food packaging up twenty steps to throw it out, rather than leave it under his seat like most people do. "That's what we call being 'over-socialized,'" I remark to him, putting on my social psychologist hat. It elicits a smile from the gentleman. I like people like that.

For the first time, a police officer initiates a conversation with me. I mention how different this game is from the tumult of Independence Day. We talk about how people just want to get out after two years of COVID restrictions. He tells me he doesn't work many games but really enjoys when he does. He's gonna bring his three kids to a game.

"How old are they?" I ask.

"Nine, seven, and four."

I give him the ball from my pocket. "Here, this'll make you a hero at home."

He smiles broadly, thanks me profusely, and walks off rubbing up the ball.

I notice a boy heading for the topiary section of the lawn area in dead centerfield. He's not supposed to go there. As I approach, I see his mother is standing guard by the sign that reads, "No admittance."

"He saw a ball hit in there and wants it," she says to me.

The boy finds the ball quickly and is out of there.

The game goes into extra innings. A host I haven't met approaches me. She is a young female host, a rarity indeed.

"Hey, do we get paid overtime if the game goes past ten o'clock?" she asks.

"Good question," I respond, "I don't know. This is my first extra inning game."

"Do they call the game after ten innings? There's no more space on the scoreboard."

Clearly, she's not a big baseball fan. "No, they just take the inning scores off the board and put the eleventh inning where the first inning is."

She is a sophomore at a state university campus. She's working at DBAP to make money for school. Her mom works in Wool E. World, where the kids can play on inflatables. She's my second encounter with a multi-generation DBAP family member tonight.

The Redbirds score a run in the top of the tenth inning, but the Bulls respond with two in the bottom half of the inning to win the game. My watch reads exactly 9:59 p.m. Sorry, we won't find out about overtime tonight.

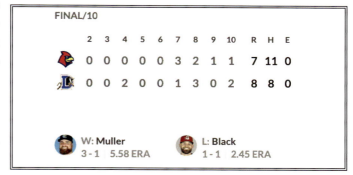

Attendance: 4,907.

SATURDAY, JULY 9

Another night where the weather is the main topic of discussion as I arrive at the ballpark.

I ask another early arriving host, Antyom G., "Gonna rain tonight?"

"Maybe. My app says about 8:30 p.m."

It seems everyone who works at the ballpark has a weather app.

"8:30 p.m.? Mine says a lot earlier than that."

"Oh yeah, My app is set to military time. I'm way off."

"Were you in the military?" I ask.

"No," he says, "I wish I could have been, but I have two steel rods in my back. I had scoliosis."

My assignment is the terrace boxes. This is my third time at these boxes but it's the first time I learn there is a list I can get that tells me who rented each box. A veteran host tells me this and helps me find the list. There's no roof over the terraces if it rains, but the bar at Jackie's Landing is wide enough that I can stake out a spot under that, if need be.

I eat dinner watching the bullpen pre-game warm up. The ballplayers are tossing plastic discs before the coaches arrive and, with regularity, the discs fly into the stands. A barefoot player hops the railing to retrieve one. With my dinner taco consumed, I help him and introduce myself.

Pregame warm up (Everyone loves Wool E.)

He asks, "How long have you worked here?"

"This is my first year."

"It's a great team," Shoeless says.

"Yep, and a great city and ballpark," I reply.

We talk about THE movie and its impact on the team. The pitcher tells me he hasn't yet walked past Annie's house.

"I better go put my shoes on."

"Certainly, before the game starts."

At 5:15 p.m. the rain and thunder arrive. Fifteen minutes later a rain delay is announced, with no anticipated start time. My weather app says to expect moderate rain until 10:00 p.m. but these estimates change about every five minutes. It's summer in North Carolina.

Taking away the tarp.

I take cover under the roof of the bar.

A bartender says, "Last night the game didn't start until eight o'clock and went until half past eleven."

She tells me she works for the concessions company.

"Are you a trained bartender?"

"No."

"Well, I guess you don't get asked for many fancy drinks."

"We wouldn't have the ingredients if we were asked, anyway."

A Fan Ambassador, one of the folks who walk around with the "How May I Help You?" signs, joins me under the roof. He's about to graduate from college as a history major but is really enjoying working at the ballpark. He tells me of another fan ambassador who they call "The Judge" because he's retired after sitting on the North Carolina state bench. I've met this guy. His name is David L.

The Ambassador then relates a story about playing ball with some friends in the rain during a thunderstorm and tornado warning.

"We were using an aluminum bat."

"That's not too smart."

"Well, the field had a chain link fence, so we thought lightning would hit that."

I roll my eyes. Is he trying to impress me with his lack of judgement?

"Anyway, I was pitching and got hit in the solar plexus by a ball, so that ended it."

I roll my eyes again.

He says his shift is over at eight o'clock and he hopes to head out then. Sure enough, at eight o'clock, he disappears. When he leaves, I'm left to be the only one patrolling the right field seats in foul territory beyond first base.

I head down to the concourse for a little leg stretch and to get out of the rain for a minute. I'm surprised at how busy the concourse is; in fact, despite the sparse crowd, you wouldn't know it was raining outside from all the activity. There are lines at the concessions and the team store is full. It occurs to me that maybe a long delay or even a postponed game isn't the worst thing for the team, economically speaking. When I mention this to another host, my observation elicits no surprise. "That's where they make their money anyway, under the seats."

I see David L., the Judge, and engage him.

"Hey, I heard you're a retired judge."

"Thirty-eight years."

I ask, "When you're a judge, do you get ratings, kinda like an umpire?"

"No, but—and I hate to brag—the lawyers named me judge of the year once. Some young judges want to build reputations as being tough on this or that. I just took 'em one at a time."

I look David L. up when I get home. He is a lifelong Durham resident. In 1979, he won election to the district court and served for sixteen years. Then, he spent eight years as a superior court judge. His special interest involved juveniles passing through the judicial system and he served on the board of directors of the Durham Child Advocacy Commission where he took a special interest in alternative mechanisms for handling juvenile delinquency in the judicial system.[4]

"And now you're living the dream, in a neon orange shirt hoisting a sign," I say to The Judge.

Big smile.

There's a break in the rain. My app says the rain will stop at 8:00 p.m. The scoreboard now reads the anticipated start time for the game is 8:10 p.m. Sure enough, that's when it starts. While the terrace boxes are all sold, they are only maybe a quarter full. Everyone is well-behaved except for some preschoolers who stand in the aisle and toss their Wool E. Bull dolls in the air. I stop them twice and talk to their parents. That didn't work; now they toss them in the air and wave at me. Sometimes, attention, regardless of whether it is positive or negative, is the best reinforcer of behavior.

At half past ten o'clock, after seven innings, I'm told I can head home if I want. This offer is made to hosts occasionally when games go past ten o'clock and someone's section has pretty much emptied out. The game lasted another hour. And then there are the post-game fireworks. The stadium doesn't clear out until near midnight.

Attendance: 7,478.

---

4   http://andjusticeforall.dconc.gov/gallery_images/david-q-labarre-district-and-superior-court-judge-1978-2002/

SUNDAY, JULY 10

More rain. We report to work at three o'clock for a game that normally doesn't start until five o'clock. Lots of standing around. To make matters worse, another game delay is announced.

I get to talking with Rob, another retiree working the game in the section next to me. Rob was a computer equipment salesperson for twenty-two years when data was stored on tapes. When he quit doing that, he sold Audis for a while then went to work part-time for Hershey's chocolate.

Steve joins us, and the conversation covers a wide range of topics. Automobiles dominate, especially the rising attraction of electric cars. I reminisce about sitting between my parents as a young child on the front seat of the family's Packard. "On the bump, no seat belt."

This allusion to car safety prompts Rob to open the topic of government regulations. It's all downhill from there. It's clear we have a variety of political opinions in our little group. Rob and Steve take opposite sides on current events and while they are not shy to express their views, they are also very respectful in the exchange. This is the first exchange of political views I've heard in my two dozen games as a host.

Thank goodness Jatovi McDuffie walks by. Jatovi is the on-field emcee for the pre, post, and between-innings festivities. Except for Wool E. Bull, he is the most recognizable face in Bulls country. Jatovi is Durham born and raised and came to this job after performing improvisational comedy. He has worked with a faith-based school for kids at risk. He's also the father of a daughter and son.[5]

Jatovi's been doing this job for about seventeen years, but you wouldn't know it from his remarkable level of enthusiasm. Last night, when there were lots of empty seats, he exuded the same excitement as on Independence Day, with an audience of over ten thousand. When not on the field, he strolls the walkway and aisles, greeting friends and strangers alike. Typically, he has a cadre of assistants, known as the Lollygaggers, following him around. They help him lead cheers, shepherd equipment on and off the field, and launch T-shirts and rubber balls into the stands.

The game is delayed an hour but then proceeds uninterrupted. I'm stationed right behind home plate, the choicest assignment. I brought my chenille mitt tonight and it works like a charm soaking up the rain from seats as fans arrive. Two guys offer me tips that I refuse.

An intern who's a senior in sports management at North Carolina State comes by and asks how things are going. He wants to make a living doing what he's doing for the Bulls and hopes to stay in North Carolina, where his parents, girlfriend, and girlfriend's parents all live. "But," he says, "if the right offer comes along . . ."

While we chat, the Redbirds score a run on a grounder to the second baseman, who chooses to go to first rather than throw home to try and get out a runner who was on third. A discussion ensues about the fielder's choice rule and its reliance on the judgement of the official scorer.[6] This leads to talk of other baseball plays that involve scoring discretion, such as the infield fly rule. For the infield fly rule to be invoked, in this case by the umpires, (a) there must be runners on first and second base or all three bases, (b) there must be no outs or one out in the inning and (c) the hit must be a fly ball or popup, not a line drive, (there's the judgement call) in the infield and in fair territory. The rule is meant to prevent a fielder from deliberately letting the ball hit the field so they can

---

5 Stephenson, S. (2014). *Bull City Summer: A Season at the Ballpark.* Daylight Community Arts Foundation: www.daylightbooks.com.

6 Rule 2, Section 14: "A fielder's choice is the act of a fielder with a live ball, who elects to throw for an attempted putout or to retire unassisted any runner or batter-runner, thus permitting the advance of another runner(s). The scorer decides whether the batter is credited with a safe hit or an extra base hit . . ."

scoop it up and start a double play. I'm surprised to learn that the runners on base are free to advance after the infield fly rule has been invoked, if they think they can avoid being tagged out. The umpire also decides whether an infielder, the pitcher, or catcher could make the catch using "ordinary effort."[7]

Finally, we turn to the discretion the official scorer has in assigning errors. This is the big one. The baseball rule for scoring errors delineates eight conditions for when an error should be charged and numerous examples of plays that are not errors. The rule says an error should be charged against a fielder "whose misplay (fumble, muff or wild throw) prolongs the time at bat of a batter, prolongs the presence on the bases of a runner or permits a runner to advance one or more bases, unless, in the judgment of the Official Scorer, such fielder deliberately permits a foul fly to fall safe with a runner on third base before two are out in order that the runner on third shall not score after the catch . . ."[8]

"This one always irked me," I offer, "we've all seen guys miss balls we think should have been gloved but, because they never touched the ball, it's scored a hit."

We agree. I'm emboldened.

"Also, the rule penalizes fielders with a lot of range. If they get to balls other guys couldn't reach and muff it, they get charged with an error and their fielding stats suffer. Why not lope over and just let the ball drop?"

The intern's radio goes off and he hustles away, promising to continue this discussion in the future.

It's Sunday night so kids get to run the bases. Timothy Troy, the manager of member relations, takes care of the folks with suites and season tickets. He has a great smile, certainly an asset in his position.

He asks me if a gentleman and his son can sit for the ninth inning right behind home plate.

"He wants to explain to his kid what a curve ball is," says Tim.

"He can explain that to me, too," I say. "I understand that how you hold the ball, it's speed on delivery, and release point will affect how it travels to the plate, but I'm amazed at how baseball announcers can identify what kind of pitch it is right after it's thrown. I certainly can't."

Tim tries to explain it all to me, throwing in the difference between lefty and righty pitchers. I'm more confused. This is gonna take some studying.

Tim stations himself by me waiting to direct the kids off the field after they've run the bases; when the kids go on the field, it's all-hands-on-deck. The game ends and the PA blares "I Want to Dance with

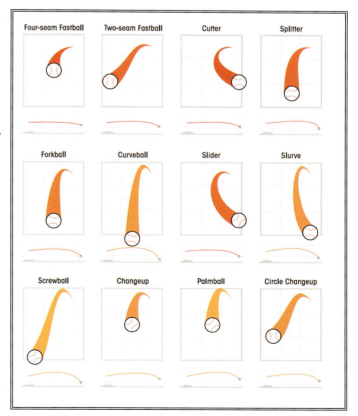

How pitches move.

---

7 https://www.mlb.com/news/the-infield-fly-rule-a-history-and-explanation
8 https://baseballrulesacademy.com/official-rule/mlb/9-12-errors/

Somebody" by Whitney Houston while the kids and their folks line up. A woman seated nearby stands to dance and moves onto the walkway. Tim joins her, to the delight of all the fans nearby. Bowing to peer pressure, I join in. Oh, the woman happens also to be my spouse, Beth, who attends occasional games, purchases a seat near my station, and practices her newfound hobby of scoring games.

Tim and I fist bump as he heads down to the field. Are we having fun, or what?

Attendance: 5,467.

Running the bases.

LITTLE LEAGUERS TAKE THE FIELD, BUT THE CIRCUMSTANCES COULD BE BETTER

Monday morning, I learn that three gunshots were fired on Sunday at a little league game in Wilson, North Carolina, an hour east of DBAP.* No one was hurt, and the children were not believed to be the target of the shooting, though the perpetrators and cause are still under investigation. Two days later, the Bulls open the field to the little leaguers, who finish their games on a professional ballfield.

* https://www.newsobserver.com/news/local/crime/article263334553.html

SUGAR

Year of Release: 2008
Rating: R
Directors: Anna Boden and Ryan Fleck
Writers: Anna Boden and Ryan Fleck
Stars: Algenis Perez Soto (pitcher), Jose Rijo (pitcher)

Plot Synopsis

From Wiki: https://en.wikipedia.org/wiki/Sugar_(2008_film)
Sugar is a 2008 sports drama film written and directed by Anna Boden and Ryan Fleck. It follows the story of Miguel Santos, also known as Sugar (Algenis Perez Soto), a Dominican pitcher from San Pedro de Macorís, struggling to make it to the big leagues and pull himself and his family out of poverty. Playing professionally at a baseball academy in the Dominican Republic, Miguel finally gets his break at age nineteen when he advances to the United States' minor league system; but when his play on the mound falters, he begins to question the single-mindedness of his life's ambition.
From IMDb: https://www.imdb.com/title/tt0990413/
Dominican baseball star Miguel "Sugar" Santos is recruited to play in the US minor-leagues.

Critic Ratings

Rotten Tomatoes: https://www.rottentomatoes.com/m/10009355-sugar
Tomatometer: 92 out of 100 (138 reviewers)
Audience Score: 79 out of 100 (10,000+ Ratings)
Critics consensus: Sugar is an exceptionally-crafted film—part sports flick, part immigrant tale—with touching and poignant drama highlighted by splendid performances.
IMDb Rating: 7.2 out of 10 (4,900 raters)
Roger Ebert: https://www.rogerebert.com/reviews/sugar-2009 , 3.5 out of 4 stars.
Ebert writes that the focus of *Sugar* is the immigrant experience in America. He writes, "The filmmakers are too observant to settle for a quick, conventional payoff." Ebert praises Algenis Perez Soto who plays Sugar "so openly, so naturally, that an interesting thing happens: Baseball is only the backdrop. This is a wonderful film."

Chapter 11
Home Series 8: *Bull Durham* Night

In baseball, democracy shines its clearest. The only race that matters is the race to the bag. The creed is the rule book. And color, merely something to distinguish one team's uniform from another's.
—Ernie Harwell, sportscaster

DiMaggio's grace came to represent more than athletic skill in those years. To the men who wrote about the game, it was a talisman, a touchstone, a symbol of the limitless potential of the human individual. That an Italian immigrant, a fisherman's son, could catch fly balls the way Keats wrote poetry or Beethoven wrote sonatas was more than just a popular marvel. It was proof positive that democracy was real. On the baseball diamond, if nowhere else, America was truly a classless society. DiMaggio's grace embodied the democracy of our dreams.
—David Halberstam, author, Summer of '49

The All-Star break is over (the minors didn't play an All-Star game this year but got the days off anyway) and it's back to work. It's also time to pay closer attention to the pennant races. With sixty games to go, a quick look at the standings for the International League East Division suggests the first ninety games have resolved nothing. Only Syracuse and Charlotte have steep hills to climb, probably too steep to make it to the top. The playoff format this season will send only the top teams in the IL East and West to a one game showdown in Las Vegas. The winner then meets the winner of the Pacific Coast League playoff in a one game winner-takes-all for the Level-AAA crown.

INTERNATIONAL LEAGUE EASTERN DIVISION					
Team	MLB	Wins	Losses	Winning Percentage	Games Behind
Lehigh Valley	PHI	49	41	0.544	-
Durham	TB	48	42	0.533	1
Jacksonville	MIA	48	42	0.533	1
Rochester	WSH	47	43	0.522	2
Worcester	BOS	47	43	0.522	2
Buffalo	TOR	46	44	0.511	3
Norfolk	BAL	44	46	0.489	5
Scranton/WB	NYY	44	46	0.489	5
Syracuse	NYM	40	50	0.444	9
Charlotte	CWS	33	57	0.367	16

IL East standings after ninety games.

> **NORFOLK**
> https://en.wikipedia.org/wiki/Norfolk,_Virginia
> https://en.wikipedia.org/wiki/Norfolk_Tides
>
>
>
> Nickname: Tide
> MLB: Baltimore Orioles (2007–present)
> Field: Harbor Park, capacity 11,856
> Population (2020): 238,005
> Economy: largest naval base in the world, defense contracting, cargo ports
> Fun fact: The Tide have been managed by several ballplayers who made their name in the majors, including Hank Bauer, Clint Hurdle, Davey Johnson, and Bobby Valentine.

FRIDAY, JULY 22

I haven't seen Josh since he told me his computer game marketing gig was drying up. When we meet tonight on the buffet line, I enquire about how the job search is going. He says not as well as he would like. He's looking for other part-time jobs like this one with the Bulls. I think to myself that he's entering that subculture of part-time sports venue employees. But compared to the others I've met, he seems "young" for joining this group.

I ask him how old he is and learn that he's in his early forties. I also learn that he has two children from his first marriage. His kids are in their late teens and early twenties. He was nineteen years old the first time he tied the knot. Brought up in a Christian environment, marriage occurred before a couple could consummate their relationship.

Josh offers that he's gonna take some course work preparing him for jobs in computer security.

"That's a field that won't go away any time soon," I opine.

"Yeah," says Josh, "As long as they need people, not computers."

It has to be a bit scary to be his age and retooling for a new profession.

At dinner, Josh and I share a table with a host who is another retired software developer and misses his former job not at all. In addition to hosting for the Bulls, he umpires for high school ballgames. He's done this for twenty-one years and loves it.

"I'm jealous," I say, "I never had the athletic chops to play baseball, any sport for that matter, and umping always interested me. I love interpreting the rule book." Really, it's what I did as a professor when I taught research methods to students. But umping was never in my future either; I've worn glasses since kindergarten and have strabismus, a malady that affects binocular vision. If I umped and was accused of being blind, I'd have to agree that it wasn't far from the truth.

I decide not to tell my table mates that as a sophomore in high school, I was the slowest runner on the worst track team in New York City. When I asked my coach if I was going to get a varsity letter, he just laughed and walked away. I got the message; I didn't come back for junior year. That's the complete history of my athletic career.

When I get home, I look up the Capitol City Umpires group but can find only business websites for it. So, I look up the North Carolina Umpires Association. Their website lists about 150 umpires available for games. It also lists areas for improvement that were discussed during its 2022 in-class training clinic:

- Approachability—All umpires should show the same respect to coaches, players, and parents, that they are given rather than animosity toward questions/appeals if approached properly.
- Balks — Balks should be called with

consistency at every age limit—excluding age nine and under (no balks called).
- Being On Time—There were VERY few instances of this in 2021, but not being on time to tournaments is not acceptable. All umpires should arrive thirty minutes before game time and check in with the site director and crew chief.[1]

Our conversation turns to the number of kids who have big time dreams and the small percentage who will actually make it to the majors. For many, I interject, the majors might not be the goal. If playing ball gets a kid a scholarship who couldn't afford college otherwise, it's a good thing. At home, I look up the stats on college baseball scholarships. The Next College Student Athlete website[2], developed to assist parents and players, tells me there are 1,650 college baseball programs and about 34,500 college ball players. "The competition for roughly 5,400 scholarships is fierce," the site informs visitors. But scholarships can be awarded fractionally, and full rides are rare.

Tonight is *Bull Durham* night at the ballpark, meant to celebrate the movie that more than anything else was the linchpin for this whole experience (in conjunction with Capitol Broadcasting, the team owners that ran with the enthusiasm the movie created, of course). The theme night includes the players wearing special jerseys; the Bulls will be the Shower Shoes, calling out a scene from the movie. Shower Shoes jerseys are available for purchase and signed ones are being auctioned off. Before the game, trivia questions about the movie are flashed on the jumbo screen and during the game Jatovi holds trivia contests with fans who can win prizes. Between innings, a foot race occurs between three ten-foot-tall figures of Crash, Nuke, and Annie. Annie trips and falls down.

Bull Durham movie night.

Before the game, I'm approached by a part-time promotions employee. She's got thick, straight reddish orange hair and is a college student working here for the summer. She's looking to recruit a young girl to shout, "Play ball!" on the field, under the guidance of Jatovi, when the game is about to start. There's a girl sitting in my section next to her father who is in a wheelchair.

"How about her?" I ask.

We approach. Her mom encourages her to do it and she says yes.

A gentleman about my age approaches me and asks, "Do the players come out of the dugout when they take the field?"

"Yep."

"I gotta get the car keys from my son."

"Who's your son?" I ask.

"Grant Witherspoon."

Grant is an outfielder drafted by the Rays in 2018, 120th overall. He's marched through the minors exactly as one would hope; a year in the rookie league followed by one in Level-A, and one in the level above. This season he started at Level-AA Montgomery and played in 49 games (194 at-bats)

---

1 https://ncuaumpires.com/2018/01/21/takeaways-from-2018-in-class-clinic/
2 https://www.ncsasports.org/baseball

batting nearly .300 with an on-base percentage of .346. When Witherspoon emerges from the dugout for the national anthem, his dad yells to him and gets his attention. Dad then raises his arm and acts like he's dangling some keys. Grant shakes his head "no" and turns away.

Dad has traveled from Colorado to watch his son play. The nine-game homestand drew him; he can work remotely. When I mention Grant's impressive rise through the minors, his dad is admirably cautious. "He'll spend some time here; the pitching gets better and better and it takes experience to get comfortable with it."

I find this realistic appraisal commendable. It takes some pressure off his son. Dad doesn't seem to be one of those sports parents we often hear about (see the movies *Fear Strikes Out* and *The Phenom*). Makes me think of my earlier conversation about the number of kids who compete for such a limited number of opportunities. Witherspoon's clearly a winner.

"Good luck; I'll be watching his career," I say to Dad, who walks away with a smile.

About halfway through the game, Timothy, my wife's dance partner, shows up in my section staring at a printout. He goes to a specific seat and engages in a long conversation with the inhabitants. He does this again with another couple. As he walks by me, I ask him what's up.

"There's no problem. I'm checking in with season ticket holders," he replies, "We interact with them a lot over the phone and by email, so it's nice to actually see them, say 'hello' in person, and ask a few questions about their experience. It gives them a face to know."

Nice touch. I'm impressed. Tim T. takes his job seriously and with a big smile.

The Bulls win the game, overcoming a 3-run deficit in the top of the first. They move into a tie for first place with two other teams.

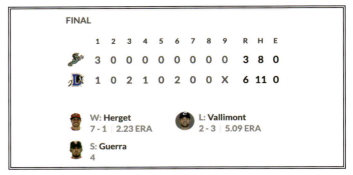

Attendance: 8,513.

SUNDAY JULY 24

The hottest day yet. It's ninety-seven degrees and the heat index is ten degrees higher. My sections are in foul territory, left field. The sun will be at my back. The game is delayed half an hour as thunder rumbles in the distance. The isolated storm misses us.

The autograph hounds are out tonight. I notice the woman I had seen before who carries her baseball card collection and wears a Minor League Baseball T-shirt. I decide to strike up a conversation. I learn her name: Kam. I ask if she's a season ticket holder.

"No, I live Winston-Salem," she offers. Winston-Salem, North Carolina, is about a ninety-minute car ride west of DBAP.

Friday night fireworks.

"You've got a team there, don't you?"

"Yes," Kam replies, "I collect autographs there too."

The Winston-Salem Dash is a Level-A affiliate of the Chicago White Sox. While looking them up after the game, I discover that a few days earlier, the Dash had a player suspended for fifty days for violation of the Minor League Drug Prevention and Treatment Program. Amphetamines.[3]

I notice she carries a neatly written list of ballplayer names and their numbers. These are her quarry. Her card collection, also neatly organized, pictures mostly major leaguers but she points out a few minor league cards mixed in. She tells me there are some players she can recognize by their faces.

"I've been collecting autographs for, oh, forty years," Kam says, proudly. Forty years!

I wonder why someone would pursue such ephemera for so long. Quickly, I'm annoyed at myself. I know exactly why she does what she does. As the Buddhists say, "It's the process, not the outcome that matters." I've done the same thing; I collected sports cards and comic books as a kid. As an adult, I collected baseball pennants from every ballpark I visited, had over forty before I realized new parks were opening faster than I could get to them. People collect shot glasses and plates from places they visit. We all have these passions that have more to do with enjoying a process than with attaining a goal. At least, the lucky among us do.

The autograph hound crowd tonight is much larger by the visitors' dugout than the Bulls' dugout. They all seem to have card collections, not baseballs, so this seems to not be a one-night passion for many of them. But why the imbalance by the dugouts? Is there someone special on the Tide?

"I've got most of the Bulls already," Kam tells me. I suppose this is true of the other hounds in my section. Mystery solved.

The host for the sections next to me is a new face. He looks very young and disinterested, mostly playing on his phone. I try to strike up a conversation but it's pretty one-sided. I ask about how he got here, and he shyly gives soft-spoken answers. He's a high school student and is switching schools for his sophomore year. That makes him about fifteen years old. His mother was contacted by the Bulls and asked if he wanted to work the games. The boy certainly increases the range of ages I find among hosts. Now it's about sixty years, youngest to oldest.

The excitement in the stadium tonight is caused by four foul balls that land around my section. One hits the walkway just a foot from a toddler and takes a big bounce. The fans are atwitter over what a close call this was. Parents should be constantly vigilant when they hear the crack of a bat. Then there is the tween-ager who stood in the middle of the walkway and tossed his cookies for about five minutes. Not the show the fans came to see. But a police officer was right there, radioed the cleanup crew, and the mess was gone with admirable speed. I've got curly-haired twin high school boys sitting in my section with a relative in a wheelchair. They eat hamburgers, funnel cakes, and soft ice cream.

Somehow, I still have an appetite. I take a break to have dinner at the taco stand just a few yards from where I'm on patrol. I sit at the bar to eat, where the drink selection is the typical limited ballpark fare (a spirit and soda), except this bar makes a specialty tequila drink to go with the Mexican food. (No, no alcohol for me while on the job.)

The T-shirt that captures my attention today reads EQU42ITY. I asked the wearer if the "42" is a reference to Jackie Robinson. Yep. The T-shirt is made by a company named Baseballism.[4] The company was formed by four former college baseball players who started a youth baseball camp that taught "the

---

[3] https://www.mlb.com/press-release/press-release-two-minor-league-players-suspended-x1257

[4] https://www.baseballism.com/pages/our-story

fundamentals of the game as well as the life lessons learned on the diamond." After the camp closed the players came back together to form the clothing company "built for love of the game."

The Bulls win again. The Sunday night run-the-bases for the kids goes off without a hitch.

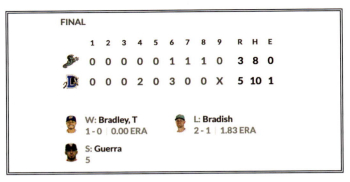

Attendance: 5,706.

HOME SERIES 8: BULL DURHAM NIGHT

BULL DURHAM

Year of Release: 1988
Rating: R
Director: Ron Shelton
Writer: Ron Shelton
Stars: Kevin Costner (catcher), Susan Sarandon (score keeper), Tim Robbins (pitcher)
Setting: Durham Athletic Park, Durham, North Carolina

Plot Synopsis

From Wiki: https://en.wikipedia.org/wiki/Bull_Durham
Bull Durham is a 1988 American romantic comedy sports film. It is partly based upon the minor-league baseball experiences of writer/director Ron Shelton and depicts the players and fans of the Durham Bulls, a minor-league baseball team in Durham, North Carolina.

The film stars Kevin Costner as "Crash" Davis, a veteran catcher from the AAA Richmond Braves, brought in to teach rookie pitcher Ebby Calvin "Nuke" LaLoosh (Tim Robbins) about the game in preparation for reaching the major leagues. Baseball groupie Annie Savoy (Susan Sarandon) romances Nuke but finds herself increasingly attracted to Crash. Also featured are Robert Wuhl and Trey Wilson, as well as popular baseball "clown" Max Patkin.

From IMDb: https://www.imdb.com/title/tt0094812/
A fan who has an affair with one minor-league baseball player each season meets an up-and-coming pitcher and the experienced catcher assigned to him.

Critic Ratings

Rotten Tomatoes: https://www.rottentomatoes.com/m/bull_durham
Tomatometer: 97 out of 100 (71 reviewers)
Audience Score: 82 out of 100 (50,000+ Ratings)
Critics consensus: Kevin Costner is at his funniest and most charismatic in *Bull Durham*, a film that's as wise about relationships as it is about minor league baseball.
IMDb Rating: 7 out of 10 (53,781 raters)
Roger Ebert: https://www.rogerebert.com/reviews/bull-durham-1988, 3.5 out of 4 stars.
Ebert thinks Bull Durham is a "treasure of a movie because it knows so much about baseball and so little about love." He finds it to be an improbable romantic fantasy, and the dynamic between the three lead characters is unsustainable. He thinks the movie ends just right, not because the outcome is plausible but because we want to believe in the power of love.

Chapter 12
Seasons Past: Club History

If my uniform doesn't get dirty, I haven't done anything in the baseball game.
—Rickey Henderson, baseball player

The other teams could make trouble for us if they win.
—Yogi Berra, quote machine

We've walked through a brief history of the city of Durham. We've read the newspapers that reported on the history of the minor leagues (okay, those were made up, but the events were true). Now we need to finish our journey through the past by following the Durham ball club on its passage from inception to my season in the stands. Luckily, when Mr. Peabody (Hector J. to friends[1]) retired his Way Back (WABAC) time machine that he used for his television cartoon "Peabody's Improbable History" (the first of its kind invented by a dog), he left it in my care. Let's think about hopping in. Where in Bulls' history might we go?[2,3]

---

[1] https://mr-peabody-sherman.fandom.com/wiki/Mr._Peabody#Peabody's_Improbable_History
[2] This history is based largely on the following sources:
Blake, M. (1991). *The Minor Leagues: A Celebration of the Little Show*, New York, NY: Wynwood Press.
Chadwick, B. (1994). *Baseball's Hometown Teams: The Story of Minor League Baseball.* New York, NY: Abbeville Press.
Holaday, J.C. (1998). *Professional Baseball in North Carolina.* Jefferson, NC: McFarland & Co.
Obojski, R. (1975) *Bush League: A Colorful, Factual Account of Minor League Baseball From 1877 to the Present.* New York, NY: Macmillan.
https://en.wikipedia.org/wiki/Durham_Bulls
Various Wikipedia pages about the ballplayers mentioned as well as their statistics pages at Sports Reference, https://www.sports-reference.com/, Baseball Reference https://www.baseball-reference.com/
[3] If you are interested in a close-up history of the Bulls since 1980, check out Rob Morris's book, *No Bull: The Real Story of the Rebirth of a Team and a City.* (2017). Durham, NC: Baseball America Books.

Mr. Peabody and his Boy Sherman enter the WABAC machine.

THE TOBACCONISTS

Depending on whose history we read, we might pick the Trinity College baseball field on April 24, 1902, as our first stop.[4] The Durham Tobacconists played on Hanes Field, named after Pleasant H. Hanes, the founder of the clothing company that still bears his name—and whose name might be on the undies you're wearing. North Carolina is known as a textile and furniture hub, as well as for its tobacco. Today, Hanes Field is used as a field hockey venue on Duke University's East Campus. At that game in 1902, we would watch the Tobacconists beat the Trinity College team 8–5 in an exhibition contest.

Or, we could go to Charlotte, North Carolina, on May 5, 1902, and see the hometown Hornets clobber the Tobacconists 12–2. This was the first game that counted in the North Carolina League standings. Doesn't sound like much fun. Maybe we'll wait another week and go to the first home game that counted, against the New Bern Truckers.

But we're getting ahead of ourselves. How did baseball get to Durham, anyhow?

The Tobacconists were a member of the North Carolina League. Durham was one of six cities to secure a spot in the newly formed North Carolina League, joining Charlotte, Greensboro, New Bern, Raleigh, and Wilmington. The owner of the Durham team was the lawyer William G. Bramham, a native of Durham and graduate of the University of North Carolina. The league played at Level-C.

For its short history, the North Carolina League was an afterthought of the minor leagues. When the minor leagues held a meeting in Chicago, Illinois, on September 5, 1901, the heads of seven professional baseball leagues formed the National Association of Professional Baseball Leagues. Four other leagues, including the North Carolina League (not yet fielding teams), were also represented, and agreed to comply with the National Association rules. Attendees planned to meet again in October in New York City. There, they developed an agreement on a grading system for the leagues based on the talent level of the players. Talent level? Who could gauge that across teams? Really, the grades were based on the size of the city the teams played in. The agreement also established the number of players a team could have on their roster, salary levels for players, and restrictions on players moving from team to team, and that wonderful reserve clause that suppressed player salaries.

We have encountered before Judge W. G. Bramham, the Tobacconists' owner, because of his involvement in minor league baseball writ large (he's got an inset on the DBAP sidewalk as you enter the stadium). In addition to his ownership of the Tobacconists, W. G. would preside over four minor leagues and go on to be the third president of the National Association for thirteen years. He's credited with stabilizing the finances of minor league ball clubs during the Great Depression and keeping minor league baseball afloat during World War II.[5] But, I don't think we'll use the WABAC to go to these meetings. Who wants to visit

---

4   https://www.milb.com/durham/tickets/durham-tobacconists

5   https://www.milb.com/milb/history/presidents

SEASONS PAST: CLUB HISTORY

William G. Bramham (center) attending the National Association of Baseball Leagues banquet in 1946.

a stuffy hotel meeting room when so many ballgames await?

The baseball dreams of North Carolinians didn't last long. On July 12, 1902, Bramham refused to let Durham play New Bern and declared the North Carolina League dead. In their only season, the Tobacconists played 48 games. They lost 27 of them and finished fifth in the six-team league.

I don't think we want to go to that last game of the Tobacconists. Too sad. And it's not like we won't have enough games to attend. After all, as of Monday, May 30, 2022, the Bulls had played 13,119 games, winning 6,759 of them. That's a .515 winning percentage accumulated over more than one hundred years. How do I know this? Look back to the Game Information Sheet in Chapter 8 that the team provides at each game. Near the bottom of the right-most column, you'll find a running total of all Bulls wins and losses.

Have the Durham teams been just average? Nope. In fact, the chance that a team that was just average (that is, should win exactly half its games) would win 51.5 percent of them over 13,000 games is vanishingly small, what we call "decimal dust" in the statistics biz.[6]

NORTH CAROLINA STATE LEAGUE (1913–1917)

A Durham team would not take the field again until 1913 when the Bulls played on Hanes Field as a member of the six team North Carolina State League. Six of the largest cities in North Carolina were represented in this Level-D league. The league lasted only four years, succumbing to the need for men to fight in World War I.

The Bulls had a successful run in the league, amassing a cumulative record of 290 wins against 214 losses. But a pennant eluded them. They finished a half game behind Winston-Salem in 1913, then a game and a half behind co-winners Winston-Salem and Charlotte in 1914. They played .570 ball in 1915 but finished second. In 1916, their 62–51 record was good only for a third-place finish. Then, 1916 looked like the Bulls' year. Early in the season, they were playing .667 ball (24–12). Snake bit, that was the year the league disbanded before it finished the season, another victim of World War I. Knowing the frustration the Bulls experienced in the North Carolina

The Durham Bulls of 1913 at Doherty (East Durham) Ballpark.

---

6 https://en.wikipedia.org/wiki/Sign_test

League, I'd put these years near the bottom of our time machine itinerary.

PIEDMONT LEAGUE (1920–1933, 1936–1943)

The Bulls returned in 1920 as members of the newly formed Level-D Piedmont League. They played at Doherty Park, a wooden structure named after the majority owner of the Durham Traction Company, until 1926 before moving to El Toro Park, later rechristened Durham Athletic Park. This league encompassed five teams from North Carolina and one from Danville, Virginia (a team that absconded with the nickname Tobacconists). In the inaugural season, the Bulls finished last. For the 1921 season, the Piedmont League moved up to Level-C and the Bulls jumped from sixth all the way to fifth place. In 1922, the Bulls tasted their first championship, defeating the High Point Furniture Makers four games to three (with one tie) in the league playoffs.

The 1922 Bulls were managed by Lee Gooch, who also played outfield and hit .350 that season. Gooch, born and raised in North Carolina, did two short stints in the majors in 1915 and 1917. He came to bat nineteen times for two different big-league teams. The highlight of his career came on June 17, 1917, when he hit his only major league home run for the Philadelphia Athletics. Gooch finished his career with ten years in the minors. Maybe that eighth game of the Bulls' first championship playoff would be worth firing up the WABAC.

The Bulls would play nineteen seasons, from 1923 to 1943, in the Piedmont League, as the league ascended from Level-D to Level-B ball. They missed two seasons when the team disbanded due to poor attendance. In their last year in the Piedmont League, the Bulls were the only representative of North Carolina and finished last. They also enjoyed affiliations with five different major league teams. Their results on the field during these years were decidedly mixed. They won four pennants but lost two playoffs. Back then, seasons were split into a first and second half with the winner of each half meeting for the championship. The Bulls finished last four times.

A ballplayer of note during the Piedmont League years was the pitcher, John Vander Meer. Vander Meer was in the minors for only three seasons, one with the Bulls. In 1936 for Durham, he compiled a nineteen and six records, with an ERA of 2.65. Impressive by today's standards, Vander Meer completed 21 of the 25 games he started. At the major league level, Vander Meer is best known for being the only pitcher to throw two consecutive no-hitters, the second coming in the first night game to be played at Ebbets Field. He was a four-time All Star and is a member of the Cincinnati Reds Hall of Fame. Bulls' fans today, at least the female fans, know Vander Meer best because a plaque commemorating his time as a Bull graces the wall in a women's bathroom (he also has a brick outside DBAP; Vander Meer and Crash Davis are the only two players honored with both a brick and a plaque).

Johnny Vander Meer plaque.

Maybe the highlight of Durham's time in the Piedmont League occurred on July 7, 1926, when El Toro Park became the new home of the Bulls. This wood structure was destroyed by a fire in June 1939 that nearly killed an employee. However, just two weeks after the conflagration, concrete stands for 1,000 fans were constructed. A new stadium on the same site, renamed Durham Athletic Park (DAP), opened for the 1940 season. At one point, the centerfield fence at DAP rested 460 feet from home plate (with trees, bushes, and telephone poles on the field) and the left field line was 390 feet long, but it was an inviting 290 feet down the right field line.[7] Its grandstand could seat 2,000 fans and had movable bleachers. DAP's capacity is now 5,000 and has held as many as 6,202 guests.[8] This venue would also provide the setting for the movie *Bull Durham*.

But it's that opening day of the 1926 season that we would want to attend. Kennesaw Mountain Landis, the commissioner of baseball, attended the ceremony. Before he became commissioner, Landis was a renowned judge who presided over numerous high-profile cases. Also, he was not averse to public attention; he played himself in a movie titled *The Immigrant* that was filmed in his courtroom. Landis was appalled at the influence of gambling on baseball, becoming commissioner just after the Black Sox scandal.[9] He also revamped the relationship between major and minor league teams but had a decidedly mixed record on racial issues in baseball.

Not only would the opening day of DAP be worth a trip back in time, but the Commish stole the show. You see, Landis rode into the park atop a bull. I want to see that.

---

7   Blake, M. (1991). *The Minor Leagues: A Celebration of the Little Show.* New York, NY: Wynwood.

8   Rosen, I. (2006). *The American Game: A Celebration of Minor League Baseball.* New York, NY: Collins.pg. 9.

9   https://en.wikipedia.org/wiki/Black_Sox_Scandal

Kenesaw Mountain Landis plays himself in a movie.

CAROLINA LEAGUE (1945–1971, 1980–1997)

Durham fielded no team in 1944, due to difficulties created by World War II. In 1945, the city found a home in the Carolina League that would last over forty years.

Because of the war, athletic young men were hard to come by, so teams sought out players who were physically unfit to serve in the military, were past their prime, or too young to serve. Among the "finds" for the Bulls was a fifteen-year-old pitcher named Tom Poholsky. Poholsky won five of eight games he pitched for Durham. Overall, he had a .597 winning percentage as a minor leaguer, even winning the International League MVP in 1950. Six years in the majors, mostly with the St. Louis Cardinals, weren't as kind to Tom; he compiled a 31–52 record with a 3.93 ERA.

Don't think playing in the same league for over forty seasons meant the Durham team had finally achieved stability. Low attendance for the Bulls and the Raleigh Pirates led the two teams to merge in 1968 and split home games between two stadiums. In 1970, the team was jettisoned by its major league affiliate, the Phillies, so it played as an independent team, the Triangles, for two seasons before disappearing completely from 1972 until 1980. The Bulls also changed major league affiliations six times.

The Durham teams were not unique. The Carolina League itself was far from a paragon of stability. You can count two dozen different cities that fielded teams for a league that rarely had more than six or eight clubs playing at any one time. If you count nickname changes, ninety different names were associated with Carolina League teams. Until recent years, "change" and "instability" would be the best descriptors of the minor leagues, especially those that play at the lower-classification levels.

On the field, there wasn't much to shout about for the Bulls during the Carolina League years. They won only two championships, in 1957 and 1967. Also, 1957 was the year the first Black ballplayers took the field for the Bulls.

THE STORIED CAREER OF FRED VAN DUSEN

Even though he didn't play for the Bulls, I must tell this story: the most valuable player in 1957 was Fred Van Dusen of the High Point-Thomasville Hi-Toms. Van Dusen's is memorable because his major league career last exactly one at-bat in 1955. He was hit by a pitch.

In 1962, the Bulls had the league's MVP. Daniel Joseph "Rusty" Staub was also nicknamed "Le Grande Orange" because of his red hair. Staub played in 140 games for the Bulls, hit .293 and walked 112 times in 640 plate appearances. He went on to play 23 seasons in the majors.

In 1981, the Bulls' Brad Komminsk won the MVP award. Komminsk played eight seasons in the majors, sixteen in the minors, and managed in the minors for nine seasons. His years in the majors were a disappointment, especially for the Atlanta Braves. Seems the Braves turned down an offer to trade Komminsk to the Boston Red Sox for Jim Rice, who entered the MLB Hall of Fame in 2009. Komminsk had a lifetime .218 batting average in the majors.

During the Carolina League years, there were other notable players whose careers were launched in Durham on their way to the big leagues. Eddie Neville, who pitched for Durham from 1952 to 1954, is still the winningest pitcher in club history (he's got a brick on the street outside DBAP). In 1936, he won 19 games for the Bulls (lost 6), striking out 295 batters.

Bob Boone, who played for Raleigh–Durham in 1969, was the son of a major leaguer and father of two boys who also played in the bigs. All four were named All-Stars during their careers.

Ron Gant, a Bull in 1986, played 16 years in the majors, and now is a host on the morning show, *Good Day Atlanta*.

Chipper Jones (1992) play only 70 games for Durham. His major league career with the Braves got his number (10) retired by the Bulls.

Joe Morgan's Bulls' number (18) has also been retired. Morgan played 95 games for the Bulls in 1963. He went on to play 22 seasons in the majors, winning two MVP awards and election to the Hall of Fame in 1990. He's also got a brick on the walkway.

Interestingly, two of the insets on the sidewalk outside DBAP commemorate ballplayers who never played for the Bulls. Jim and Joe Mills were twin brothers and native to North Carolina who "had a tremendous impact on high school baseball in the state."[10] Jim played and coached in the minors for various teams in the state, but he never played for the Bulls.

And then there's the inset for Roger Craig. Craig pitched for twelve seasons, coached, and managed in the majors. He compiled a 368–186 record as a pitcher with an ERA of 3.86. He was born in Durham and

---

10 https://www.nchsaa.org/news/2019-7-8/jim-mills-joe-mills

attended North Carolina State University but never played for the Bulls. However, he was the team's batboy. I suspect he's the only batboy honored in this way.

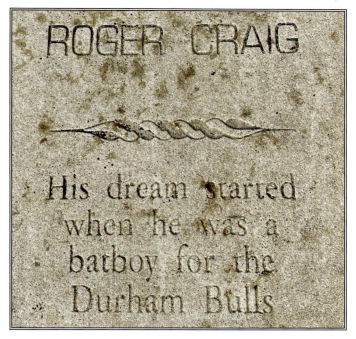

Batboy Roger Craig's inset outside DBAP.

The list of impressive ballplayers who passed through Durham could go on. But you get the idea; lots of memorable ballplayers passed through the Level-A Bulls. I guess it goes without saying that, since they were clearly elite ballplayers, they didn't stay long before marching up the minor league team ladder.

If we're gonna go to DAP during the last half of the twentieth century, we could pick a game to watch any of these players. But it's hard not to consider stopping the WABAC machine to watch the filming of the movie *Bull Durham*. We could be among hundreds of extras populating the stands on a cold October night in 1987, sitting on our coats while the cameras rolled.[11] We would be the only ones in the stands who knew what the film would mean to the Bulls, indeed, the city of Durham. That peek into history appeals to me.

THE INTERNATIONAL LEAGUE (1998–)

The popularity of the movie wouldn't truly pay off for another decade, though attendance at the DAP would climb well before the movie's release and as the facility fell into disrepair. In 1987, 217,012 fans attended Bulls home games. By 1990, attendance had climbed to over 300,000, averaging over 4,000 fans a game in a ballpark meant to handle 5,000.[12] Miles Wolff, who purchased and restarted the Bulls franchise in 1980, when DAP was around fifty years old, wanted a new ballpark (Wolff also was publisher of *Baseball America* for eighteen years) so he could attract a Level-AAA ball club.

In Chapter 2, I gave a brief history of the Bulls' present-day ballpark. Here's a bit more detail. In 1988, the city of Durham put a bond issue on the ballot.[13] It was rejected by voters who were skeptical that anything could be done to save downtown Durham. Citizens felt money would be better spent on education and public transportation. Disillusioned by the lost public vote, Wolff put the Bulls up for sale.[14] Meanwhile, Jim Goodmon, the owner of Capitol Broadcasting Company, was planning a sports complex that would sit between Durham and Raleigh and unite the two cities. He thought the Bulls would be a great anchor for his complex and he optioned land. He bought the Bulls.

Suddenly, the Bulls leaving Durham was a real possibility. Like Durham, there was skepticism in Raleigh about using public money for a minor league ball team. So, the elders in the state capitol gave

---

11 Shelton, R. (2022). *The Church of Baseball: The Making of Bull Durham: Home Runs, Bad Calls, Crazy Fights, Big Swings, and a Hit.* New York, NY: Alfred A. Knopf.

12 Morris, R. (2017). *No Bull: The Real Story of the Rebirth of a Team and a City.* Durham, NC: Baseball America Books.

13 Rice, E.S. & Anders, R.S. (2017). *Becoming Durham: Grit, Belief, and a City Transformed.* Raleigh, NC: Verdant Word Press.

14 Wolff, M. (2023). *There's a Bulldozer on Home Plate.* Jefferson, NC: McFarland.

Durham thirty days to approve a plan for a new ballpark. A unanimous Durham City Council voted to use certificates of participation, a mechanism that allowed the city to borrow money that would be paid back with tax dollars, to put DBAP plans back on the drawing board. On April 6, 1995, DBAP opened to rave reviews.

Since the Bulls moved out, DAP has served as home of the North Carolina Central University Eagles (a Historically Black College or University), a professional women's softball team (the Durham Dragons), and blues and beer festivals.[15] DAP was renovated in 2008 and is in great shape today. It is a pilgrimage site for fans of baseball and the *Bull Durham* movie. If you visit almost any day of the week, you will see others visiting as well. Regrettably, NCCU has abandoned its baseball program, leaving a hole in DAP's tenant line-up.[16]

The Bulls were still in the Carolina League when

Present-day DAP, site of the movie *Bull Durham*.

DBAP opened, feeding higher-level minor league teams for the Atlanta Braves. But not for long. In 1998, the Bulls were elevated to Level-AAA and became an affiliate of the American League expansion club in Tampa Bay, the Devil Rays (now just the Rays). This arrangement hasn't changed in twenty-five years. And, the Bulls attendance is always near the top of minor league baseball, hovering around 500,000 fans a season.

According to that May 30 Game Information Sheet I got from Guest Services, the Bulls International League record sat at 1,710 wins and 1,476 losses. The team has won seven (count 'em, seven!) league championships since 2002. As you can imagine, as a Level-AAA affiliate the list of Bulls players to ascend to the majors is long; besides players acquired through trades, nearly every Rays player will pass through Durham at some point in their career. Interestingly however, only one of the three numbers that have been retired since the Bulls ascension to the International League has been a player; that was Crash Davis' number (8) retired in 2008. The other two numbers were worn by managers. William Evers (20) was the Bulls' manager for eight seasons. Evers teams won 613 games, made six playoff appearances, and won the IL championship twice. After coaching for many years in the majors, Evers retired at the end of the 2021 season. Charlie Montoya (25) managed the Bulls for eight seasons and shepherded the team to 1148 wins (.551 winning percentage) before taking the job of manager for the Toronto Blue Jays.

If I had my druthers, I'd use the WABAC to visit another opening day, this time for DBAP. I'd also love to be in that crowd crammed into the ballpark in July 2019 to see Aaron Judge and Giancarlo Stanton of the Yankees visit when rehabbing with the Scranton-Wilks-Barre RailRiders. The seating hosts who were there relate the experience with a broad smile on their face. Let's go.

Uh oh. The WABAC seems to be malfunctioning. It took me to the year 802,701 AD, and I met a race of people called the Eloi. Nice people, but they don't play baseball. And I like Durham in 2022 better. Maybe we'll just go to tomorrow night's ballgame. . . .

---

15 https://en.wikipedia.org/wiki/Durham_Athletic_Park
16 https://indyweek.com/news/ninth-street-journal/the-future-of-durham-s-old-ballpark-more-baseball/

Chapter 13
Home Series 9: The Stakes Get Higher

More than any other American sport, baseball creates the magnetic, addictive illusion that it can almost be understood.
—Thomas Boswell, sports columnist

I called the Seattle runner out, and Pinella came storming out of the dugout and said, "Jesus Christ, Al." I said, "Louie, the play wasn't even close." And he said, "I don't give a damn about the play. My club is so flat that I don't know what to do." I was a veteran umpire by that time so I knew what was happening. "Louie," I said, "what do you want me to do?" And he said, "I don't know, you tell me." So I said, "All right, let's just stand here and jaw. Let's bob our heads back and forth. I'll turn around, take a few steps. You follow me. I'll turn around, take a couple of steps. You follow me. I'll turn around again, and I'll jerk your ass." He threw up both is hands and said, "That's a great idea." So we started bobbing our heads left and right and up and down. His arms flailing up and down and left and right. Finally I turned around and took a couple of steps. He followed me, unfortunately a little too close. When I turned around, he accidentally bumped me.
Lou was going to get ejected anyway, but when he bumped me, I had to eject him hard–and make it look good. . . .
The whole thing was a setup.
—Al Clark, former major league umpire[1]

TUESDAY, JULY 26
It's the opening game of a six-game series against the Lehigh Valley IronPigs. The Bulls and IronPigs are tied for first place in the IL East. This series is the first really important one of the season.

---

1   Clark, A. (2014). *Called Out but Safe: A Baseball Umpire's Journey.* Lincoln, NB: University of Nebraska Press.

> **LEHIGH VALLEY**
>
> https://en.wikipedia.org/wiki/Allentown%2C_Pennsylvania
>
> https://en.wikipedia.org/wiki/Lehigh_Valley_IronPigs
>
>
>
> Nickname: IronPigs
> MLB Affiliate: Philadelphia Phillies
> Field: Coca-Cola Park, capacity 10,100
> Population (2020): Allentown, PA, 125,485
> Economy: Formerly heavy industry, now service-oriented
> Fun fact: In 2011, the IronPigs were managed by Ryne Sandberg, a Hall of Fame player for the Chicago Cubs. He led them to their first playoff appearance.

Talking with Josh before the game, I see he is wearing a Durham Bull Sharks cap, another item associated with a special night at the park.

"I couldn't pass it up," he says. He then informs me that for his birthday his wife bought him three minor league caps from teams with names guaranteed to bring a smile to your face. He has about forty hats in his collection.

Josh also tells me that Wool E. Bull has COVID. After a moment of trepidation, he reassures me that the previous Mr. Bull was recruited to take his place until he recovers. Heaven forbid there would be a Bulls game without Wool E.!

After washing my hands from my seat cleaning, I spot a family with two boys wearing Phillies jerseys, the parent club of the IronPigs. On their jerseys, one boy has the name Harper (Bryce Harper, number 3) and the other Lee (Hao-Yu Lee, number 33). Standing next to each other on the line for a hot dog, the T-shirts read "Harper Lee." I approach Dad and ask if he knows who Harper Lee was. He knows she was a writer but guesses the wrong book. She wrote *To Kill a Mockingbird*.

I also learn tonight that autograph hound Pete is known by many employees. Seems he's first in line to enter the park when the gates open and leaves as soon as the game is over, often standing by the visiting team's bus to gather more signatures. I also learn that he has met the real Crash Davis. Later, when he wanders by my station, I ask Pete if this is true. He confirms it is. He met him when Davis attended the groundbreaking for DBAP. I'm getting the sense that Pete is something of a legend around here, everybody seems to know him, like him personally, and talking about him brings a smile to the face.

Dave H., the friendly season ticket holder says hello. "I've been expecting it to rain." He says, "I was sitting in my car reading a book."

"What are you reading?" I inquire, "*See Dick and Jane?*"

Not missing a beat, Dave retorts, "I didn't get to finish coloring it in." Big smile as he walks away.

A member of the clean-up crew pushes his cart by me and asks me what league the Bulls play in? Are they any good? I explain to him the International League lineup of teams and that the league is just a step from the major leagues. I think back to the host who thought the game might be called after the tenth inning because there was no more space on the scoreboard. Comparing these two with the knowledge of Josh, host Dave, and the fervor of Pete, I'm amazed at the variability of relationships to the game you can find among the folks at the park, even the employees. For some it is just a job, for others it's a passion.

Ugly clouds gather. Suddenly seven members of the ground crew descend on my section, which is near an entrance to the field close to where the rolled-up tarp hugs the wall. The crew takes up seats. Other staff join them.

"Can I see your ticket?" I ask one crew member in jest.

HOME SERIES 9: THE STAKES GET HIGHER

"Please throw me out!" he responds, jokingly.

Mike, the club's general manager, joins and sits with the crew. Mike's my boss's boss's boss. I ask to see his ticket, hoping it will elicit a grin. It does.

Mike is staring at a radar image on his phone "It's gonna rain."

I see the image on his phone is very detailed and he tells me it's the best weather app around.

"Nah, it's not gonna rain," I say looking up at the sky.

An inning or two later, the threat has passed.

"You were right," Mike says as he walks by.

"My back wasn't aching," I say.

Later, I purchase the weather app Mike uses. Unlike the app I've been staring at, the description you get uses weather lingo I do not understand at all. It looks real cool, though. Maybe I'll learn.

There are two balks in the game, an unusual occurrence. I note that the actions of the pitcher seem to be different in each case. I'm surprised to find that the rules of baseball define twenty different actions by the pitcher that result in a called balk:

- Interrupt the pitching motion;
- Fail to come to a complete stop during the set position;
- Fail to step toward and ahead of a throw;
- Fail to have both hands on the ball once he is in set position;
- Pitch while his pivot foot is not touching the rubber;
- Pitch while his head is not facing the batter;
- Fake a throw to first or third;
- With runners on first and third, step toward third without throwing;
- Fail to complete a throw to an unoccupied base;
- Commit to a pitch without completing the pitch;
- Make a quick pitch;
- Fake a pitch;
- Drop the ball while on the rubber;
- Disengage the rubber improperly;
- Delay the game;
- Come to the set position twice;
- Change from one pitching position to the other without disengaging the rubber;
- Pitch using a tampered ball;
- Take a second step;
- Step off the rubber for a third time during the same at-bat.[2]

Who am I trying to kid. I never could have been an umpire.

The Bulls are down by one run and have the bases loaded in the bottom of the ninth with no outs. There's a putout at the plate, a line drive caught in shallow left field, a ground out to the second baseman. Game over.

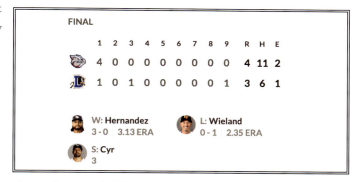

Attendance: 4,062.

FRIDAY, JULY 29

To combat the heat, I'm trying out a new water bottle that I'm carrying in a backpack I'll use for the first time. The backpack will also include a Bulls raincoat, the seat-wiping glove my friend bought me, a baseball, some energy bars, and my cheat sheets for DBAP seating and concessions. I've seen other hosts with

---

2 Formosa, D. & Hamburger, P. (2023). *Baseball Field Guide*, New York, NY: The Experiment.

backpacks that they secure to the railing by their station with a carabiner. I feel like I'm getting this job wired but I discover that, when I get to the ballpark, by breaking my prep routine at home, I've forgotten my badge and cap. My neon green shirt gets me in the stadium, and I suspect no one will notice. Still, I feel naked. Beth, my accommodating spouse, brings me my missing garments. Luckily, we live about a ten-minute drive from the park.

Tonight is "Defenders of the Diamond" night, celebrating Marvel Comics superheroes. The players wear special jerseys and, as on other special nights of this sort, signed jerseys are put on auction on the Bulls' website. This time I notice that the proceeds netted from the sale will go to the United Way.

A defender of the diamond.

My assignment is in the Diamond View seats, facing directly into the sun. I guess because of the heat, there is no batting practice. Before the game starts, I investigate the goings-on at Wool E. World, the playground for kids in the upper deck of right field. It's just a few yards from my position.

Wool E. World has a batting cage where parents can toss plastic balls to their kids swinging plastic bats, an inflatable T-ball cage, an obstacle course, a skee-ball game, and a slide. The attendants use an electric pump to blow up the stations and at the seventh or eighth inning deflate them for storage. Parents buy tickets they hand to young employees who monitor each station. It looks like fun for preschoolers, who are the principal users. Fun for most parents, too—but maybe not the dad whose preschooler has decided that, rather than play the games as intended, throwing the balls over the fence would be even more fun. Dad is not amused, and junior hears about it.

Wool E. World T-ball.

The first arrival in my section is an older couple. They sit in the top row, corner seats, the farthest place you can sit and watch the game.

"We like to have the whole field in front of us," the woman tells me.

They sit in those seats the entire game.

The next arrivals are three tweeners with gloves who stand by the outfield wall, jump up and down, and yell to the centerfielder who is warming up. Success! He tosses them a ball and the boys scurry away delighted.

At about seven o'clock the clouds roll in and the temperature drops nearly twenty degrees. At half past seven o'clock we're on a rain delay that lasts about twenty-five minutes. There's no hiding from the rain out here. Most folks head for other parts of the stadium. I have to stay, and I stand against a wall that offers minimum protection.

A surprising number of fans return when the delay ends. But I learn something from the host stationed next to me that I hadn't noticed in my earlier assignments out here.

"I've had to warn four fans about vaping," she says.

Seems when the Diamond View seats are largely vacant, these seats become a favorite of fans who want to sneak a smoke and don't want to leave the ballpark or get turned in by fans occupying nearby seats. Sure enough, a few minutes later I see a puff of smoke go up in my section.

An older man walks by who has a cast on his foot. He initiates a conversation about the fielding shift happening in front of us.

"Four outfielders! Do they think this guy's Lou Gehrig? He's hitting below .200."

"Maybe the shift is why he's hitting so bad."

My new friend will traverse the outfield walkway at least seven times. Each time he stops to talk. I look forward to his visits. He's here from Annapolis, Maryland. He comes once a year and stays a month at a health center, mostly focused on diet but also other health-related behaviors.

"Are you retired?" I ask.

"No, I own a law firm but don't do much."

"You just tell others what to do, eh?"

"Don't do much of that anymore either."

He's a life-long Orioles fan and can't believe his team is playing respectable ball this year.

The REAL show.

"It's been so long."

He checks the O's game score every time he stops by.

Tonight's attention-grabbing T-shirt sums up the wearer's life priorities in five words. On his back, the shirt lists, "Faith, Family, Friends, Freedom, Firearms."

But the real winner tonight is Mother Nature, with an assist from the ballpark.

Attendance: 7,259.

SATURDAY, JULY 30

Ron Shelton, the writer and director of the movie *Bull Durham*, has just published a book retelling his experiences in getting the movie to the screen, called *The Church of Baseball*. An hour before the game starts, he's at the park to sign copies. I'm second in line and, no big surprise, Pete is fourth. Shelton knows how to sign books. He makes eye contact with the requestor, exchanges pleasantries, asks a question. He doesn't just look down, sign, and push the book away.

Tonight is also Campout Night. Kids and adults can take part in a pre-game parade along the warning track and sleep the night on the field in tents. Most of the participants appear to be here as part of scout troops. Campers also get a post-game snack and Sunday morning breakfast. As curious as I am (especially about how they will secure their tents without destroying the turf), I decide not to stay to watch how this goes off.

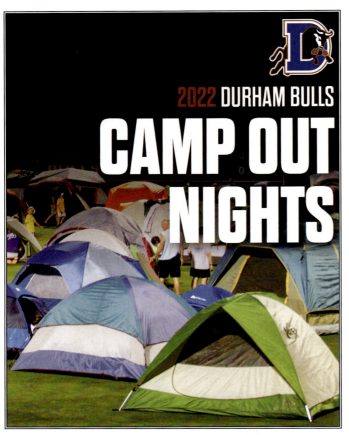

Camp Out night.

I talk with Steve and Josh before the game. They tell me that today Duke University had an orientation for prospective hosts for home football and basketball games. They both attended. They saw other Bulls hosts there and anticipate they will get jobs. My list of members of the Professional Sports Host Federation of the North Carolina Research Triangle (I made that up) continues to grow.

Before the host meeting, Lisa recounts an incident that happened last night in the upper-level seats behind home plate. Seems a belligerent male fan got into a confrontation with a female fan. He was a bit inebriated and was shouting offensive language. There were kids in the vicinity. He got into an argument with a woman sitting nearby who asked him to quiet down. Little did the guy know the woman was a coach's wife. A few cops showed up, stood nearby for a while, and the guy calmed down, then left. Later, the guy's wife apologized to the coach's wife. These kinds of incidents, which seriously worried me after my orientation, have been remarkably infrequent; I've heard of just two so far. Infrequent enough that they are news at the host meetings when they occur.

I'm hosting right behind home plate tonight and Dave H. is working next to me. In addition to displaying a knowledge of the game well beyond my own, he tells me about his daughter. She's a senior in high school and also works at the ballpark as a Lollygagger, an assistant to Jatovi. Dave proudly tells me she is a free safety and split end on the Chapel Hill High School football team. The only girl ever to play on the Chapel Hill football team.

Nicole, the mother of a host named Cody, who has special needs, stops by to talk to Dave. She's carrying a signed copy of Shelton's book. Immediately, Dave rats on her.

"She hasn't seen the movie," he tells me.

"Let's get her escorted from the park," I jest.

"It's true," she replies. "The movie's a bit risqué and I couldn't watch it when my kids were young."

We agree this is a weak excuse and talk some more about other baseball movies.

Nicole mentions a report she had seen on Albert Pujols, the Cardinals and Angels slugger. He has put out a press release that he was divorcing his wife of twenty-two years ("irreconcilable differences") just days after she underwent successful surgery to remove a brain tumor.[3] Pujols was one of Nicole's favorite players until this happened. The kicker for her was that one of their children, from a previous marriage of his wife, had Down Syndrome from birth.

On a lighter note, Nicole says, "I'm gonna go

---

3 https://nypost.com/2022/04/05/albert-pujols-irreconcilable-differences-in-divorce-from-wife/

watch the movie now on my phone." She leaves to get back to Cody.

Behind me, there's a guy with a dog on a leash. A wrap on the dog says she is in training to be a guide dog. Her handler tells me he is down from Washington, DC, where he helps train the dogs. He's in the process of moving to the Durham area. He takes the dogs on field trips, including outdoor events like baseball games, and even rides with them on the DC Metro. The dog rests attentively on the walkway next to him, calm as can be as a multitude of people walk by.

The big event at the game is when a twelve-year-old boy with autism wanders away from his parents. Apparently, he was missing for a while before his folks let anyone know, about the fourth inning. It's now a few innings later and he is nowhere to be found. An announcement is made on the PA system asking fans to please be on the lookout for a lost boy in a purple jersey and purple hat.

As I look around the seating bowl, it seems impossible that the boy could be among this crowd of over nine thousand people and not be spotted, even if most fans' attention is directed elsewhere. If the boy is still in the park, he must be on the concourse, I think, maybe in a bathroom. I ask Dave if I can take a break. I walk through the men's rooms (I suspect I'm not the first to do this). No sign of the boy. My guess is he's wandered outside the park. In all, four announcements are made to the crowd, the last two including pictures of the boy. The search lasts about forty-five minutes. Thankfully, the boy is found outside the park.

In all, it seems to me the response of the club and its employees to this episode was well thought out and about as effective as it could have been. The employees were alerted quickly, and when the affair persisted, the entire crowd was enlisted to help. The psychologist in me thinks that the wording of the announcement could be a little different. It should include a behavior prescription, something like "please look around you, to your left and right, and if you see a boy in a purple jersey and hat, please keep an eye on him and let a game employee know." When given these kinds of prescriptions people do them, even without thinking. While this might be a slightly better message, today it wouldn't necessarily have been any more effective.

I also think about parenting. The first responsibility for a child's safety lies with the parents. The vast majority of parents maintain appropriate control of their kids in the ballpark. They permit their children the correct amount of autonomy, given their age, disposition, and assessment of the circumstance. Typically, when I see kids on the walkway without an adult, they are in groups of two or more. Still, not only do kids occasionally get lost but they also do dangerous things (gymnastics on the handrails, run and play catch on the walkway) while their parents, sitting nearby, are engrossed in conversation with other adults. What are they thinking?

The Bulls lose the game. Despite the starting pitcher, Taj Bradley, being a hot prospect, tonight is not his night. He gives up six hits and three runs in two innings of work. The Bulls are two-hit until the sixth inning. A valiant comeback effort falls short (okay, maybe not so valiant: eight players were left on base, hitters were only two for nine with runners in scoring position). We're still tied for first at the day's end.

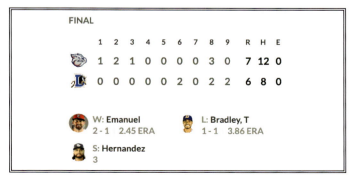

Attendance: 9,098.

SUNDAY, JULY 31

I'm delighted to learn at the host's meeting that my assignment has changed from the Diamond View seats to the section directly behind home plate! Shade! And I can call balls and strikes, second guessing the umpire! While cleaning my seats, I discover a penny on the concrete and put it in my pocket.

At dinner I meet a new host, Rich H., who joined the crew in June. The dinner talk is about last night's lost child. Several hosts talk about a group of three Durham police officers we saw eating and talking behind home plate. They seemed oblivious to the drama unfolding in front of them. Another host and I had pointed them out to folks we thought should know. Josh approached the officers and learned they were off duty.

"Then why the heck were they standing on the walkway in uniform?" I ask, rhetorically.

"Exactly!" responds Josh. "It just didn't look good."

We learn that the boy was found by some police officers on a street about *two miles* from the ballpark. We wonder whether an all-points bulletin was put out, or they just thought it odd for the boy to be out walking alone after dark.

I meet David L., The Judge, on my way to my station. I notice he wears two bracelets on one arm and two electronic devices on the other.

"One is an emergency medical alert, the other is my activity monitor," he tells me.

"What about this bracelet with the skulls and red eyes," I ask, "I'm guessing you're a motorcycle rider."

"You got it," The Judge responds, "but I haven't ridden since January. Rotator cuff. Can't play golf either. Spending too much time at home." The Judge has a custom Harley Softail. I tell him I rode a Harley for a few years, but my life was in danger; my mind wanders too much for that kind of activity.

Outside the park, the Bulls are hosting "Touch the Trucks" night. There are fire trucks, construction vehicles, and the police's mobile command unit. Apparently, their presence was instigating questions from some fans entering DBAP about whether something was wrong.

Police Mobile Command Unit.

At my station, I see Rich H. is stationed just a few sections away. I learn that he is a recently retired journalist. We discover we have common friends and share outrage over the recent demise of the North Carolina Central University baseball team. Rich asks me questions about what the expectations are for hosting—checking tickets, walking the aisles—and I'm able to answer them all. Feels good; I'm getting the hang of this job.

Behind my sections, there is a policeman who arrives before game time and stands nearly motionless in the exact same place for seven innings. Then a mom and dad with a babe-in-arms comes by to talk. Suddenly, the police officer is animated and wears a big smile. They talk for about ten minutes and the baby gets a sticker the policeman pulls from his breast pocket. When the family leaves, the officer reassumes his motionless demeanor. Later, I learn the dad was an off-duty officer.

The Bulls lose, but so do the Jacksonville Jumbo Shrimp, the team the Bulls are tied with for first place. We split the series 3–3 with Lehigh Valley. The homestand ends with these three teams tied atop the IL East.

As I leave the stadium, I toss my found penny into the fountain by the entrance.

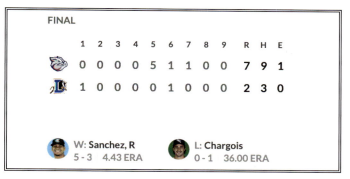

Attendance: 5,283.

MILLION DOLLAR ARM

Year of Release: 2014
Rating: PG
Director: Craig Gillespie
Writers: Tom McCarthy (screenplay)
Stars: Jon Hamm, Bill Paxton, Asif Mandvi, and Alan Arkin

Plot Synopsis

From Wiki: https://en.wikipedia.org/wiki/Million_Dollar_Arm
The film is based on the true story of baseball pitchers Rinku Singh and Dinesh Patel who were discovered by sports agent J. B. Bernstein after winning a reality show competition.
From IMDb: https://www.imdb.com/title/tt1647668/?ref_=fn_al_tt_1
A sports agent stages an unconventional recruitment strategy to get talented Indian cricket players to play Major League Baseball.

Critic Ratings

Rotten Tomatoes: https://www.rottentomatoes.com/m/million_dollar_arm
Tomatometer: 64 out of 100 (149 reviews)
Audience Score: 68 out of 100 (25,000 + ratings)
Critics consensus: Pleasant to a fault, *Million Dollar Arm* is a middle-of-the-plate pitch that coasts on Jon Hamm's considerable charm without adding any truly original curves to Disney's inspirational sports formula.
IMDb Rating: 7 out of 10 (46,000 raters)
Roger Ebert: https://www.rogerebert.com/reviews/million-dollar-arm-2014. (Written by Susan Wloszcyna, May 16, 2014), 2 out of 4 stars
Ebert thinks "This supposedly uplifting true-life baseball tale never quite strikes the necessary emotional sweet spots."

Chapter 14
Home Series 10:
The Surf & Turf Series

You don't realize how easy this game is until you get up in that broadcasting booth.

—Mickey Mantle

I'm glad I don't play anymore. I could never learn all those handshakes.

—Phil Rizzuto

My penny in the fountain didn't pay off, (never thought it would, really) but it wasn't disastrous either. The Bulls split their away series against the Worcester Red Sox (known to fans as the WooSox), but the Jacksonville Jumbo Shrimp won five of six from the Memphis Redbirds and the Lehigh Valley IronPigs took four of six from the Syracuse Mets. So, we start a crucial set against Jacksonville, billed as the "Surf & Turf" series, two games out of first.

INTERNATIONAL LEAGUE EASTERN DIVISION					
Team	MLB	Wins	Losses	Winning Percentage	Games Behind
Jacksonville	MIA	59	46	0.562	-
Lehigh Valley	PHI	58	47	0.552	1
Durham	TB	57	48	0.543	2
Buffalo	TOR	54	50	0.519	4.5
Scranton/WB	NYY	54	50	0.519	4.5
Worcester	BOS	54	51	0.514	5
Norfolk	BAL	48	56	0.462	10.5
Rochester	WSH	47	58	0.448	12
Syracuse	NYM	47	58	0.448	12
Charlotte	CWS	40	65	0.381	19

> **JACKSONVILLE (AGAIN)**
>
> https://en.wikipedia.org/wiki/Jacksonville,_Florida
> https://en.wikipedia.org/wiki/Jacksonville_Jumbo_Shrimp
>
>
>
> Nickname: Jumbo Shrimp
> MLB affiliate: Miami Marlins (2009–present)

TUESDAY, AUGUST 9

My assignment tonight is the first base tunnel and the two sections in front of it. This is my first time manning a tunnel. It means I'll be directing traffic as fans emerge from the passageway while they stare at their tickets wondering where their seats are. It will be a true test of how well I've learned the ballpark's layout. I estimate maybe 1,500 people will come through the tunnel.

This will also be my first experience with a radio. Before the game, I head to the recesses of the stadium to get my equipment. The radios are kept in a storeroom under the concession stands down the first base line. The room is filled with groundskeeping vehicles, protective tarps, rakes, brooms, and turf seed. A metal stairway leads to a small room where charging cradles sit for thirteen radios. Each is labelled with the position it is meant for. Most are gone when I get there but "First Base Tunnel" is still charging.

There are ten channels on the radio. The back of my ID badge lists who is to use each channel. There's one each for sponsors and promotion, tickets, parking, grounds, operations (that's me), food and beverage, security/Durham Police/EMT. Three are marked "DO NOT USE." This is the first time I've looked closely at the back of my badge. I discover it also contains a Rain Hotline phone number and a Bulls mission statement ". . . to present baseball, 'The Great American Pastime,' as an affordable family entertainment with a commitment to customer and community service, ethical business practices, and professional growth of our employees." Can't argue with that.

Among the first fans to emerge from the tunnel is a family visiting from Charlotte, North Carolina. The first word out of the father's mouth as the field comes into view is "Beautiful."

"First time here?" I inquiry.

"Yes," then quickly, "the ballpark at Charlotte is nice too."

"Maybe, but nothing like this," I kid.

As traffic picks up, I realize I'm standing with my arms crossed. The social psychologist in me kicks in again. I know this pose is viewed as defensive, insecure (that's me tonight), and closed off—not friendly at all. I consciously remind myself not to stand like this. Hands-on-hips (akimbo), at my sides, and behind my back will work better. And a smile can work wonders.

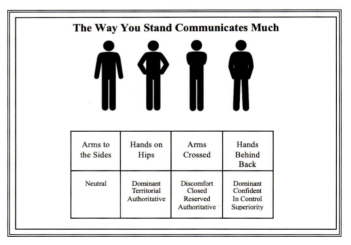

A group of Lollygaggers is standing by the tunnel waiting to help Jatovi do an on-field performance. I notice two 'gaggers taking a selfie. With an exaggerated stern face, I approach and question why they're staring at an app on their phones rather than attending to their jobs, which at the moment appears to be "just wait around until we're needed."

"It's BeReal," one of them tells me, although I'm oblivious to what that means. "It's just two minutes."

At home, I learn BeReal is the latest hot phone app among Gen Zers. The website LifeHacker[1] tells me:

> Every day at a different time, users get a push notification from the app. They have exactly two minutes to open BeReal and snap a picture of what they're doing. The app activates both the front and back cameras on a user's phone, so actually, the person takes *two* photos, which are uploaded simultaneously . . . You may scroll through the BeReals posted by your friends to see their largely mundane activities, which makes this a much different experience from scrolling through Instagram, where users have a tendency to upload the very best pictures of themselves at the very coolest moments in their lives.

So, this app captures you being real, warts and all—no photo doctoring, and must be taken in the two-minute window.

A survey by Common Sense[2] tells me that in 2021 teenagers spent about eight and a half hours and tweenagers five and a half hours a day staring at screens. The 'gaggers are older than this, but they have grown up with screens. Me? I have absolutely no desire to download this app. I quickly lose interest when Wool E. Bull walks by and pulls my beard.

On the walkway, I meet the executive director of Real-Life Works.[3] Real-Life Works provides employment and training for adults with developmental disabilities. The organization runs a thrift store in Raleigh. Her team is recognized on the field between innings.

A dad walks down my aisle with his four-month-old daughter strapped to his chest.

"Is it her first ballgame?" I ask facetiously.

"Actually, it's her second," he replies.

His two boys are sitting politely right by the dugout, pleading for balls.

"If they misbehave, chase them away," Dad says.

The boys have scavenged two balls so far tonight.

The game ends in a Bulls win. I return my radio and head home.

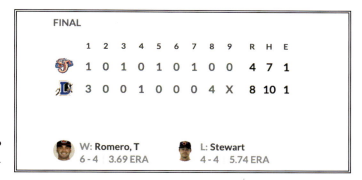

Attendance: 4,152.

THURSDAY, AUGUST 11

The vast expanse of the Diamond View Seats is my territory tonight. As I survey the twenty rows of twenty-three seats searching for bird poop to clean, two things catch my attention. First, I find one of those cork stoppers that flies off the fireworks. It must have been in the stands since last Saturday. It traveled close to the length of a football field to get here.

Then, I'm amazed to find a bit of greenery protruding from the concrete beneath a seat. How the heck did this get here? It's growing out of a small crack in the cement just beside the step. This is a small wonder. It makes me think of the song "Spanish Harlem" that Ben E. King made a hit in 1960, when I was nine. It has the lyric, "It grows up in the street/Right up through the concrete." Great song.

---

1 https://lifehacker.com/what-is-the-new-social-media-app-bereal-and-do-you-r-1848780094

2 https://www.commonsensemedia.org/research/the-common-sense-census-media-use-by-tweens-and-teens-2021

3 www.real-lifeworks.org

A bit of greenery.

I have dinner with John, the former criminal lawyer who uses a voice amplifier. Prior to moving to Durham, he practiced law in Florida and tells me he won about seventy percent of his cases. He is in his fifth year as a host. He is complimentary of the changes in the workplace atmosphere at DBAP he's witnessed.

"When I first arrived," he says, "I worked three-quarters of a season before someone talked to me."

Although John wishes there was more training for hosts, he still heaps praise on Scott. He relates to me that when he lost his voice, he went to tell Scott he needed to quit. Scott would have none of it. He suggested that John work the K-Wall and the scoreboard, two positions that would limit his need to converse with fans. John accepted the arrangement.

As I head to my station after dinner, I see a guy in his twenties with a glove getting chased away from collecting balls that go into the stands. As soon as the gates open, a kid about eight years old takes his place for a few minutes. This kid shows up at the park with a clear backpack. I count seven balls in there before his new hunt even starts.

During batting practice, a Jacksonville player launches several balls onto the walkway in front of the Tobacco Road restaurant. As the game starts, an intern stops by to ask how things are going. I notice he has ice cubes wrapped around the palm of one hand. He offers that one of the homers was headed close to an older woman, so he stuck his hand out to deflect it.

I ask the intern what his favorite part of the job is.

"Clubhouse," he says, "lots going on and you get to meet the players."

"And your least favorite?"

"Parking! No doubt about it."

"Easiest."

"Suite cleanup."

Later, he walks by pushing a cart and collecting garbage bags. I notice his ice compress is gone.

"Gonna tough it out," he says with a smile.

The game is delayed forty minutes by a passing storm. This means I'll need to offer to wipe down seats for fans in my section when they arrive. In all, I'll have sixteen people sitting in over four hundred seats. Among the sixteen are three friendly high school students. One offers his name and asks me mine, a rarity.

"You guys from Durham?" I inquire, using the monosyllabic local colloquialism.

In near perfect unison the boys shout, "We're Durmites!"

I love it. I'll adopt that response when asked where I'm from.

For the first time tonight, I notice that the outfielders on both teams look at cards they carry in their back pockets. They look at them before each batter gets up. It tells them where they should position themselves based on the batter's frequency of hitting the ball to different areas of the field.

The gentleman I had met the week before from Baltimore who is in Durham for a month at a health clinic ambles by.

"You still here?" I ask.

"I went back home for three days to attend to some business, but I'm back now."

Clearly, his earlier claimed disengagement from his law practice was less than the complete truth. As seems to be true among the hosts, this guy just wants to be a baseball fan when he's at the ballpark, thank you.

We talk about the unexpected resurrection of his beloved Orioles. They're in playoff contention. With a big smile on his face, he shakes his head in disbelief. Like before, each time he walks his circuit around the stadium he stops by me and checks the O's game score. I'm gonna miss this guy when he goes home.

I surveil the lawn area tonight, though it is closed. It's open for Bark in the Park and when attendance reaches a certain level. You must have a specific ticket for the lawn; otherwise, stay off.

The Bulls are down 5–4 going into the bottom of the ninth. Runners on first and second with two outs. A single to right sends the runner on second around third, headed home. Out at the plate. Game over. Bulls lose.

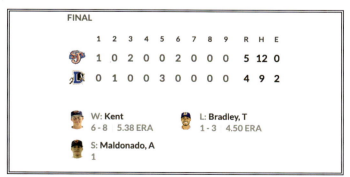

Attendance: 4,689.

FRIDAY, AUGUST 12

The weather is perfect for a night of baseball. Summer temperatures in the low eighties and little humidity. The aisle railings are decorated with paper palm trees. Tonight's theme is "Margaritaville." Special margarita cocktails are available. Hosts are given leis with plastic flowers to wear. I get my neckwear while in line for dinner, but later in the stands I'm asked where I got it. Without a word, I remove it and place it around the neck of the inquiring host.

"Aloha," I say.

The crowd will be large, especially because the weather is nice and Friday night means fireworks after the game. I'm hosting the section next to the visitor's dugout so an eye must be kept on the aisle which, of course, is filled with a half dozen or so autograph hounds before the game starts. Also typical, this early crowd is well-behaved and disperses before the game begins.

The hounds are out.

The first fans I meet are five gentlemen taking a selfie in the walkway. I ask if I might be of assistance. They take me up on the offer. Three are wearing identical polo shirts and two are in different but identical shirts. This is a dead giveaway that it's a business get-together. Sure enough, I learn that the three guys in polos are from Spain, and they are attending their first baseball game ever. They have no idea how the game is played, the locals tell me. The two businesses are in information security and one company is acquiring the other. I make the assumption that the local company is doing the acquiring, but I'm wrong. The locals assure me that their company will retain its autonomy.

"I suspect the need of your services won't disappear any time soon," I offer, to recover from my mistake.

"Recession-proof," is the response.

Along with what feels like the endless playing of Jimmy Buffet songs over the PA system, many of the on-field antics between innings take on a topical island theme. In addition to the "Race Around the Bases" that Wool E. loses to a preschooler when he stops to hug a cow mascot (where did she come from?), there is a ring toss on the necks of flamingos, two games that involve tossing plastic parrots, and a limbo contest. This night also seems to have more than the usual non-baseball entertainment; there's a tug-of war, Wool E.'s drive of a go-cart and ATV around the warning track, and musical chairs. Of course, as happens at every game, fans salute the military, get their big smiles projected on the jumbo screen, and sing "Take Me Out to the Ballgame" and "Sweet Caroline" (a local favorite, of course). The nightly toss of T-shirts into the crowd also delights the fans. It's always a pleasure to watch this stuff going on, but tonight it seems even more fun; maybe it's the weather.

A gentleman arrives in my section with a group of teenaged boys all wearing USA baseball caps. He asks for a food recommendation. I don't mind this as much as others seem to. I do have two favorites.

"My favorites are the tacos and pizza," I offer, and take the opportunity to make an inquiry of my own, "You here for USA baseball in Cary?"

"Yes, we're here from the Bay Area. Under-15 ball."

"It's a wonderful experience for the boys. Something they'll never forget."

"Agreed."

Later the boys tell me they're from Livermore, California.

I begin to notice lots of teens with USA baseball hats and T-shirts in the crowd. Psychologists call this "cognitive priming." It happens when exposure to one stimulus leads to greater recognition of related stimuli. Have you ever thought about buying a particular make or color of a car then suddenly start to see more cars of that make or color on the road? You know you have. It's only human.

The game lasts just two hours and twelve minutes. The Bulls win and are back into a tie for first with Jacksonville. Next morning, the Bulls website heralds, "BULLS BATTER SHRIMP."

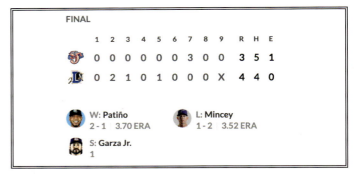

Attendance: 8,292.

SUNDAY, AUGUST 14, 2022

Talk about the pennant race is picking up at the pregame host meeting.

"How many games we got left?"

"Who's here on rehab assignment from the Rays?"

"Brady (Williams, the Bulls' manager) must be getting serious; Sunday games are usually 'bullpen day,' when pitchers down the priority list get a chance to throw a few innings. But tonight, he's put our ace on the mound."

I'm stationed at the third base dugout again. The autograph hounds are out in force. I see the woman from Winston-Salem is here again and decide to strike up a conversation with her. Kam was a librarian in Memphis for many years but is now retired. I tell her librarians are among my favorite people. It's one of those jobs I would have seriously considered myself had my life taken a different path. I even served on the library board for a few years in my old hometown. We talk about all the services libraries now provide. Along with sharing books and videos, there are the homeless people who come in for warmth and the bathroom, the latchkey kids who arrive after school, people without access to a computer, and the "activities" that teenagers sometimes act out in the distant stacks.

"In a way," Kam says, "my hobby draws on the same skills I used in my work." She's right, of course. She's still sorting and cataloging.

Kam gets a big score when a Jumbo Shrimp catcher, Payton Henry, comes by to sign. Henry has been playing professional ball since being drafted in the sixth round in 2016 by the Milwaukee Brewers (with a $550,000 bonus). He got traded to the Marlins in 2021 and made his major league debut that September, when the major league team's rosters expand to more than twenty-six players. For 2022, he has a Topps baseball card that Kam pulls out and he signs.

"Having a card must be a real treat for him," Kam opines.

My next stop is to chat with "Third Base Greg," the guy who tends the bar out on the walkway. Seems he's a collector, too, but not autographs. He has a collection of Marvel comic books that he's proud of. He also prides himself on his knowledge of comic books. This leads to a trivia contest and a discussion of the comics Silver Surfer and Sgt. Fury and his Howling Commandos. I had the first issue of both but tossed

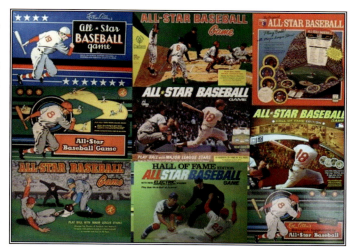

The cause of my misspent (?) youth.

them, never thinking how much they might be worth some day.

It seems like this is nostalgia night when fan Dave H. walks by wearing a T-shirt with a picture the Strat-O-Matic Baseball board game on it. He says he loved playing it as a kid, rolling the dice. I tell him I favored All Star Baseball, a spinning game.[4] I played this game for hours, by myself, managing both teams. I discovered that I could turn an out into a hit depending on the angle I looked at the card when the spinning stopped. The Yankees won a lot.

My favorite fan tonight is also the youngest I've seen in the ballpark. She is five and a half weeks old.

I ask her mom, "Is she here to run the bases after the game?" Mom laughs.

Two young boys come by and ask me to sign a baseball.

"You want my autograph?" I ask incredulously.

"Yes, sir, we're trying to get all the hosts."

The ball probably has about four signatures on it and I'm glad add mine. I learn that the night before the boys were taking pictures of the hosts.

A group arrives that includes a man using a

---

[4] https://boardgamegeek.com/boardgame/3157/all-star-baseball

motorized wheelchair. They park his chair directly behind his seat in the last row, across from the trash and recycle bins on the other side of the walkway. This leaves about four feet of space for the hundreds of fans who'll walk by during the game. I ask if I can move the wheelchair against the wall when it's not being used. This is where people safely park similar chairs and baby strollers. Granted the man is disabled, but this would be no inconvenience to him or his party. My request is refused. I move the receptacles but am annoyed that I'll have to stand beside his vehicle the whole game, so no one accidentally walks into it. I'm relieved when his party leaves to go up to the suites around the second inning, apparently an accommodation they asked for, and his wheelchair goes with him.

The game is a back-and-forth affair. The bulls lead early, get tied, get the lead back, get tied again, then fall behind by three runs in the top of the seventh. Things look bleak. But a six-run outburst in the bottom of the seventh puts them ahead for good. In the eighth, an ad for Tums antacid tablets runs on the PA and scoreboard. Good timing.

Tonight's attention-grabbing T-shirt reads "Whiskey and yoga." That's a combination I'd never thought of before.

I'm asked to help monitor the kids when they run the bases. My job is to usher them (and their folks) off the field at the dugout, so they don't run on the grass or head for the outfield. There are three attempts at escape, two kids dart by for the outfield, and one ducks under the rope and heads for the infield. An embarrassed mom corrals her daughter and makes a big apology.

It seems there are some baseballs sitting in the dugout for all to see.

One young boy asks, "Can I get a ball."

"Nope. The dugout is off limits."

Another boy takes matters into his own hands. I don't see him head down the dugout steps but do see him emerge and run by me with his souvenir held in the air. It's time to see how much forbidden fruit is down there before this gets out of hand. I find only one more ball. As I climb the dugout steps, I'm greeted by a cherubic toddler with a pleading outstretched hand. No! Oh, hell. Here's the ball, kid.

Attendance: 7,767.

TROUBLE WITH THE CURVE

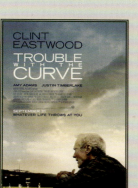

Year of Release: 2012
Rating: PG-13
Director: Robert Lorenz
Writer: Randy Brown
Stars: Clint Eastwood (baseball scout), Amy Adams, John Goodman, Justin Timberlake

Plot Synopsis

From Wiki: https://en.wikipedia.org/wiki/Trouble_with_the_Curve
Trouble with the Curve is a 2012 American sports drama film directed by Robert Lorenz and starring Clint Eastwood, Amy Adams, Justin Timberlake, Matthew Lillard, and John Goodman. The film revolves around an aging baseball scout whose daughter joins him on a scouting trip. Filming began in March 2012, and the film was released on September 21, 2012.

This was Eastwood's first acting project since 2008's *Gran Torino* and his first acting role in a film he did not direct since his cameo in 1995's *Casper*. A year after its release the film became the subject of a plagiarism lawsuit by a producer alleging that his former partner had taken an unfinished script after a dispute and conspired with his agent and Warner Bros. to present it as the work of a relative unknown.

From IMDb: https://www.imdb.com/title/tt2083383/?ref_=fn_al_tt_1
A daughter tries to remedy her dysfunctional relationship with her ailing father, a decorated baseball scout, by helping him in a recruiting trip which could be his last.

Critic Ratings

Rotten Tomatoes: https://www.rottentomatoes.com/m/trouble_with_the_curve
Tomatometer: 51 out of 100 (205 reviewers)
Audience Score: 66 out of 100 (25,000+ Ratings)
Critics consensus: Though predictable and somewhat dramatically underwhelming, *Trouble with the Curve* benefits from Clint Eastwood's grizzled charisma and his easy chemistry with a charming Amy Adams.
IMDb Rating: 6.8 out of 10 (64,000 raters)
Roger Ebert: https://www.rogerebert.com/reviews/trouble-with-the-curve-2012, 3 out of 4 stars.
Ebert extols actor Clint Eastwood's professionalism. While the story "has certain foreseeable moments" they appear at appropriate times. Ebert finds it a pleasure to watch a good story told expertly.

Chapter 15
Home Series II: A Playoff Preview?

Baseball fans—the radicals—are so anxious to get a baseball that has history attached to it, that they are willing to risk arrest for petty theft. They are willing to fight amongst themselves for such a ball if necessary. A blacked optic or a busted breezer in their opinion, is a mere incident—if they can only get that pellet.

—*Sporting Life* magazine, July 22, 1916

When Steve and I die, we are going to be buried in the same cemetery, 60-feet 6-inches apart.

—Tim McCarver (Steve was his catcher.)

INTERNATIONAL LEAGUE EASTERN DIVISION					
Team	MLB	Wins	Losses	Winning Percentage	Games Behind
Durham	TB	66	52	0.559	-
Lehigh Valley	PHI	65	53	0.551	1
Buffalo	TOR	62	55	0.53	3.5
Jacksonville	MIA	62	55	0.53	3.5
Scranton/WB	NYY	62	55	0.53	3.5
(5 Teams Not Listed)					

Another big series opens in Durham. The Nashville Sounds, the leaders of the IL West, come to town with the best record in the league, 70–46. The Bulls had a successful road trip, taking four of six games from Norfolk and stretching their lead in the East to two games. But they lose the first game of the series with the Sounds, 10–7. Their lead is down to one game as I arrive for work.

> **NASHVILLE (AGAIN)**
>
> https://en.wikipedia.org/wiki/Nashville,_Tennessee
> https://en.wikipedia.org/wiki/Nashville_Sounds
>
>
>
> Nickname: Sounds
> MLB: Milwaukee Brewers (2021–present)

WEDNESDAY, AUGUST 23

I have dinner with Rich H. and Steve. I learn that Richard is the former Durham editor for the *Raleigh News & Observer*, the paper of record in North Carolina. Last homestand, I subbed for him for two games when he was "summoned" out of town. Richard's trip was instigated by a call from a buddy who invited him to Boston to attend a three-game series at Fenway Park between the Red Sox and Yankees. I'm jealous. He talks with more enthusiasm about the new Ford 150 Lightning electric pick-up truck he and his friend tooled around Boston in than he does about the games. We all agree electric cars are here to stay, but charging stations and times are the limiting factor at the moment.

Dave H. is hosting the sections next to mine. Our talk turns to the music blaring out of the PA system before the game starts. We agree Nashville country music doesn't appeal to us and whoever chooses the playlist includes too much of it. We wonder who and how the music is chosen. We know that some players have snippets of particular songs played as they enter the batter's box. Beyond that, how the music played over the PA is selected is a mystery to us.

This Bulls game is the venue for a team-building night for the chemical giant BASF, whose North American headquarters (it's a German-owned company) is located in the Cary, North Carolina, Research Triangle Park. I take a smart phone picture for three young ladies who are attending the event. They hail from Texas, Louisiana, and Indiana, and have known each other only a month but are now "besties." Baseball is new to them; one had been to a high school game but other than that, no games come to mind.

I finally meet two guys who I see constantly circling the stadium with camera equipment around their necks. Patrick Norwood does video and co-hosts the podcast "Hit Bull Win Steak" with Scott. Paxton Rembis does photos.

Paxton tells me, "I take photos for fun. I'm the graphic designer for the Bulls." He sweeps his hand in front of us. "I designed anything you see in the stadium that has a Bulls logo on it. I also do the designs on the clothes and the uniforms." The number and complexity of graphics in a stadium like DBAP and its swag store is no small matter. But who'd think about the amount of work that goes into creating them until it's pointed out to you? I'm really impressed.

Today is Ukraine Independence Day and the Bulls honor it by having Ukraine night at the ballpark. The walkway is draped in Ukraine flags and artificial flowers in the nation's colors, yellow and blue. The Ukraine national anthem is sung by the Ukraine Choir of North Carolina before the game begins. Commemorative T-shirts are available. Many fans

The Ukraine flag, Bulls style.

are decked out in traditional garb (except the one guy who is wearing a T-shirt with a picture of Ukrainian president, Volodymyr Zelenskyy, that reads "I need ammunition, not a ride"). This is another intrusion of the outside world on the baseball cocoon. Still, this one has a different feel. The fans seem to appreciate the opportunity to express their solidarity with the Ukrainian people, especially their community neighbors from Ukraine.

As the game starts, a woman in my section heads down to the dugout, walks on the field and gives Jonathon Aranda, our first baseman and a star of the team, a big kiss. When she returns to her seat, I approach her and ask how she knows the ballplayer.

"Mother," she responds.

Mom is here on vacation from Mexico. She speaks about as much English as I speak Spanish, which ain't much. We can agree her son is a great ballplayer. She shows me a Facebook page with photos and videos of her son playing in the big leagues (he batted 16 times for the Rays earlier this year, his first stint in the bigs, and batted .375, with two RBI). She is clearly very proud of her son.

The attention-grabbing T-shirt tonight has a map of the United States that has two arched baseball stitching's, one running down the length of the Rocky Mountains and the other the Mississippi Valley. The shirt reads, "United by The Game."

In the fourth inning, the Sounds score five runs, four on a grand slam. I go over to Dave H.'s section to commiserate with him. The game is lost. But a young boy, maybe eight years old, who sat quietly in my section the whole game pounding his baseball glove, and his dad leave happy when I pull a ball out of my backpack to give it them. In return I get a big smile and hearty handshake.

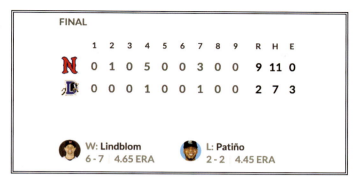

Attendance: 4,366.

THURSDAY, AUGUST 23

I have dinner tonight with two hosts who also work at other sports arenas. The conversation inevitably turns to working rules and regulations and how they differ from one venue to the other. I point out that, depending on how fans get their tickets—on paper, electronically, at the box office—the cryptic abbreviations used to indicate the same seating sections seem to be different. I've stared at these on occasion, almost clueless, and had to give it my best guess. I've even joked with fans that once they walk all the way to the other side of the stadium and can't find their seats they can come back, and I'll try again.

"Why don't they standardize these?" I muse.

"And why don't they put the abbreviations on the back of our IDs, instead of putting the radio stations there?" says one of my tablemates.

"And give us a suggestion box!" says the other.

More talk with John tonight. I learned his career adventures went well beyond practicing criminal law. After he said goodbye to the courtrooms, he went into production for NBC and Fox Sports, working mostly on auto racing. He tells me of meeting James Caan, the actor, in a garage before a race and interviewing him for forty-five minutes. He was clearly pissed off when not a second was used on the air, even during a rain delay. John rolls his eyes and says he quit sports broadcasting "when they learned I believed in evolution."

My station is under the Snorting Bull, a first for me. Working next to me at the Tobacco Road restaurant entrance is a host who describes himself as another refugee from working at home who needed to get outside. This is his third season with the Bulls, fourth if you count the one cancelled by the COVID pandemic. He's a tech guy who works on the software that provides people their health information. These are the websites that keep track of our medical records, appointments, billing, and messaging for clients and their doctors. He builds features and fixes bugs in the software.

As people start to arrive, I learn what my job will be tonight. Lots of folks walk up here to take their picture beneath the Snorting Bull. The bull is so big, however, that to get it all in the shot you need to move so far back the humans in the picture get decidedly small. We figure out that you get your best pictures from the side of the bull or by moving just a bit away and pointing your phone up at an angle.

Lots of people, especially kids, come to stand against the railing above left field and hope to catch a home run. Or they can yell and wave at the players as they toss the ball in warm up between innings. Maybe they'll throw a ball to you. I need to make sure they don't do this during play. Most fans understand this and are polite in this way. No homers to left tonight, but two kids get balls tossed up to them.

The first recipient is a tweenaged girl who leans on the railing beside a boy about the same age.

"Where do you go to school?" I ask.

The boy goes to Trinity School, an independent Christian school in Durham and Chapel Hill.

The girl goes to Durham School of the Arts.

"What's your art?"

"I play trombone and theater."

"Wanna be on Broadway?"

"No, I like music better."

She has come equipped with a fancy glove.

"Do you play?" I inquire.

"No, but my friend does, and I want to."

About the fifth inning, their cajoling of the players pays off. A Sounds player launches a ball that lands inside the restaurant gate. The guy who catches it is kind enough to give it to me so I can give it to the young musician.

The second recipient is a lanky young boy who lives a few towns away. I ask where he goes to school.

"I'm homeschooled," he says.

"Do you play ball?"

"I'm starting. I signed up this year but only eight kids showed up."

He leaves for a while but later returns with his mother.

He waves at a player who sends a ball his way. He makes a perfect catch.

Another railing-leaner has on a T-shirt that displays the Snorting Bull, but the words "Hit Bull Win Steak" are written in Korean. I'd love one of these, but I can't find any on the internet.

The fan's relay race tonight includes some unexpected drama. The relay requires two teams of three runners to circumnavigate the entire length of the warning track. As the third and final leg starts, the second runner on one team gets in the way of the final runner on the other team. A collision ensues and the guy who just passed the baton face plants on the warning track. A mixture of gasps and laughs go up among the crowd. Luckily, no damage is done. The runner he interferes with ends up winning the race, so Jatovi needn't make a decision about disqualification.

Sitting at a bar stool of the restaurant that faces out to the field is a gentleman who informs me that he is a former coach of a high school traveling team. He also was a high school ump for a while. He gave it up during the pandemic. His son is now a high school baseball coach. Finally, he reveals that his grandfather played in the minors of the Negro Leagues.

"Mom still has the bat he used," he says with wistful eyes.

HOME SERIES 11: A PLAYOFF PREVIEW?

The game is tied at five runs apiece going into the bottom of the eighth inning. The inning starts with a single. Then the Sounds pitcher walks two batters, hits two more, and throws a wild pitch. Classic minor league action I haven't seen in a while. One HBP call is vigorously protested by Rick Sweet, the Sounds' manager. To the delight of the crowd, the ump ejects him from the game. I swear Sweet came one more bulging vein on his forehead short of kicking up the dirt. I'm disappointed. No matter. The Bulls win.

Attendance: 4,721.

FRIDAY, AUGUST 26

I share the dinner line with Steve and a host I meet for the first time, Tom G. Talk turns to our section assignments. Tom tells us that a few years back a host was assigned to stand at the end of the dugout.

"You met the players. It was great. Some were real friendly, others ignored you," Tom says, "And you had to watch out for foul balls."

We agree this was a real treat. Tom thinks it only lasted two years.

On my way to my station, I run into Josh. He tells me he's very tired. He's been working as a host for a company that puts him on a bus to work out of town. He's not looking forward to next weekend, when he'll work a Duke football game as well as take two round trip bus rides, three hours in each direction, to work some auto races.

"How's the computer security class going?" I inquire.

"I finished the intro classes but the tuition for the next class is $17,000. Not sure I can afford it. I might have to put this on hold for a while."

My section is the Terrace Boxes. The first arrivals are the employees of Environment Resources Management, an international company headquartered in Raleigh that consults with businesses about creating sustainable solutions for protecting the environment, health, and safety. They've purchased four boxes that quickly fill up with employees and their families.

Tonight is another Cervezas de Durham (Beers of Durham) night. The Bulls are serving beers in a hard plastic cup in the shape of a baseball bat, about two feet tall. Since I'm stationed in front of the bar at Jackie's Landing, I can tell you the souvenir cups are a big hit. Not only are the two lines at the bar each thirty yards long, but the cups are sold out by the fourth inning.

In the top of the third inning, next to me there is a family with three kids, a boy maybe five years old, a girl maybe three, and a babe-in-arms. The boy takes his dad's empty beer bat and starts pounding it on the railing. It breaks and the top part lands on the head of a woman in the seat below. No damage, but she looks angry and confronts the father. Dad asks junior to apologize. The boy hides behind his father, wraps his arms around his leg, and begins to wail. The woman's demeanor softens, and order is restored. While dad gently lectures and consoles his son, I collect the shattered pieces of the cup for the trash can.

The Bulls fall behind by four runs in the top of the first and, despite several valiant efforts to overcome weak pitching, they lose the game 11 to 8.

For the rest of the game, the tearful boy sits quietly as Dad explains to him different aspects of the game. In the bottom of the ninth, I approach and ask the boy if he'd like a baseball. Dad tells him to say thank you. He does, shyly.

"Say it louder," Dad insists.

A louder "thank you" follows, as does an expression of appreciation from dad.

After the fireworks, junior approaches me yet again, by himself, with another thank you.

Baseballs really do contain magic.

Attendance: 8,855.

SATURDAY, AUGUST 27

I'm assigned the first base tunnel tonight and the two sections that flank the entrance to the seats, just behind the home team dugout. As I arrive, a mom and three kids are walking up the aisle after hawking autographs.

"Get anybody?"

The boy runs over to show me his card collection and which ones are autographed.

"Hey, these are Bulls Topps cards! Where'd you get them?"

"In the team store."

I didn't know this set existed. I walk down to the store. Scanning the checkout area, I spot the card sets. I'm disappointed when only sets from 2019 are available. I guess there was no set in 2020.

"This year's cards sold out in three days," says the clerk.

At home, a visit to eBay scores me a 2022 set, at four times the store price.

Richard, hosting the section next to me, calls me over to meet Tony Riggsbee. Riggsbee is the award-winning PA announcer for the Bulls and has been for over twenty years. He was born and raised in Durham (a Durmite!) and also does news and sports on two local radio stations. He is the executive director of the Raleigh Hot Stove League, an organization that holds a charity banquet each year.

A family of four emerges from the tunnel. Mom and dad have on matching baseball jerseys that have "Clemente 21" on the back and "Cangrejeros" on the front. Roberto Clemente was a Hall of Fame ballplayer and humanitarian who perished in a plane crash at the age of thirty-eight. Dad tells me the uniform jerseys are replicas of Clemente's from when he played in the Puerto Rican League. The family is from Puerto Rico and comes to Durham through Tampa, Florida. They love it here.

Not long after the game begins, it dawns on me that I am probably hosting the busiest intersection in the stadium, maybe for the busiest game of the season. Nearly nine thousand fans will fill the stadium and thousands will emerge through my tunnel, dozens with questions about their seats. Since it's Saturday, Ripken the bat dog will be at the dugout gate. This means people will stream down my aisle to get a picture with the pooch.

"He's right there!" yells one youth.

I'll have to make sure they don't linger. Also, next to where I stand, Jatovi and his crew of Lollygaggers will set up their staging area before they go on the field for between-inning entertainment. Dozens of people will come by to say hello to Jatovi. He knows many of their names and greets them all with an enthusiastic smile.

And a busy staging area it is. Here's a list of the folks I share my hosting spot with as the game progresses:

- The singer of the national anthem
- The guest "play ball" announcer
- The runner who races around the outfield warning track competing with an image of Wool E. projected on the wall
- The kid who races Wool E. around the bases
- The contestants in the Homestretch Tug-of-War

HOME SERIES 11: A PLAYOFF PREVIEW?

- Wool E., before he launches T-shirts from a giant hot dog
- The kid who tosses Angry Birds into three buckets
- Jatovi and his minions on the dugout tossing balls out to the crowd.

Later, Jatovi engages the crowd in a competition between the first and third base stands. The contest is to see which fans can sing the loudest. Jatovi warns the fans that booing will lead to their side being disqualified.

At the end of the fifth inning, Ripken's handler leads the canine up the aisle. I'm relieved that the stream of folks crowding the aisle might finally be over. Not so. As Ripken passes me, I get handed his signed baseball card. Even the bat dog has a baseball card! How come the Seating Ball Hosts don't have cards? I'm gonna lodge a protest. Anyway, Ripken takes up residence on the walkway by my station and is immediately surrounded by fifty or so fans wanting to take photos, get cards, pet him. The walkway is absolutely packed, and the dog is calmer than I am. This will go on for two innings.

A benefit of the evening is that I get a chance to learn more about Jatovi. I learn that in addition to his work for the Bulls, he does personal computer consulting, and also emcees for the Carolina Hurricanes hockey team. He is spearheading an effort to provide an eSport facility in downtown Durham that will serve as a springboard for city youth to become interested in and find employment in the media and computer sector.

"Durham companies recruit from out of town when there's so much potential talent right here," he tells me.

Only two other incidents during the evening demand my attention. A man approaches me about the fifth inning and asks politely if he and his son can come sit in my section. There is a loud fan behind them that's ruining the game for those around him. "Sure," I say and point out some empty seats. Then a host from a few sections away comes by to tell me that there is a spill in her section. I get to use the radio for the first time.

"Nacho spill in 202," I say in a super serious voice.

"Got it," is the reply.

At this point, I realize that this will be the last homestand before the kids go back to school . . .

The Bulls outhit the Sounds but can't deliver the big hit with runners in scoring position. When the night ends, they have fallen out of first place.

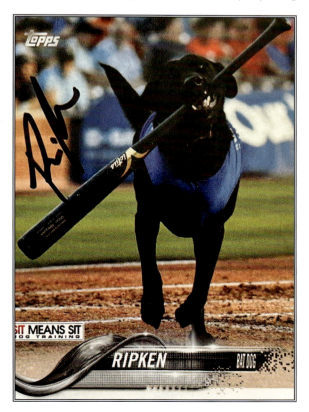

Ripken the Bat Dog's baseball card.

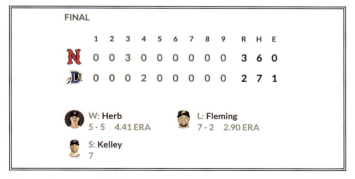

Attendance: 8,882.

THE PHENOM

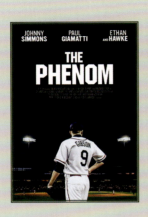

Year of Release: 2016
Rating: Not Rated
Director: Noah Buschel
Writer: Noah Buschel
Stars: Johnny Simmons (pitcher), Ethan Hawke (father), Paul Giamatti (therapist)

Plot Synopsis

From Wiki: https://en.wikipedia.org/wiki/The_Phenom_(film)
The Phenom is a 2016 American sports drama film written and directed by Noah Buschel, starring Johnny Simmons, Paul Giamatti, and Ethan Hawke. The film was released on June 24, 2016, by RLJ Entertainment, and is loosely based on the early life and professional struggles of former Major League Baseball player Rick Ankiel.
From IMDb: https://www.imdb.com/title/tt3885524/
A rookie pitcher undergoes psychotherapy to overcome the yips.

Critic Ratings

Rotten Tomatoes: https://www.rottentomatoes.com/m/the_phenom_2016
Tomatometer: 79 out of 100 (47 reviewers)
Audience Score: 38 out of 100 (500+ Ratings)
Critics consensus: Powerfully acted and emotionally affecting, *The Phenom* proves a baseball movie can step away from the mound and still deliver a heater down the middle.
IMDb Rating: 5.2 out of 10 (2300 raters)
Roger Ebert: https://www.rogerebert.com/reviews/the-phenom-2016, 3 out of 4 stars.
Ebert contrasts *The Phenom* with *A League of Their Own* comparing Tom Hanks' pronouncement that "There's no crying in baseball!" with Hopper Sr.'s "Pain is weakness leaving the body" when he attempts to console his distressed son. Ebert suggests the film's director "recognizes the tragedy within Hanks' once-funny line, and the toxic nature of believing it."

Chapter 16
Who's On First?

There are three types of baseball players—those who make it happen, those who watch it happen, and those who wonder what happens.

—Tommy Lasorda

Baseball players are smarter than football players. How often do you see a baseball team penalized for having too many players on the field?

—Jim Bouton

We've walked through the history of the city of Durham, read the "newspaper articles" that heralded important events in minor league history, and considered visiting noteworthy past Bulls' ballgames using a time machine. We've met dozens of fans and employees of the team. So, what's left? Oh yeah, what about the ballplayers?

As a Seating Bowl Host, I have no more access to the ballplayers than an average fan. I met one player before a ballgame when he retrieved a flying disc that landed in the section I was hosting. I met the parents of several players. That's it. But still, minor league ballplayers lead a unique existence and it's essential that I give a shout-out to the guys whose skills fans come to watch.

September 2 is as good a time as any to learn a bit about who the players are and take a peek at how they are performing. Every September 1, the major league teams expand their rosters from 26 players to 28 (and can add an additional player on days they play doubleheaders).[1] Only 14 players can be designated as pitchers, though position players can pitch if the score of the game favors one team by more than six runs. Until 2020, MLB rosters could be expanded in September to 40 players, essentially meaning that all players in the minors who were on the major league team's active roster could be called up. That would have been something to see; a dozen new guys filling the locker room, cramming into the dugout. Talk about messing up team "chemistry."

---

1   https://www.mlb.com/glossary/transactions/26-man-roster

Major league teams can also have a "taxi squad" of five players that travels with them, players who can practice with the team but can't play in games that count.

> ### WHERE DID THE TERM "TAXI SQUAD" COME FROM?
>
> It seems Arthur McBride, the owner of the Cleveland Browns football team from 1945 to 1953, also owned a taxi company. He gave his surplus players jobs driving cabs. Hence, the taxi squad actually did drive taxis!

Team chemistry raises the question of how much money minor league ball players get paid. The pay scale depends on the league's level. According to Advocates for Minor Leaguers[2], the standard salary for Level-AAA ballplayers is $700 a week and they are only paid during the season. That's about $17,500 for five months. They must cover their own housing expenses. Off-season they're on their own. However, for those players who are on the 40-man major league roster, the minimum salary is $700,000.[3] And for early-round draft picks, the signing bonus can be significant. It is estimated that the median minor league ballplayer salary is $44,680 and the range is from $19,910 to $187,200.[4] I can't help but wonder how this disparity plays out in a locker room, though I suspect resentments are held in check. And the disparity is even greater in a major league locker room.

It's important to note that the ball players are "owned" by the major league teams and not by their minor league clubs. Their salaries, comings and goings, ups and downs, even how long they stay in a game (for example, pitch counts) can be dictated by the affiliated major league club. Everything else about my experience as a host in the ballpark is controlled by the Bulls. Not the players though, the Rays control them.

Talking about the minor league experience, Clint Barnes, who played seventeen seasons with four major league clubs and about a dozen minor league teams, put it well[5]: "It's all about getting to your dream of playing in the Big Leagues. You have to play at your best every day and it is definitely not easy. You have to go through the aches and pains. The tough thing is how short your career can be. If you can be in this game in pro ball for ten years, you are pretty blessed. You are expected to be at your best every single day. There are no sick days. There are no excuses."

Missing from Barnes's description is what must be a constant sense for many ball players that where you are is only a temporary stop. Keep your bags packed, not just for the next road trip but for your next assignment, whether it be up or down the levels of play, or out completely. To give an idea for how pervasive this sense must be, I compared the opening day roster of the Bulls with their roster on September 2. This is a snapshot that could have produced different results most any other day. A count of the number of "transactions," or movement of a player for the Bulls up or down, or out, reveals 245 such moves were made between April 5 and September 1.

Let's start with pitchers. The Bulls had 32 pitchers listed on their roster on opening day and 23 on September 2. Fifteen pitchers appear on both rosters. That means 25 pitchers were on one list but not the other. This statistic also doesn't take into account a pitcher who might have been promoted or demoted and then came back to the Bulls. Of four catchers on the opening day roster, three were with the Bulls as September began. Infielders? The opening day roster

---

2   https://www.advocatesforminorleaguers.com/

3   https://www.statista.com/statistics/256187/minimum-salary-of-players-in-major-league-baseball/

4   https://www.comparably.com/salaries/salaries-for-minor-league-baseball-player

5   Ibid.

Position Player	Games	At-Bats	Runs	Hits	Home Runs	RBI	Walks	Strike Outs	Stolen Bases	Batting Average	OBP	SLG	OPS
Luke Raley **Infield**	43	148	26	44	10	34	20	47	5	0.297	0.407	0.527	0.934
Jonathan Aranda **Infield**	104	403	71	128	18	85	45	100	4	0.318	0.394	0.521	0.915
Josh Lowe **Outfield**	60	224	37	68	10	51	31	79	13	0.304	0.388	0.527	0.915
Vidal Brujan **Infield**	47	186	43	56	4	16	23	31	15	0.301	0.385	0.462	0.847
Miles Mastrobuoni **Infield**	118	464	82	137	16	58	52	87	21	0.295	0.366	0.466	0.832
Rene Pinto **C**	64	244	32	63	13	50	21	71	1	0.258	0.318	0.512	0.83
Grant Witherspoon **Outfield**	52	173	27	42	9	23	25	50	3	0.243	0.348	0.451	0.799
Tristan Gray **Infield**	105	383	61	86	30	82	22	132	3	0.225	0.278	0.501	0.779
Jim Haley **Infield**	97	329	58	75	18	41	32	110	15	0.228	0.304	0.453	0.757
Xavier Edwards **Infield**	74	280	41	77	5	29	34	48	5	0.275	0.352	0.382	0.734
Cal Stevenson **Outfield**	57	170	29	45	2	17	31	42	9	0.265	0.376	0.353	0.729
Ruben Cardenas **Outfield**	68	238	32	46	12	29	25	82	4	0.193	0.272	0.412	0.684
Ryan Boldt **Outfield**	67	250	39	59	7	31	18	78	8	0.236	0.299	0.38	0.679
Ford Proctor **C**	79	268	27	57	6	28	44	95	3	0.213	0.329	0.306	0.635

Abbreviations:
OBP: On Base Percentage. Total number of hits, walks, and hit by pitch divided by the total number of at-bats, walks, hit by pitch, and sacrifice flies.
SLG: Slugging Percentage. Total bases (e.g., a double counts as two bases, a triple three, and a homer four) divided by at-bats.
OPS: OBP plus SLG. Of all the batting statistics, OPS shows the highest correlation with the number of runs a team scores.[6]

---

6 Law, K. (2017). *Smart Baseball*. New York, NY: Morrow.

listed six, four of whom were in the Bulls dugout on September 1. We'll learn more about the two who went up to the majors shortly. Of the eight outfielders who started the season with the Bulls, four were still in Durham as the final month of the season began.

So, who are the Bulls? Well, first we have to decide what credentials you need to wear the manteau of a "full-time" Bulls player. For position players (not pitchers) the minor leagues require that a player have 2.7 at-bats per team game played to qualify for the batting leader rankings. By this measure, four Durham players qualified: Jonathon Aranda, Miles Mastrobuoni, Tristan Gray, and Jim Haley. Four players ain't enough to field a team. So, let's "draft" for our team the 14 players who had the most at-bats for the Bulls. This works pretty well. We end up with five outfielders, seven infielders, and two catchers. On September 1, the Bulls had sent about 5,600 batters to the plate. Our 14 position players accounted for about 4,100 of those appearances, about 72 percent of the total. Not bad. Our team's position players are listed in the table above.

What pitchers make our Bulls team? For a pitcher to qualify for the IL leader board, he needs to pitch .80 innings per team game. By that standard, nary one Bulls pitcher qualified. Still, the Bulls ranked seventh out of the 20 IL teams in earned run average (they were third in hitting, based on OPS). Pitching is a little trickier when it comes to picking a team because relief pitchers won't have as many innings as starting pitchers, but they are a necessary (some might say the most necessary) component for the pitching staff. So, the best criteria for deciding who comprised the Bulls' go-to pitchers through September 1 would probably be the number of games the pitcher appeared in. Through September 1, 52 pitchers had taken the mound for the Bulls. To compose a staff of pitchers, we need to include all pitchers who appeared in 19 contests or more. This comes to 15 hurlers (making our complete roster of 29 players, or one more than the minor league limit[7], but the Bulls had two pitchers with the minimum 19 innings, so let's pretend one pitcher is on the disabled list). The pitchers on our rosters pitched only about 340 of the 1130 inning the Bulls had played, or about 30 percent. The pitchers and their stats are listed on the next page.

How old are they? Most of our Bulls are between the ages of twenty-four and twenty-eight years old. The youngest player on the team is Xavier Edwards, a shortstop born in 1999 in Mineola, NY. Xavier was drafted out of high school—North Broward Prep High School in Coconut Creek, FL. His high school has seven players listed as having played professional baseball. The North Broward Eagles baseball team won the 2022 Florida High School Athletic Association 3A championship.

Xavier Edwards #2.

At the ripe old age of thirty-three, Seth Blair is the oldest Bull. He's a pitcher who graduated from Arizona State University and he has played professionally since being drafted in the first round (number 46 overall) of the 2010 draft. He's not made it to the majors. He pitched in relief in 20 games for the Bulls this season before he was released.

---

7   https://en.wikipedia.org/wiki/List_of_International_League_team_rosters

Pitcher	Wins	Loses	ERA	Games	Starts	Saves	Innings Pitched	Strike Outs	Whip
Javy Guerra	1	0	1.37	41	0	9	39.1	50	0.86
Ben Bowden	4	0	2.45	21	0	0	22	24	1.5
Dalton Moats	1	0	3.13	42	1	0	46	48	1
Dusten Knight	3	3	3.23	41	1	9	47.1	56	1.23
Tommy Romero	6	5	3.51	23	13	1	66.2	58	1.23
Calvin Faucher	3	3	3.73	32	4	0	41	50	1.49
Cristofer Ogando	2	1	4.13	36	0	3	48	48	1.21
Ralph Garza	3	2	4.5	20	3	1	30	22	1.07
Joel Peguero	2	1	4.58	32	4	0	39.1	33	1.55
Luke Bard	0	0	4.88	19	1	0	24	27	0.96
Chris Muller	4	3	5.25	42	1	2	48	58	1.69
Easton McGee	5	7	5.34	22	18	0	94.1	73	1.3
Phoenix Sanders	0	0	5.4	25	1	1	30	36	1.37
Zack Erwin	4	5	5.79	32	2	0	37.1	29	1.58
Seth Blair	0	3	7.61	21	2	1	23.2	17	1.86

Abbreviations:
ERA: Earned Run Average. Earned runs allowed per nine innings pitched.
WHIP: Walks and Hits per Innings Pitched.

Seth Blair #86.

Where are they from? Our Bulls have been born in fifteen different states, with Texas (five players) and California (four players) contributing the most players. Five other countries have contributed players: three from the Dominican Republic, and one each from Panama, Mexico, Venezuela, and Germany. The player born in Germany is Phoenix Sanders, a right-handed pitcher. He grew up in Florida, where he pitched for Daytona State College, having received no scholarship offers. He transferred to the University

Phoenix Sanders #52.

of South Florida, an NCAA Division I school, as an upperclassman. Another short timer for the Bulls (25 games), he now pitches for the Norfolk Tide.

How much education do they have? Twenty of our players attended college. Of the nine players who didn't attend college, six came to the Bulls from south of the border. Three were drafted out of US high schools. We've already met Xavier Edwards, so let's meet Josh Lowe. Josh attended Pope High School in Marietta, GA, a suburb of Atlanta. He was the first round, 13th overall draft pick by the Rays in 2016. Josh received a signing bonus of $2,597,500. As of September 1, Josh had played in 60 games for the Bulls and 52 for the Rays, having been called up twice to the majors.

Josh Lowe #11.

When were they picked in the draft? For a player to be eligible for the baseball draft, he must have attended at least three years of college and be a resident of the United States, one of its territories, or Canada, or have attended an institution therein. Any college player who has turned twenty-one is also eligible.[8] There are 50 rounds in the draft and each MLB team picks in each round. That's 1,500 possible draftees each year. Unlike other sports, baseball players drafted after their junior year of college can decide to return to school full-time and get drafted again after their senior year.

Of our 23 players who were picked in the baseball draft, 10 were picked by Tampa Bay, and 13 were picked by other teams then traded to the Rays. We've already met the two players on our team that were picked earliest in the draft; Josh Lowe was picked 13th in the 2016 draft and Xavier Edwards was picked 38th in the 2018 draft. The player picked lowest in the draft is Dusten Knight, picked in the 28th round, 852nd overall, by the San Francisco Giants in 2013. He's also among the "long in the tooth" at age thirty-two. Dusten has been "owned" by five different major league teams and has pitched in the majors for both Tampa Bay and the Baltimore Orioles. In 2019, he played in the Mexican League for the Diablos Rojos del Mexico—in English, the Mexico City Red Devils—before he returned to the states and played for the Pensacola Blue Wahoos of the Level-AA Southern League.

Dusten Knight #35.

How many have major league experience? Of our 29 Bulls, 15 have seen major league action. For most this experience can be described as "going up for a cup of coffee." Players can be called up to fill

---

8 https://fansided.com/2022/07/15/mlb-draft-rules-explained/

a slot when another player is on the disabled list or for one of those double headers. But four of our pitchers have at least five decisions in the majors and three position players have been to bat over 100 times. One of these is Josh Lowe. Another is Vidal Brujan, one of the players called up by Tampa Bay with this September's roster expansion. He was then sent back to Durham a week later. Hailing from the Dominican Republic, he's seen service in seven minor league seasons with more than a half dozen teams. He plays winter ball in his home country.

Miles Mastrobuoni #3.

Vidal Bruján #7.

Who's batted the most for the Bulls? Before we leave the team, four more players deserve recognition. These four had played in over 100 of the Bulls first 130 games. So, you might say they were the backbone of the team I watched.

Miles Mastrobuoni hasn't had a major league at-bat in his six-year professional career, but he has had his swings for the Bulls with over 500 plate appearances in 2022. He was drafted by the Rays in 2016. In 2019, playing for the Rays Level-AA, Montgomery Biscuits, Miles was named a Southern League Mid-Season and Post-Season All Star, and the Best Utility player.

Tristan Gray leads the IL in home runs with 30. Drafted by the Pittsburgh Pirates in 2017, Tristan started out in Level-A ball. In 2020, when the pandemic shut down minor league baseball, Tristan played in 12 games for the Sugar Land (Texas) Skeeters of the Constellation Energy League (Sugar Land now has a Level-AAA ball club). The league was created to give minor leaguers, former major leaguers, and walk-ons an opportunity to play during the pandemic. There were four teams in the league, and each played 28 games. It was in operation for only one year and all games were played at Constellation Field in Sugar Land. Roger Clemens and his son Cody managed Team Texas. It finished last (11–17).

Tirstan Gray #9.

Sometimes, even if you know nothing about the players on the field, just watching allows you to know who stands out. I remember watching a Level-A ball game when a batter hit a lazy bloop single to right field. By the time the ball was retrieved and thrown in the batter was at third base. I promise you the batter wasn't playing Level-A ball for long.

Jonathon Aranda is one of those stand-out ball players. He comes in third for the most at-bats for the Bulls. He was called up to the majors in the September roster expansion for his second stint with the Rays this year. We met his mother earlier in the season when she came from Mexico to watch her son play. Isaac Paredes was another stand out for the Bulls early in the season. He plays second baseman for the Rays now and has over 300 plate appearances for them. We met him earlier this season as well. He's the guy who hit three home runs against the Yankees and then was hit by a pitch his fourth time up.

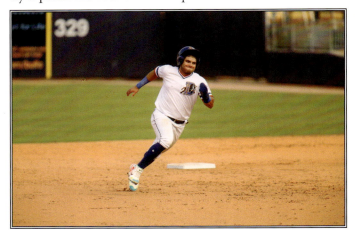

Jonathan Aranda #62.

Finally, let's spend some time with Jim Haley. Born in Pennsylvania, he played three seasons of college ball for Penn State, appeared in 146 games, and had a .801 OPS in his final season. Haley hasn't visited the majors yet in his seven-year career but he's an everyday infielder for the Bulls.

Jim Haley #17.

Who is coaching the team? Brady Williams became the manager of the Bulls in 2019, when Charlie Montoya got the job managing the Toronto Blue Jays. Brady was drafted in the 45th round of the 1999 draft and played five seasons in the minors with 978 plate appearances (.218), but never made it past Level-AA ball. He was promoted to the Bulls' coaching staff after five years as manager of Tampa Bay's Level-AA team, the Montgomery Biscuits. Before that, he managed the Hudson Valley Renegades (Short Season Level-A, 2009), Bowling Green Hot Rods (Level-A 2010–12), and Charlotte Stone Crabs (Level-A 2013). Baseball runs in his family's blood. His father was an infielder turned manager and his son is now managing in the minors as well.

Williams coaching staff is rounded out by bench coach Reinaldo Ruiz. The MLB glossary describes a bench coach as someone "typically considered the right-hand man to his team's manager. Bench coaches assist their managers in decision-making and will sometimes relay scouting information from the team's front office to the club's players. Many bench coaches go on to become managers or are former managers. The bench coach typically steps in to act as manager when the regular manager is unavailable (often as a result of being ejected from the game)."[9] Ruiz spent just a short time as a player in the minors.

Will Bradley is in his first season as the Bulls' hitting coach. He previously held the same position in the California Angels' minor league organization.

Brian Reith is the Bulls' pitching coach. He was drafted by the Yankees in 1996 in the sixth round. He pitched in 2001, 2003, and 2004 for the Cincinnati Reds. Reith spent the 2021 season on the Rays staff as a major league pitching fellow, helping with the development of pitchers.

If you think the coaches' stories sound similar to those of ballplayers—traveling up and down the minor league ladder, hoping to reach the majors—you're right.

So, that's the best I can do to introduce you to the core of the Durham Bulls, 2022 edition, the team that drew me and hundreds of thousands of fans to watch them play. They are younger than the average American. Their educational attainment is indistinguishable for the United States population. They have called more cities "home" than most people.

But what truly sets them apart from the rest of us is that they play damn good baseball.

---

[9] https://www.mlb.com/glossary/positions/bench-coach

Chapter 17
Home Series 12: Yankees Invade North Carolina

I was such a dangerous hitter I even got intentional walks during batting practice.
—Casey Stengel, baseball pundit

The way to catch a knuckleball is to wait until the ball stops rolling and then to pick it up.
— Bob Uecker, another baseball pundit

| INTERNATIONAL LEAGUE EASTERN DIVISION ||||||
Team	MLB	Wins	Losses	Winning Percentage	Games Behind
Durham	TB	73	56	0.566	-
Jacksonville	MIA	69	59	0.539	3.5
Scranton/WB	NYY	69	59	0.539	3.5
Lehigh Valley	PHI	69	60	0.535	4
Worcester	BOS	67	62	0.519	6
(5 Teams Not Listed)					

With just four series left to play, things are looking pretty good for the Bulls. They come home on a four-game winning streak and have a three-and-a-half game lead in the IL East. But this homestand is against the Scranton/Wilkes-Barre RailRiders, one of the teams on their heels. The team will also enter that final 20-game period during this homestand. The best record in the last 20 games of the season is the second tie-breaker (after head-to-head competition) should two teams finish the season with the same record atop the division.

SCRANTON/WILKES-BARRE

https://en.wikipedia.org/wiki/Scranton,_Pennsylvania

https://en.wikipedia.org/wiki/Scranton/Wilkes-Barre_RailRiders

Nickname: RailRiders
MLB: New York Yankees (2007–present)
Field: PNC Field, capacity 10,000
Population: 567,559
Economy: health care, academic, and manufacturing sectors.
MLB: New York Yankees (2007–present)
Fun Fact: The RailRiders nickname is in recognition that Northeastern Pennsylvania was the home of the first trolley system in the USA.

TUESDAY, SEPTEMBER 7

I'm stationed behind home plate for this matinee game on Labor Day. After dinner, on the walkway, the conversation turns to "horror stories." One host relates an encounter he had with a woman who was "in her cups" as Ben Franklin would have said.[1]

"She moves from seat to seat during the game," he says, "none of which are on her ticket. If you question her, she says the seats are empty and gets in your face to let her sit there. She was carrying a beer can that you can't buy in the stadium."

Sure enough, as the game begins the woman appears. I note that she doesn't have a beer in her hand, which is good, but she does walk by the premium seats several times during the game, often stopping on the walkway to watch the action for a while. For this game, at least, she is well-behaved.

There is also a guy in a section over from mine, a season ticket holder, with a permanent scowl on his face. He can be a real pain, my neighbor host says. I've had a run-in with him as well. A few nights back he asked me if I had a knife on me. He had a small bandage on his finger that was coming loose and wanted to cut it off. I don't carry a knife, so I suggested he go to Guest Services. The look he gave me suggested that wasn't the answer he wanted. Did he want me to go to Guest Services and get a knife for him?

"That guy's an example of why it's important to smile as much as you can when you're young," I say, "That scowl is stuck in place."

"It gets frozen there," my co-worker responds.

Don't let your face get stuck like this!

But the story that leaves me truly saddened is told by John, the host who breathes through a tracheotomy tube. He was working the K-Wall when he saw a guy who had come out of the Tobacco Road restaurant and was smoking a big cigar on the walkway. The smoker was clearly "jagg'd and jambled," as Ben Franklin might have put it. When John told him smoking was not allowed, the guy took a deep tug on the cigar and blew it at John's breathing tube.

"'You're just jealous you can't smoke anymore'," John recounts the guy saying, then adds, "But I was never a smoker."

Later, the smoker re-emerged from the restaurant and lit up another stogie. John approached him again. This time the guy threatened to "get" John. John was shaken. When the game was over, he asked one of the more muscular hosts to accompany him to his car. The smoker was nowhere to be seen.

---

[1] https://www.openculture.com/2014/10/ben-franklins-200-synonyms-for-drunk.html

The way some people behave is inexplicable to me. This guy was a classic bully. The dictionary defines a bully as "a blustering, mean, or predatory person who, from a perceived position of relative power, intimidates, abuses, harasses, or coerces people, especially those considered unlikely to defend themselves."[2] Studies suggest bullying is as common among adults as children. Some common explanations for why people bully others include that the bullies have experienced emotional trauma, they are insecure, they've been bullied themselves, they lack empathy, and they have poor social skills. John's story will stick with me for a long time.

As the fans file in, it's clear that there are lots of Yankee faithful in the Durham area. While every game brings out fans of the major league team the visitors are affiliated with, tonight the Yankee T-shirts and jerseys are more prominent than is typical. Many sit behind the visitor's dugout. You can tell because when something good happens for the RailRiders a cheer goes up in that section.

A local joke is told about the derivation of the name of the city of Cary, North Carolina, just down the road from Durham, and the home of the Research Triangle Park where numerous science and technology companies have facilities. Supposedly, Cary stands for "Containment Area for Relocated Yankees" (no, not the ball team). Over the course of the evening, I talk with several Yankee fans and get to tell them of my misspent youth in the bleachers of Yankee Stadium.

The game is a thriller. The Bulls take a 1–0 lead but then give it up on an error. The home team takes the lead again but the RailRiders re-tie the game at 2–2. The game goes into extra innings. In the top of the tenth, the RailRiders "ghost runner" (the player who starts an extra inning on second base) scores on a single. The Bulls are down 3–2 going into the bottom of the tenth. Not to worry, Miles Mastrobuoni hits a triple to right field driving in the tying run, his fourth hit of the game. Luke Raley's single to center produces a walk-off win for the Bulls. The team streams out on the field to congratulate Raley. It's the most exuberant demonstration by the Bulls I've seen all season.

A walk-off win leads to an on-field celebration.

My baseball give-away tonight goes to a girl, maybe four years old, and her younger brother. She's wearing a tutu and has glitter on her face. These kids were incredibly well-behaved for the eight innings they were at the game. Her dad is wearing a T-shirt inscribed "I Bleed Carolina Blue." That makes him a sworn enemy of Duke, but I gave his kids the ball anyway.

Keep that smile on your face, ballerina.

Attendance: 6,005.

THURSDAY, SEPTEMBER 8

Queen Elizabeth of England passed away today. My job is checking tickets at the gate between the Tobacco

---

[2] https://www.dictionary.com/browse/bully

Road restaurant and the walkway in left field, where the flagpoles are. Before the game starts, a member of the ground crew arrives.

"I need to lower the flags," he says, "Can you help me make sure the flags are an even height?"

Dave H., who's manning the Snorting Bull to my right, comes over to help. The four flags are lowered. But then another ground crew member standing out on the field yells up that they are all too low. Up they go about four feet. There is discussion about whether the American flag should be a bit higher than the others.

"Nope," says the crew member, "I was in the Army for twenty-five years, I know."

After the game, I learn a bit more about lowering the flag as an act of respect or mourning. There seems to be consensus that the practice is described as "half-staff" when the flagpole is on land and "half-mast" on a ship. How far down the pole the flag should go is a bit more controversial. Some sources say it should be lowered only the width of the flag (what do you do when, like in our case, the flags are of different size?)[3], others say it should be halfway down the pole.[4] Protocol also says that the flag should be raised to the top of the pole, its finial, before it is lowered to half-staff and first raised back up before the flag is removed from the pole.

Pete, the autograph seeker, walks by. I learn that he has returned from a trip to the Northwest where he attended baseball games in Seattle (a day game) and Vancouver (the same night) as well as two other cities in eastern Washington state.

"It's dirty work," he says, "but someone's gotta do it."

About the sixth inning, a customer at a table in the restaurant stands up. He says the Ks being draped on the K-Wall are blocking his view of the action. He begins complaining loudly to the K-Wall guy who is a young man with both physical and cognitive challenges. I approach him and see he can't get the words out to defend himself.

"I couldn't see the home run!" says the diner, who clearly "sees two moons" (yep, Ben Franklin again).

"Technically," I inform him, "you're not at the ball game, you know."

"Yeah, but why can't the Ks be hung over there?"

I check where he is pointing and find that part of the wall is opaque so the Ks couldn't be seen from the field.

Two operations interns walk by. We discuss the situation. They confirm that the number of Ks on the wall now are accurate and agree that if another strike out occurs it will go up right where it's supposed to, the diner be damned. Remarkably, this guy is attending the game with a friendly young woman in a wheelchair, who is at her first baseball game ever. She's the kind of person who asks you your name and offers her own, even though your encounter will be fleeting. Didn't the angry diner see the K-Wall guy had trouble walking and couldn't respond to his complaint? I watch this bully carefully for the last three innings of the game. He consumes a beer each inning. There are no more strike outs.

In the top of the ninth inning, a RailRiders player hits a long home run that lands on the roof over the restaurant's outdoor seating. A man with a dog wins the ball as it rolls off the roof. Dave H. and I note that this guy has just showed up. The winner gets on his phone and talks and waves at his friends who are sitting on the third base side of the park, displaying his trophy.

"Where'd that dog come from?' Dave asks me. Neither of us saw how he got to the walkway.

We approach the man and ask why the dog is in the park.

"It's a service dog," he says, "It's my daughter's. She's sitting over there." He points into the distance.

Dave and I agree this is probably hooey. The dog

---

3   https://en.wikipedia.org/wiki/Half-mast
4   https://writingexplained.org/half-mast-or-half-staff-difference

doesn't have on a vest, sniffs us, and tugs on the leash. How he got in the park is beyond us.

As I leave the park, I decide that the earlier warning I received regarding assignments in left field was accurate. Alcohol-related problems in the ballpark are exceedingly rare. But there's more drinking going on at the restaurant and a disproportionate number of alcohol-fueled difficulties seem to spill over from this venue. It's my job to see that these problems don't get out of hand.

My favorite T-shirt tonight has "Unionize the Minors" across the front. I ask the wearer where he got it.

"Tipping Pitches," he says. Tipping Pitches is a "baseball podcast with a pro-labor bent."[5]

The game is a downer. The Bulls fall behind 2–0, tie it up, then give up five runs and lose 7–2. The Bulls pitchers gave up 15 hits and the home team's hitters only got 4. Our lead in the IL East is shaved to 2.5 games, only two in the loss column.

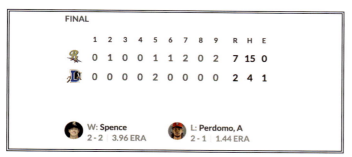

Attendance: 4,806.

SATURDAY, SEPTEMBER 10

As I leave for work, it starts to rain. My two weather apps both suggest it will rain light to heavy until around eleven o'clock at night. Will this be my first rain out? The heavy downpour doesn't materialize, but a steady misting persists for four hours. The game starts a half hour late and proceeds uninterrupted, in the mist, until the weather clears up around the fourth inning.

At dinner, conversation centers on the scoreboards again. Three nights ago, none were functioning. Now, the large electronic scoreboard is operating but not at full functionality.

"Maybe the renovation money has some funds for improving the scoreboards," I offer. "I know the money is for the internal workings of the stadium, to improve the ballplayers' experience, but sometimes those kinds of items are tucked away in there." I'm quickly disabused of this thought.

Not necessarily a company kind of guy, still, I propose a defense of the Bulls. "Just to give the Bulls' side of the story, maybe the loss of revenue the last two seasons due to the pandemic has made money tight." This goes over about as well as my renovations suggestion. All agree the team could fix the scoreboards if they made it a priority.

There is more discussion of other ways the fan experience might be improved. Most of these suggestions are offered by a tablemate who doesn't walk the aisles. He is satisfied when I point out that, in fact, most of these things are done—for example, radios at the tunnels and emptying of trash on the walkway during the game.

At my station, the host next to me and I talk about the rule changes the major leagues adopted yesterday. The pitch clock will go into effect in the next major league season. I've become a big believer in this rule change, watching it in action this season. The bases will get bigger. Good. The shift will be outlawed. Teams will have to have two players on each side of second base. I still don't like this rule. Batters should learn to bunt or hit to the opposite field. Then the shift will go away.

A young woman and a man I suspect is her father approach me with *that* question, "What's good to eat?" They are both wearing Bulls gear, but I learn that they are not from the area. She's a trainee at Fort Bragg. Fort Bragg is an Army base near Fayetteville, North Carolina, and is one of the largest military installations in the

---

5   https://tippingpitches.myshopify.com/pages/about

world.[6] Named after a Confederate general in the Civil War, Braxton Bragg, it has recently been proposed and approved that the name be changed to Fort Liberty.

It occurs to me that many of the fans may be coming to watch a game from the military installations around the area. Perhaps this is why there is a recognition of current and former members of the military each game. I'll have to look closer next time when soldiers are asked to stand and be recognized. Why didn't this occur to me earlier? I'm disappointed it took me so long to pick up on this.

I respond to the soldier and her dad, "I can tell you what *I* like, but please don't come back later and tell me how awful the food was."

They agree to my terms, I make three recommendations, and the two head off to the taco stand.

There were no attention-grabbing T-shirts tonight, but that doesn't mean all the garb is unremarkable. A man comes to sit in my section wearing a Scottish kilt and a baseball jersey. The colors clash dramatically. Unconventional attire to say the least.

The only crisis this evening occurs when a young boy "tosses his cookies." He somehow manages to do this once at his seat and twice on the walkway. The burly cop standing near me does not like this at all; he quickly moves away. In a flash, a special sawdust is applied, and Scott arrives with a broom and dustpan. Remarkable how fast this was handled. This kind of incident is extremely rare—impressive considering the way kids eat at a ballpark—it's only the third I've witnessed the entire season.

The family sitting in front of the boy's seat get a baseball from me. Smiles all around. Is it a good idea for hosts to have a stash of giveaways, maybe not baseballs but wristbands? I rest my case.

The Bulls lose a heartbreaker. They enter the eighth inning clinging to a one run lead. Two walks (one of which includes a called ball for delay of game)

---

6   https://en.wikipedia.org/wiki/Fort_Bragg

and a bloop single that falls between three Bulls reverses the ultimate decision.

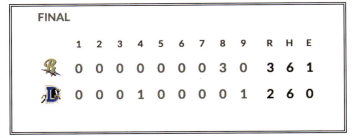

Attendance: 7,723.

SUNDAY, SEPTEMBER 11

The football season has started. The Carolina Panthers game is playing on the jumbo screen. It will be gone before the gates are open for arriving fans.

It's the twenty-first anniversary of the attack on the World Trade Center. The Bulls honor first responders with a short but solemn ceremony after we sing the national anthem. Wool E. Bull spends the night dressed in firefighting gear. On the field between innings, there is a competition involving police and firemen in which the responders put their upper bodies in soft, transparent globes about six feet in diameter then try to knock each other down. The firemen win.

My station is out at the right field Diamond View seats. One of my sections is the Hurricanes Party Deck. This section requires a ticket check and a wristband to gain entry. There is a buffet table for fans as well as a private bar. The deck has been rented by Precision BioSciences, a company that is headquartered just a few blocks from the ballpark. The company has a proprietary genome editing technology that inserts, deletes, and repairs DNA. Put simply, it has therapies in development for preventing and treating cancer. The technology was developed at Duke and is one of those examples of how a university can contribute to the local community as well as the health and well-being of people worldwide. There are at least one hundred people on the party deck, not counting a slew of kids, mostly in strollers. Two nine-month-old twins win the award for cutest duo of the evening.

The ticket checkers for the party deck are two sisters who work for the concessioners, not for the Bulls (this is the second sister act working concessions I've met). They are working their first homestand. They ask me for help passing out complementary sunglasses. I'm happy to oblige and model a pair myself. They fit nicely over my prescription glasses. And, showing people I have "six eyes" elicits lots of smiles.

Throughout the evening, I have no more than fifteen people sitting in the other section I monitor. This section has two large electric fans that help cool the patrons in the seats. Nice touch on a steamy night. But the electric fans give off a whirring sound that makes it hard to hear the PA announcer if you're sitting in the ten or so rows of seats in front of them. That said, it's rare to see folks sitting this high up in the outfield seats, so it's no big deal.

The closest thing I have to a crisis tonight occurs when a gentleman approaches and asks if I have seen some boys.

"No, how many?"

"Six or seven. They're a ball team. Maybe they went to the playground," he says, unconcerned.

"I'll keep an eye out."

A few innings later the gentleman walks by again, unaccompanied.

"Did you find the boys?"

"No, they found me. They wanted ice cream."

I was wrong. There was another crisis tonight. The RailRiders scored four runs in the top of the first. The Bulls claw back to 4–2 after five innings but then the roof falls in. The visitors score 10 more runs and finish thrashing the Bulls with 17 hits, both marking Durham's worst performance of the year. As the Bulls hit the road, their lead has shrunk to 1.5 games, with four teams separated by only two losses. Is there a bright spot? Well, the Bulls are still in first, there are only 15 games to go, and their last three series are against sub-.500 teams.

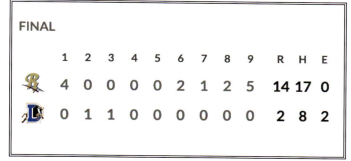

Attendance: 5,896.

Tonight is special for me because for the first time I have been invited to post-game Sunday beers and pizza with a group of hosts who gather regularly.

On my way to the pizza joint, I pass Pete standing with a few other autograph hounds beside the bus that will whisk the RailRiders from the ballpark.

There are seven other guys around the table chatting, imbibing, and eating pizza. The talk is all about sports, especially memorable experiences of games that went into extra innings. I ask the group what they think the best baseball movie is. The answer I get is . . . I think I'll save this for the final chapter.

FEAR STRIKES OUT

Year of Release: 1957
Rating: Approved
Director: Robert Mulligan
Writers: Ted Berkman and Raphael Blau; based on the story by Jimmy Piersall
Stars: Anthony Perkins (outfielder), Karl Malden (Piersall's father)

Plot Synopsis

From Wiki: https://en.wikipedia.org/wiki/Fear_Strikes_Out
Fear Strikes Out is a 1957 American biographical sports drama film depicting the life and career of American baseball player Jimmy Piersall. It is based on Piersall's 1955 memoir *Fear Strikes Out: The Jim Piersall Story*, co-written with Al Hirshberg. The film stars Anthony Perkins as Piersall and Karl Malden as his father, and it was the first directed by Robert Mulligan.

The film was a box office success, grossing $33 million on a $9 million budget.

From IMDb: https://www.imdb.com/title/tt0050383/?ref_=fn_al_tt_1
True story of the life of Jimmy Piersall, who battled mental illness to achieve stardom in major league baseball.

Critic Ratings

Rotten Tomatoes: https://www.rottentomatoes.com/m/fear_strikes_out
Tomatometer: 83 out of 100 (24 reviewers)
Audience Score: 76 out of 100 (1000+ Ratings)
Critics consensus: Based on the true story of troubled baseball star Jimmy Piersall, *Fear Strikes Out* is an emotionally compelling drama featuring excellent performances from Anthony Perkins and Karl Malden.
IMDb Rating: 6.8 out of 10 (1,900 raters)
Roger Ebert: https://www.rogerebert.com/features/zombies-in-the-outfield (star rating NA; *Fear Strikes Out* is #5 movie in review))
Ebert writes that Anthony Perkins' performance as a ballplayer is uncomfortable but does add tension to his performance. Ebert thinks Karl Malden steals the movie playing Piersall's father, who "pushes his son to glory and then to madness." Ebert feels the movie is a cautionary tale to parents who place undue expectations on children to excel at sports.

Chapter 18
Home Series 13:
The Season Comes to an End

As the final homestand begins, there are only three teams with a legitimate chance to win the IL East pennant.

Team	MLB	Wins	Losses	Winning Percentage	Games Behind
Durham	TB	79	62	0.56	-
Scranton/WB	NYY	77	63	0.55	1.5
Jacksonville	MIA	75	65	0.536	3.5
(7 Teams Not Listed)					

INTERNATIONAL LEAGUE EASTERN DIVISION

The road trip wasn't friendly to the Bulls. Their lead shrunk to just 1.5 games with nine games to play. Scranton and Jacksonville have played one less game than the Bulls. The Bulls won the first game of the series against the Norfolk Tide, but so did the RailRiders and Jumbo Shrimp. As I head to the ballpark, the Bulls' lead remains the same.

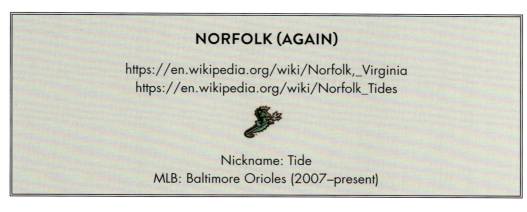

NORFOLK (AGAIN)

https://en.wikipedia.org/wiki/Norfolk,_Virginia
https://en.wikipedia.org/wiki/Norfolk_Tides

Nickname: Tide
MLB: Baltimore Orioles (2007–present)

WEDNESDAY, SEPTEMBER 21, 2022

Wayne, G., Artyom, Tom, F., and I watch the Bulls batting practice together. After an assessment of the Bulls' playoff prospects, talk turns to our seating assignments. But unlike other conversations that begin with "Where are you working tonight?" this one is about which sections we worked most this season. I think I've been assigned to every section, but most frequently has been my assignment tonight, behind third base.

This is my second brush with the impending end of the season. Tom C. came by at the end of the last homestand to exchange well-wishes; he'll be out of town for the final homestand. Tonight, the friendly guy on the clean-up crew comes by my station to say goodbye. He's still looking for work to fill his time once the season is over and is hoping to get a job at a local hospital. I'm gonna miss this job, the talks with fans, and especially the folks I've worked with, many of whom I may never see again. It reminds me of the last few days at summer camp.

Dave H. provides the antidote to my melancholy. As he walks past my station while I clean my seats, he shouts, "I don't care what anybody says, I think you're doing a great job!"

"Thanks," I reply.

Wait. He's teasing me. How'd I miss an opportunity to jab him back? Oh well, at least my wistful thoughts were interrupted. Thanks, Dave.

I take my dirty rag to Guest Services and toss it toward the basket that contains the other dirty ones. I hit the rim, but the rag falls out.

"No points for you," says the attendant.

"The only point I have is on the top of my head," I reply.

I get a slap on the back and another smile.

In the Men's room, while washing my hands I run into another employee who is shuffling from one sink to another. He complains, "Half the sinks don't work." I've noticed this on occasion as well, though half is certainly an exaggeration, but I thought it was happening because of where I placed my hands, the sinks being activated without touch, and I too would shuffle on down the line until I found one that responded to my waving palms.

Third Base Greg, the bartender, is missing from his station. I ask his substitute where he is.

"He's in Canada, closing his cabin for the winter."

"I suspect the leaves are changing up there. Maybe he's getting ready to do some ice fishing," I propose.

The sub is a native North Carolinian and a golfer. Ice fishing holds no attraction for him. It's on my bucket list, though.

A man in an Orioles jersey (Norfolk's parent team), is standing behind me, next to where my backpack dangles from the railing. When I walk over to retrieve my water bottle, he introduces himself. He's the father of Connor Norby, the starting second baseman for the Tide. Connor is playing in only his second game at Level-AAA, having just been promoted from the Bowie Baysox of the Eastern League. He was drafted in 2021 in the second round out of Eastern Carolina University. He received a $1.7 million signing bonus. Dad says Connor now has a nicer car than he does. Connor batted leadoff for the Tide the night before and hit a homer his first time at bat. By the time this night is over, he'll hit a second home run and have six hits in his first eleven at-bats. Clearly, he's the real deal. I now have three players on my watch list because I've met their parents.

Connor's dad is a nice, talkative gentleman, clearly living out a dream for himself and his son. He's from Minnesota and had been a lifelong Twins fan until his boy was drafted by the Os. He keeps up a colorful commentary that includes not only his son's exploits (and advice he would give him if he could) but that of numerous other Tide players. He will share his status as a proud parent with anyone who walks by and glances in his direction. About the fifth inning, Dad is joined by Connor's mother (Dad's ex-wife), her boyfriend, and Connor's girlfriend. When the game

HOME SERIES 13: THE SEASON COMES TO AN END

ends, the family heads down to the field. Connor emerges from the dugout; his girlfriend joins him on the field and photos are snapped of the two of them. Not gonna see that in the majors, are you?

Tonight's eye-catching T-shirt reads, "Jesus Loves Good Beer." This one might offend some folks and takes nerve to wear.

The between-inning entertainment tonight includes a video of two Bulls' players, Miles Mastrobuoni and Jim Haley, telling each other "Dad Jokes."

"Why did the man name his dogs Rolex and Timex?" Because they were watchdogs.

"Why is the calendar scared?" Because its days are numbered.

"Why was the computer late for school?" Because it had a hard drive.

The jokes are groaners but seeing the players crack up while they read them is the real entertainment. Watching those serious and hyper-focused figures on the ballfield make each other laugh turns them into human beings.

As the game ends, a fan who shuffled into the handicapped seats using a cane is not having as much success in his exit. His friend asks if I might get him a wheelchair. I head off to Guest Services and retrieve one. Upon my return, an EMT sees me and takes charge of the chair. When we reach the man, four employees are already with him. We get him into the chair, and he heads for the elevator. I'm impressed with the speed of everyone's response.

The game itself is a downer. Norfolk scores 10 runs before the Bulls get on the board. All is lost! But wait, both Scranton/Wilkes-Barre and Jacksonville lose as well. The Bulls hang on to their game and a half lead.

On my way to car, I pass a mom, dad, and two kids all wearing Pittsburgh Pirates jerseys with the name Madris on the back. Bligh Madris is a Bulls outfielder who the team picked up on waivers from the Pirates. Madris played in 39 games for Pittsburgh.

I take a guess, "You related to Madris?"

Dad responds, "No," with a big smile on his face. "He's the first Palauan to play major league baseball. We're also from there."

The Republic of Palau is a country in the western Pacific Ocean comprised of around 340 islands with a population just over eighteen thousand. No ice fishing there.

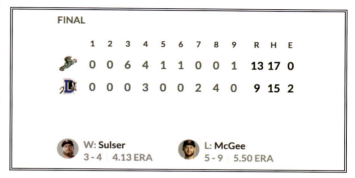

Attendance: 4,131.

THURSDAY, SEPTEMBER 22, 2022

The Rays promoted Miles Mastrobuoni to the majors. Miles is the utility player who holds the distinction of having come to the plate more frequently than any other Bulls player this season. Mastrobuoni is a favorite around the Bulls ballpark for his reliable play at multiple positions in both the infield and outfield and his solid performance at the plate (batting .300, with 16 home runs). This is his first trip to the majors.

"I suspect he'll have a big steak tonight," says Wayne as we wait on the dinner line.

"I hope he does great," I respond, "but this is a bad time for the Bulls to lose such a quality player."

I'm surprised to see posters taped around the ballpark asking for help locating "Eddie Munson" in connection with the disappearance of Chrissy Cunningham. Oddly, the posters are cartoon drawings. What up?

The mystery is soon solved when I realize tonight is "Stranger Things Night." Mr. Munson is one of the characters in the popular cable TV show. As fans

Have you seen this man?

Is that Eddie Munson?

arrive, I'm surprised at the number who have arrived in show-related T-shirts and even full character regalia. There are at least a half dozen fans wearing Hawkins (the fictitious town where the show's action takes place) High School cheerleader outfits. Others are wearing Hawkins Middle School AV club T-shirts. Still others are dressed up to look like Eddie Munson. For the entire game, Jatovi carries a stuffed doll of the character Eleven. Even Wool E. Bull gets in the act—or is that Munson himself?

I've got the first base tunnel again tonight. This is the station that's most active for directing people to their seats. For that reason, it's also my favorite assignment—and because the walkway is the staging area for Jatovi and the Lollygaggers. More work but also more fun.

I ask an operations person his assessment of the season, operations-wise.

"Not too much trouble," he says, "Just long." The Level-AAA schedule was expanded this year.

"Do you get any time off now?"

"Not next week but the week after is vacation."

He tells me that as part of the stadium renovations (that have already started under the left field stands), the Bulls dugout will move from the first base to the third base side.

"It's a little larger."

The grumpy guy sits in my section. He wants me to watch his bag while he goes to get a hot dog. I can do this but it's risky, given my attention needs to be focused on the fans emerging from the tunnel. I find a willing fan already seated to watch his bag. When he returns with dog in hand, he almost has a smile on his face.

Still, he has a complaint.

"It's twenty degrees warmer in there," he informs me about the temperature on the concourse.

HOME SERIES 13: THE SEASON COMES TO AN END

I check my weather app. It reads seventy-three degrees with a light breeze. Maybe the heat is over. I can even see light jackets and sweatshirts (some just purchased from the team store) around the stands. I'm delighted.

A season ticket holder I have never seen before sidles up to me. He also starts with a weather report.

"Too cold. This isn't baseball weather."

"I'll take it," I respond, "It sure beats standing in the Diamond View for four hours in 105-degree heat."

He tells me that season ticket holders have been asked if they want to change their seats for next season, since the Bulls will be switching dugouts.

"Why would I do that?" he muses, "The third base dugout faces into the sun. I sat in lots of seats before picking the ones I got. I'm right where I want to be."

I wonder if the ballplayers weighed the extra space the switch will give them relative to looking into a North Carolina sun in August. Maybe there were other considerations as well.

Before sitting back down, the season ticket holder tells me he wants the Bulls to clinch their playoff spot soon. He and a friend will go to Las Vegas to watch the playoff games.

The game was everything a baseball fan could ask for. Lead changes, ties, an extra inning. The visitors take a one-run lead in the top of the tenth. But a two-run homer by Luke Raley in the bottom of the tenth brings victory to the Bulls. Good thing too; both the RailRiders and Jumbo Shrimp win their games as well. The Bulls lead stays at 1.5 games.

When the game ends, there is a fireworks display to make up for the one that was cancelled last homestand due to rain. Jatovi tells the fans in the Diamond View seats they should move to the right field foul area because of the direction of the wind. I'm glad to hear this. Safety first.

FRIDAY, SEPTEMBER 23, 2022

Wayne and Josh are watching batting practice. I join them. The first topic of conversation is Mastrobuoni's promotion to the Rays. He didn't bat in his first game but was used as a defensive replacement.

We head to the food line and agree the food seems better this week. The menu appears more closely to resemble the fare available in the PNC Triangle Club suites. Wayne asks Josh if he is still looking for work. Josh says yes and Wayne shares a connection he has with a sports media outfit. Josh writes it down.

I ask Josh, "Would you work for the Bulls full time?"

"In a heartbeat!"

After the hosts' team meeting, Wayne says goodbye. There is talk about how we might all gather during the off season. I suspect I might see him at Duke basketball games where he is also a host. I'll surely look for him.

My assignment tonight is in left field under the Snorting Bull. On my left, checking tickets at the Tobacco Road restaurant gate is a fourteen-year veteran host who also works other sports arenas in the area.

"Working the Bull is pretty easy," I say.

"You just gotta watch out for people trying to sneak in. There are two gates over there that have chairs in front of them, but people try to push them out of the way," I'm advised.

Later, my neighbor will give a baseball to the parents of a six-year-old boy who is pressed against the

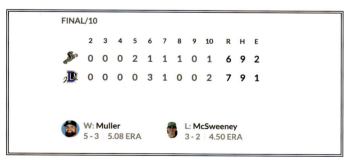

Attendance: 7,167.

left field wall hoping to get a prize. This host knows how to do his job.

Next to my station, sitting in the restaurant's outside area is a large party, maybe thirty people. They are in Durham at a leadership training conference hosted by Duke's Nicholas School of the Environment. They are all rising stars with expertise in the area of clean water preservation. One of the conference organizers, a professor at Duke, hears that I'm a retired Duke professor.

"What do I need to do to get a job?" he asks.

"Apply. I got recruited while attending a Duke baseball game here. It's a great gig."

I meet two former ball players on the walkway. One is a self-described former "poor" Division II college pitcher who got interested in baseball as a seventh grader when he served as the batboy for the Fort Worth Cats, an independent team founded "as a means to provide greater opportunities for baseball players in Texas to receive optimal exposure, publicity and notoriety from both college coaches and professional scouts."[1] The other was a high school teammate to the Tides' outfielder Brett Phillips when he played for Seminole High School in Florida.

The Bulls squander an early three-run lead and lose the game 6–3. This one hurts. The RailRiders win their game and are now just one win behind the Bulls in the standings. The Bulls have five games to play and the RailRiders have six.

As the game ends, the operations crew comes through to clear the walkway of people before the Friday night fireworks begin. I ask if this is a precaution that happens every Friday and Saturday night before fireworks begin.

"Yes," I'm told, "last night the Diamond View seats were cleared because of the wind but the restaurant walkway is always cleared."

I'm asked to stand far back on the walkway in an alcove (for my own safety), watch the side of the restaurant to make certain no one tries to get in to see the fireworks, and be sure the Snorting Bull area is clear of people. Sure enough, as the show is about to begin, a woman starts pushing the chairs that block the side entrance from the restaurant to enter the ballpark. I notice she has a drink in her hand.

"If you have a ticket, you need to enter through the gate over there, but you still can't stand on the walkway," I tell her. I notice her eyes are nearly completely shut.

"I'm a Bulls employee," she says.

"Good, then you know you can't do this. Please enter through the proper gate."

Annoyed, she mumbles, "Enter through the gate," and walks off.

I watch her walking through the restaurant patio and follow along, walking out of the alcove.

FINAL

	1	2	3	4	5	6	7	8	9	R	H	E
S	0	0	0	0	0	3	1	2	0	6	12	0
D	0	0	3	0	0	0	0	0	0	3	5	1

Attendance: 8,453.

Suddenly, an operations person is running toward me waving me back to where I was supposed to be standing. Oops, I forgot that was for my own safety. I head back. Another mistake on my part; I let my curiosity get the upper hand.

SUNDAY, SEPTEMBER 25, 2022

"Happy last game!" shouts Lisa as we pass each other on the concourse.

"Boo!" I respond.

She acknowledges also being a little sad with a head nod.

Talk among the hosts centers on a near melee

---

[1] https://www.fortworthcats.org/contact-1

that occurred on the field the night before. The Bulls were behind 4–1 entering the bottom of the seventh inning. Tristan Gray hit a two-run homer to narrow the gap. The bases were reloaded for a grand slam by Luke Raley. On the next pitch, Ruben Cardenas hit his second dinger of the game. And the pitch after that hit Bligh Madris, not his bat. The benches cleared but no punches were thrown. The Tide pitcher, Blaine Knight, was ejected from the game. I hear about this on the food line, at the host's meeting, and while cleaning my seats. Darn, although I was watching the game at home, I turned my TV off right after the third homer of the inning and missed the high jinks. Coupled with a RailRider loss, the Bulls lead is back up to 1.5 games.

There are photos and hugs all around at the final host meeting of the season. The hosts take pictures of themselves rather than take them for fans. It brings a smile to my face. My first hug of the day goes to Josh, who looks tired again. He informs me his daughter is in the hospital, but on the mend. It's kept him up at night. We talk about ways to get together after the season. Maybe we'll watch the world series at a sports bar?

On the walkway, I meet another family of a player, Brett Maverick Phillips of the Tide. Brett was drafted ten years ago and has played for four different major league teams. But what gets me is his middle name.

"Brett Maverick! Was he named after the TV character?" I inquire. *Maverick* was one of my favorite shows growing up.[2]

All I get is a head shake and a facial expression suggesting it's not the first time the question has been asked.

I can't resist. I sing the first few lines of the theme song, with a little alteration.

"Luck is his companion, *baseball* is his game."

I asked if they know the Norby family. They say yes. The Norbys will also stand behind my sections today.

I'm stationed by the visitors' bullpen. One of my sections has a back row for fans with mobility concerns. A Guest Services employee brings by a family of four with a baby carriage. They asked to be relocated so the baby carriage can stay with them. No problem. At first. But as the stands fill, I've got fourteen people, not counting the seven-week-old baby, two strollers, and one wheelchair stuffed into twelve seats. A nice couple, not serious baseball fans ("Can the runner on base run after a fly ball has been caught?") offers to move.

"That would be great!"

"Where can we sit?"

"Anywhere you want in my sections."

Bless their hearts. A few innings later, I give the couple my last baseball of the season. They're thrilled, maybe as much as I was when they helped solve my problem.

My spouse, Beth, is sitting in one of my sections. She has tolerated my love of baseball for nearly fifty years. Beth's father was a West Point graduate, who served two tours of duty in Vietnam. His family, of French Huguenot origin, came to these shores to fight for the good guys in the American Revolution. Beth's mom was a graduate of a Georgia finishing school. (Me? My grandparents got off a boat at Ellis Island, fleeing poverty and persecution in Eastern Europe.) The season started with a kiss goodbye at our doorway when I left for work. Then, Beth started buying an occasional ticket, arriving late and leaving early. By season's end, she's at the games a half hour before the first pitch and stays to the very end. She's got a scorebook now. She answers questions from the less-educated fans who sit around her. I think we may now share yet another interest.

Beth loves funnel cakes but refuses to eat them. Health food it ain't. However, she promised herself to have one during the last game. Upon her arrival, she is crestfallen when the funnel cake stand is closed. But wait . . . she goes back after the game has started to check again. It's open!

---

2 https://en.wikipedia.org/wiki/Maverick_(TV_series)

Beth scores her funnel cake.

The game is over early. The Bulls score five runs in the first three innings and the Tide submits. Scranton/Wilkes-Barre also wins and remains 1.5 games behind the Bulls. It's a two-team race now with just three games to play in Charlotte against the Knights.

At beers after the game, I sit next to John. He tells me he is headed for more surgery next week to help restore his voice. I tell him his impaired voice can't hide his glowing personality, humor, and bright smile. As I get up to leave, we hug.

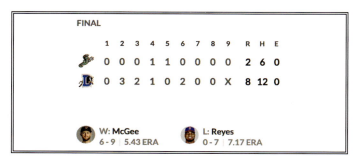

Attendance: 7,742.

CODA

The Bulls go to Charlotte for the last three games of the season. They win the first game on Monday, 6–2. Scranton splits a doubleheader, so the Bulls are up by two games. But Scranton holds the tiebreaker, so the race is still on. Not for long. On Tuesday, the Bulls win 10–1. The IL East pennant is theirs. When the season is over, the Bulls record is 86–64, three games better than the RailRiders.

With anticipation, it was on to Las Vegas for the IL championship game against the Nashville Sounds. These two teams played 18 times during the regular season and the Sounds won 10 games. Nashville's final record is 5.5 games better than the Bulls. But that doesn't matter in Vegas; the Bulls silence (Muzzle? Gag?) the Sounds, with a cacophony of runs, 13, and hits, 15, led by Vidal Brujan (four hits, three runs), Luke Raley (3 RBI), and Bligh Madris (4 RBI). Meanwhile, four pitchers, each working two or three innings, toss an eight-hit shutout. Calvin Faucher gets the win, striking out five of the six batters he faces. The music is over for the Sounds. This is the Bulls eighth International League title since joining Level-AAA ball in 1998.

In the Level-AAA championship game, the Bulls face the Reno Aces, winners of the Pacific Coast League Western Division, who beat the El Paso Chihuahuas 6–2 in their championship game. The game starts as though the Bulls would pull off another rout, scoring a run in the top of the first inning and three more in the second. But the Aces respond with three in the bottom of the second and two in the third. The Bulls tie the game in the top of the seventh but a 450-foot homer by Dominic Canzone in the bottom of the eighth puts the Aces back up by one. Not to worry. In the top of the ninth, the Bulls score five runs, capped by a three-run blast by Tristan Gray, hit on a three balls, no strikes pitch. The Aces go quietly in their last at-bat.

The Bulls are champions of Level-AAA baseball.

HOME SERIES 13: THE SEASON COMES TO AN END

Level-AAA champs.

FIELD OF DREAMS

Year of Release: 1989
Rating: PG
Director: Phil Alden Robinson
Writers: Phil Alden Robinson (screenplay), W. P. Kinsella (book author: *Shoeless Joe*)
Stars: Kevin Costner (devoted baseball fan), Amy Madigan (his wife), James Earl Jones (fictionalized author), Ray Liotta (outfielder).

Plot Synopsis

From Wiki: https://en.wikipedia.org/wiki/Field_of_Dreams
Field of Dreams is a 1989 American sports fantasy drama film written and directed by Phil Alden Robinson, based on W. P. Kinsella's 1982 novel *Shoeless Joe*. The film stars Kevin Costner as a farmer who builds a baseball field in his cornfield that attracts the ghosts of baseball legends, including Shoeless Joe Jackson (Ray Liotta) and the Chicago Black Sox. Amy Madigan, James Earl Jones, and Burt Lancaster (in his final film role) also star. It was theatrically released on May 5, 1989.

The film received generally positive reviews from critics, and was nominated for three Academy Awards: Best Picture, Best Original Score, and Best Adapted Screenplay. In 2017, it was selected for preservation in the United States National Film Registry by the Library of Congress as "culturally, historically, or aesthetically significant."

From IMDb: https://www.imdb.com/title/tt0097351/?ref_=fn_al_tt_1
Iowa farmer Ray Kinsella is inspired by a voice he can't ignore to pursue a dream he can hardly believe. Supported by his wife, Ray begins the quest by turning his ordinary cornfield into a place where dreams can come true.

Critic Ratings

Rotten Tomatoes: https://www.rottentomatoes.com/m/field_of_dreams
Tomatometer: 88 out of 100 (65 reviewers)
Audience Score: 86 out of 100 (100,000+ Ratings)
Critics Consensus: *Field of Dreams* is sentimental, but in the best way; it's a mix of fairy tale, baseball, and family togetherness.
IMDb Rating: 7.5 out of 10 (118,000 raters)
Roger Ebert: https://www.rogerebert.com/reviews/field-of-dreams-1989, 4 out of 4 stars.
Ebert thinks that *Field of Dreams* isn't for the grouches and realists among us: "It is a delicate movie, a fragile construction of one goofy fantasy after another. But it has the courage to be about exactly what it promises. 'If you build it, he will come.' And he does."

Chapter 19
Postseason Wrap Up

No matter the sport, all professional athletes possess the fundamentals of exceptional strength, foot speed, reaction time, and hand-eye coordination. Beyond that, each sport requires successful athletes to excel at slightly different sets of physical abilities. And different player positions in each sport refine further what those needed abilities are. For example, hockey players need greater balance than most other athletes to remain upright on the ice. Soccer players need leg dexterity more than almost any other athletes.

Earlier, I contended that hitting a round baseball heaved at 90 mph with movement meant to deceive you while you swing "a smooth, rounded stick"[1] is the most difficult challenge in all of sports. How baseball players do this as well as they do astounds me.

Another baseball talent I gained a new appreciation for this season is the speed and accuracy with which baseball players throw the ball. (And my elbow is fully healed, thanks for asking). I can't count the number of times I thought a runner would easily be safe at a base but then saw a laser beam emerge from a fielder's arm to make the play close. Quarterbacks in football need to throw perfect darts, but there is only one QB on the field at any given time. In baseball, there are always nine flamethrowers on the field. Before warm-ups, a favorite activity of minor league baseball players is to toss around a football or a plastic disc. Now I know why. I wonder how many professional baseball players were quarterbacks for their high school football teams. I bet quite a few.

Below are some reflections on my experiences as a Durham Bulls Seating Bowl Host during the championship season of 2022. On occasion, I make claims that are based on no evidence other than my own observations. My sample of observations is small and not likely to represent any population that would interest anyone other than me. And maybe you.

---

[1] Official Baseball Rule, 2019, Section 3.2(a)

MY FAVORITE PARTS OF HOSTING

I was drawn to become a seating bowl host because I wanted to watch baseball, meet people, and enjoy the outdoors. But there were pleasures in the job I didn't anticipate. Now, whenever I see someone with a stretched-out arm holding a camera, I'm drawn to ask if they would like me to take the picture for them. I must have done that two hundred times as a host.

"That's the picture for your holiday card!" I humbly suggest.

And giving away baseballs. I could make a kid's day, and mom's and dad's day too.

MY LEAST FAVORITE PARTS OF HOSTING

Wiping down seats.
Chasing kids from the aisles.

THE CAST OF CHARACTERS

Who are the seating bowl hosts? They are a judge, a graphic designer, educators, a newspaper editor, a physical therapist, a criminal attorney, a small business owner, a TV crew member, an enterprise architect, a freelance writer, a marketing executive, a software developer or debugger, a construction or warehouse worker, a rehab center director, a college financial aid officer, a sports event coordinator, a kitchen manager, a worker for a health-care non-profit, a career soldier, a computer equipment or car salesman. Some are retired, some still employed. Some are looking for full-time work.

These are the people helping you find your seat and decide what to eat. They make sure your tush stays clean and dry. They take your picture. They answer your questions about the stadium, the team, and the game of baseball. They return your smile. They keep you safe. Does that sound like your parents, aunts and uncles, or grandparents? It should. Most hosts have plenty of experience in those roles as well.

Then there are the groundskeepers, EMTs, police, traffic controllers, salespeople, concession stand workers, and custodians. Let's not forget Ripken, the bat dog. The teenagers operating the video feeds. There are interns who corral the fans participating in the between-inning high jinks, launch T-shirts into the stands, or help the operations gurus insure everything runs smoothly. Many interns are college students, majoring in sports management or a related field. Most want to make a career in sports operations.

I was impressed by the complexity of the organization that was needed to put on a minor league baseball game; the number of moving parts. But equally impressive was the Bulls' full-time staff. It takes a competent and devoted team of managers and executives to pull this off. Of course, they love the game of baseball. But that's not enough. Their jobs are rarely fun. Miles Wolff, the former owner of the Bulls, pointed out, "If you get in this game for fun, you've gotten in for the wrong reason. It is not fun. It is sixteen hours a day of hard work. If you don't put in the time, you'll be out of business in two years."[2]

Finally, there's the most remarkable group of all: the fans. Most impressive are the fans who overcome age or immobility to watch a live game, and the families who arrive with newborns only weeks old. I met a five-week-old baby and a ninety-four-year-old man. The fans' skin color can be white, Black, or brown and every shade in between. The fans come dressed in shirts that display their philosophy of life and represent the entire spectrum of political beliefs. Everyone is welcome here. In 2022, fans turned the turnstiles at DBAP over 470,000 times.

Oh yeah, there's also those guys who dress alike and run around on the grass.

THE LEVEL OF PLAY

You may assert that "the minor league ballplayers don't play as well as the guys in the majors!" True,

---

[2] Blake, M. (1991). *The Minor Leagues: A Celebration of the Little Show.* New York, NY: Wynwood Press. P. 57.

some don't. But the quality of play, at least in Level-AAA and AA ball, isn't *that* much different from the big leagues. More bonehead plays? Yes, a few, but I saw numerous impressive displays of athleticism as well, in almost every game. Monster home runs. Fielding gems. Impressive pitching performances.

A major league team has 26 active players on its roster from opening day until August 31. Of those players, I'd guess that 18 to 20 will never see the minor leagues again, except maybe on a rehab assignment. For the other six or eight, there are players in the wings itching to take their place. Those minor leaguers will become major leaguers when their performance can't be denied, or when a player in the big leagues doesn't perform up to snuff or gets hurt. For the 2022 season, the Rays' post-season wild card roster had six (of fourteen) position players I saw play in Durham. And remember, rehab assignments will bring some big stars to your team's intimate stadium. Aaron Judge rehabbing in Durham? Wanna go?

If your team's best players can get called up in a flash, how do you form an allegiance with your hometown heroes? We've seen that the core of a Level-AAA minor league club is pretty stable. 15 players accounted for over 70 percent of the plate appearances for the Bulls during my season hosting. So, let's flip the script. The fact that some players will get promoted can add to your involvement as a fan rather than detract from it. Player traffic goes up and down, adding complexity to your relationship with the club and the daily melodrama. Who is this guy just promoted from Montgomery? Is he on the fast track? The seating bowl hosts were dismayed when our best players got promoted to the Rays, but we followed their performance in the bigs diligently and always wished them the best.

It's also true that major media outlet coverage of the minors is anemic, nowhere near the coverage you'll find for the majors. But a little effort, using the internet and all that social media stuff, can satisfy even the most voracious fans' desire for information on their team. And then there's the MiLB First Pitch app. For the cost of a major league ticket or two, you can watch the games of any minor league team from Level-AAA to Low-A.[3] I learned how to mirror my phone screen so I could watch the Bulls on my TV. Are the production values the same? No, but the announcers know their stuff.

THE SURROUNDINGS

Do you enjoy taking your kids to the state or county fair, or an amusement park? Then I've got a great idea: take them to a minor league baseball game. It's safer. Your kids are less likely to get lost, and less likely to get sick from eating the food they will consume. They won't be immune from a tummy ache, or course, but those carnival rides can't help digestion.[4] Bring your baseball gloves. Getting a ball or meeting a ballplayer is a matter of strategy and persistence[5]. A souvenir ball or a player's John Hancock may not provide quite as much of an immediate adrenaline rush as a roller coaster ride, but the thrill will last longer.

If you're planning a date, an outing with friends, or a workplace social event, consider a minor league game rather than a trip to a monster stadium or arena. Parking is much easier and it's cheaper all around. All of the seats give you an intimate view of the action. The between-inning antics are guaranteed to bring a

---

3 https://apps.apple.com/us/app/milb-first-pitch/id508217833

4 I don't want you to think that upset tummies are a frequent occurrence at a minor league ballpark. They're not. In fact, they're very rare and isolated. It may seem otherwise because I mentioned every instance I encountered. From the fans' point of view, the probability that such an event will intrude on your enjoyment, for a few moments, is exceedingly low. I mentioned them here for exactly that reason.

5 If you want to learn some techniques for hawking baseballs, take a gander at: Hample, Z. (2011). *The Baseball*. New York, NY: Anchor.

smile to your face, no matter how sophisticated you think you are. And you're less likely to encounter belligerent spectators (mentioned in my recountings because of their rarity). A minor league ballpark is a great place to bond with those who matter to you.

> **YOU CAN ATTEND A MINOR LEAGUE GAME FOR LESS THAN A THIRD OF THE COST OF AN MLB GAME**
>
> Robert Bruce, a senior writer for the Penny Hoarder reports that according to Team Marketing Report, the average cost for four people to attend a major league baseball game, including tickets, parking, and concessions was $257. For a family of four, according to Minor League Baseball Fan—Cost Survey, the cost of four tickets, four hot dogs, four drinks and parking was $70.*
>
> * https://www.thepennyhoarder.com/save-money/minor-league-baseball-on-a-budget/

If you just want to watch people, I've found no better venue than a minor league baseball park. Minor league baseball attracts Americans from every walk of life, every age and ethnic group, every political persuasion. Say "hello" to the folks sitting next to you. They're there for the same reason you are. Share your thoughts about the action on the field. Sometimes, your neighbor will ask you a question you can answer. That'll make you feel good. Sometimes, your neighbor will recite statistics and trivia that will blow you away.

THE MOVIES

If you have watched the movies profiled at the end of chapters, you've seen how America's pastime can serve as the stage for playing out the human drama, how baseball fits into American culture, childhood, and family life. But, on occasion, you need to cast a skeptical eye on how baseball is depicted in films. For example, Keith Law, a sportswriter and former special assistant to the general manager of the Toronto Blue Jays, wrote this in his book *Smart Baseball*:

> The execrable film *Trouble with the Curve* . . . was rife with inaccuracies, but perhaps none was as absurd as the idea that [Clint] Eastwood, playing a local scout, was the only employee from his team to see the player they were considering for the number two pick in the entire draft. A team picking second would likely have a dozen people go watch every candidate for that pick.[6]

You also may be wondering how I could possibly have left a particular movie off the list. True, there are several sequels to *Bad News Bears*. Then there's *Hardball*, in which Keanu Reeves plays a miscreant whose punishment is to coach an inner-city little league team, and *Everybody Wants Some*, about a college baseball team's off-field antics. I'm sure there are others I'm not aware of. I don't suspect aficionados of baseball movies will be terribly upset, though.

There are also two documentaries that I left off, not because they're bad but I decided to stick with scripted movies. *The Battered Bastards of Baseball* is a great retelling of the saga of the Portland (Oregon) Mavericks, a Level-A short-season club in the Northwest League that played from 1973 to 1977. Owned by Bing Russell, actor Kurt Russell's father, this independent team was so successful it rankled the feathers of major league baseball. The movie is entertaining and provides a lesson on what happens all too often when Jack meets the Giant. Another documentary is *50 Summers*, a film that follows the history of minor league baseball

---

6 Law, Keith. (2017). *Smart Baseball: The Story Behind the Old Stats That Are Ruining the Game, the New Ones That Are Running It, and the Right Way to Think About Baseball.* New York, NY: William Morris.

POSTSEASON WRAP UP

in Omaha, Kansas. It contains some excellent background on minor league baseball but bogs down a bit in local interests (though the Durham Bulls play a supporting role). Maybe that's why it has no reviews on Rotten Tomatoes and gets a 6.8 (out of 10) as an IMDb rating.

And just to court some controversy, I present my preferred results of a tournament involving the twelve surviving movies. At one time, I had the idea of choosing the winners by counting the number of times the plot of each film hinged on action taking place on the field and how much of each movie takes place in a locker room or on the field. Thank goodness I abandoned these notions in favor of just picking my favorites.

I've divided the movies into four categories that capture the main themes of the movies. A love of baseball begins in the tweenage years, the budding baseball fans my job required me to police (Little League). Baseball can create a special bond between fathers and sons, for better or worse (Dads: Good and Bad). Reflecting the society around it, baseball has used prejudices to exclude talented players from the ballfield (Those Left Out). The minor leagues remind us that baseball isn't all glitz and green stuff; it requires talent, determination, patience, learning from failure, and luck (The Minors).

I won't go through all of the films, but want to steer you to a couple of the more obscure gems that will help get you through the offseason. *Sugar* is worth

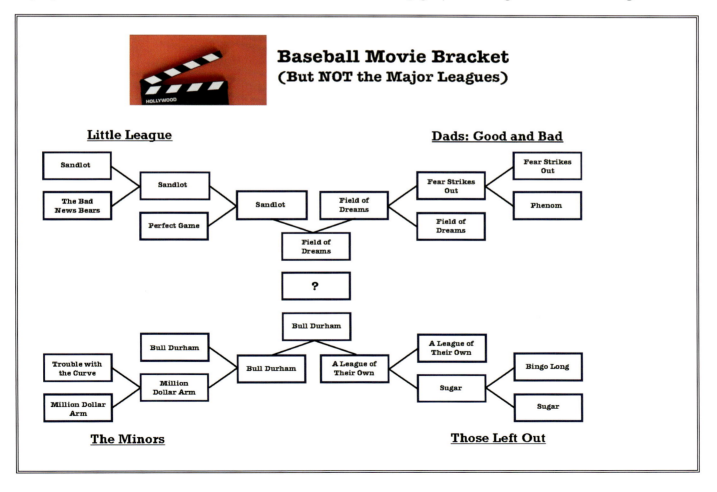

HEY! DAD. YOU WANT TO HAVE A CATCH?

I have some personal sentiment attached to that ballfield in Iowa. Back some twenty-five years ago, Beth and my two kids, Seth and Emily (fifteen and eleven at the time), humored me and we took off on a Father's Day baseball pilgrimage in the family van. Louisville, Kentucky, was the first stop (we missed the Redbirds, who later would become the RiverBats, then just the Bats), followed by Cleveland (Indians vs. Brewers at Jacobs Field); Fort Wayne, Indiana, (the Wizards, now the TinCaps); South Bend, Indiana, (Silver Hawks); Chicago (Cubs vs. Brewer at Wrigley), Cedar Rapids (the Kernels), and Ames, Iowa (the Cubs).

But the highlight of the trip was our stop in Dyersville, Iowa, to visit the Field of Dreams. This was well before major league baseball had embraced the myth. There was a small store, a dispute over ownership, and not a soul on the field, save the Cooper family. The next crop of corn was just beginning to appear. Still, we took the field. My father passed away not long after our trip to that World Series game in Yankee Stadium. At the time, I was about the same age as Ray Kinsella when he loses his dad in the movie. I got to play catch with my son and daughter on the Field of Dreams.

The Cooper family sneakers emerge from the corn at the field of dreams.

a watch because it tells the story of a poor, aspiring Dominican ballplayer and vividly depicts his struggles with cultural assimilation. *Perfect Game* follows the first team from outside the United States to win the Little League World Series. It is inspiring and contains much culture-clash.

My choice for the tournament winner came down to two films, *Field of Dreams* and *Bull Durham*. I couldn't choose between them. So, I raised the issue over beers with a group of fellow seating bowl hosts. I asked them what they thought was the best baseball movie of all-time. *Field of Dreams* was quickly dismissed. Perhaps it's no surprise that *Bull Durham* was the winner. (It also won two awards for the screenplay and was named the best sports movie by both *Sports Illustrated* and Rotten Tomatoes) Their other choices were all about the big leagues. *The Natural* ran a close second, followed by *Eight Men Out* and *Major League*.

Okay, *Field of Dreams* is easy to poke fun at, but I'm not alone in my love of this movie. *Field of Dreams* finishes fifth among the Rotten Tomatoes critics (with a rating of 87 out of 100), behind *Bull Durham* and *Bad News Bears* (both got 97 ratings), *Sugar* (92), and *Bingo Long* (89). Among viewers, *Field of Dreams* (86 rating) finishes second behind *Sandlot* (89). All together, *Field of Dreams* finishes fourth. *Bull Durham* wins. Only *A League of their Own* has more viewer ratings than *Field of Dreams*.

THE FINAL SCORE

The basics of baseball are the same whether it's played as T-ball or Moneyball. Hit the ball and try to beat it to a base. Catch the ball on the fly or have your throw beat a runner to a bag. But the nuances of the game change with each level of play. The rules of the game and even the equipment used is different if you are watching a game at little league, high school, college, semi-pro, or the minor and major league levels.

And a fan's experience is qualitatively different at each level. Two dozen parents and friends anxiously watch a T-ball game and hope their kids remember to run to first base, not third, after they hit the ball. Parents watch their kids play high school ball with a couple hundred other fans and dream that maybe this will lead to a college scholarship. Minor league fans, in the thousands now, watch for the love of the game, the ambiance, the friendships they make at the ballpark, and even out of civic pride. In the majors, some 57,000 fans have watched the Dodgers play a home game.

A chance encounter at a college baseball game led to my season as a Durham Bulls Seating Bowl Host. I think I found much more than baseball games to watch. I think I found America at its best. Personally, I found the sweet spot.

Will you join me at the ballpark?

Acknowledgments

My journey into minor league baseball land relied on the cooperation and assistance of many people along the way. First and foremost, there was the entire Durham Bulls organization and its full-time employees. It's a class organization. For me it was personified by George Habel, vice president for special projects, and Tyler Parsons, the team's general manager. When I approached them about the project, they were cordial, then receptive, then helpful. They were confident that their operation and the product they put on the field would shine under the scrutiny of an outsider. They were correct. My admiration for all the Bulls employees only grew as the season progressed.

Then there were the other Bulls seating bowl hosts. I have sung their praises throughout the pages of this book. They come from far and wide with remarkably diverse personal histories. But they know they have at least one thing in common; a love of baseball. From there, good times and friendships are just a step away. So many smiles, stories, helping hands.

My spouse, Elizabeth Cooper, is aways by my side. She provided encouragement every step of the way. She became a baseball fan herself. She sat and watched over forty baseball movies with me; above and beyond the call of duty! She employed her prodigious photography skills to brighten the pages of this book.

At Skyhorse Publishing:
- Hector Carosso, project editor
- Reed Miller, editor
- Kirsten Dalley, production editor
- Brian Peterson, creative director

My literary agent, Steve Harris, CSG Literary Partners, Syosset, NY. I thought he was treating me special, for what reason I couldn't say. Then, I discovered he treats all his writers the same way.

Finally, I want to thank John Burness, the former vice president for public affairs and government relations at Duke University. John not only provided encouragement as I wrote the book, but he also introduced me to the Bulls' brass and in doing so made my task of gaining their trust so much easier. John was a great friend and devoted fan of baseball. He passed away while the book was being written.

Book References

Blake, M. (1991). *The Minor Leagues: A Celebration of the Little Show*, New York, NY: Wynwood Press.
Chadwick, B. (1994). *Baseball's Hometown Teams: The Story of Minor League Baseball*. New York, NY: Abbeville Press.
Clark, A. (2014). *Called Out but Safe: A Baseball Umpire's Journey*. Lincoln, NB: University of Nebraska Press.
Feinstein, J. (2014). *Where Nobody Knows Your Name*. New York, NY: Anchor Sports. P. 215.
Formosa, D. & Gilbert, T.W. (2020). *How Baseball Happened*. Boston, MA: Godine.
Hamburger, P. (2023). *Baseball Field Guide*, New York, NY: The Experiment.
Hample, Z. (2011). *The Baseball*. New York, NY: Anchor.
Hogan, L.D. ((2006). *Shades of Gray: The Negro Leagues and the History of African-American Baseball*. Washington, DC: National Geographic.
Holaday, J.C. (1998). *Professional Baseball in North Carolina*. Jefferson, NC: McFarkand.
Irvine, A. ((2018). *The Comic Book Story of Baseball*. New York, NY: Ten Speed Press.
Law, K. (2017). *Smart Baseball*. New York, NY: Morrow.
Morris, R. (2017). *No Bull: The Real Story of the Rebirth of a Team and a City*. Durham, NC: Baseball America Books.
Obojski, R. (1975). *Bush League: A Colorful Factual Account of Minor League Baseball from 1877 to the Present*. New York, NY: Macmillan.
Pietrusza, D. (1995). *Minor Miracles: The Legend and Lore of Minor League Baseball*. South Bend, IN: Diamond Communications.
Rice, E. S. & Anders, R. S. (2017). *Becoming Durham: Grit, Belief, and a City Transformed*. Raleigh, NC: Verdant Word Press.
Rosen, I. (2006). *The American Game: A Celebration of Minor League Baseball*. New York, NY: Collins.
Shelton, R. (2022). *The Church of Baseball: The Making of Bull Durham: Home Runs, Bad Calls, Crazy Fights, Big Swings, and a Hit*. New York, NY: Alfred A. Knopf.
Stephenson, S. (2014). *Bull City Summer: A Season at the Ballpark*. Daylight Community Arts Foundation: www.daylightbooks.com.
Wolff, M. (2023). *There's a Bulldozer on Home Plate*. Jefferson, NC: McFarland.
Zoss, J. & Bowman, J. (1996). *Diamonds in the Rough: The Untold History of Baseball*. Chicago, IL: Contemporary Books.

Image Credits

1. Pregame Warm Up

A Baseball Ashram: Courtesy of Henry Haggart
https://9thstreetjournal.org/2020/07/31/the-bull-durham-house-then-and-now/
PNC Triangle Club Overlooking the Ballfield: Courtesy of Capitol Broadcasting Co.
https://www.milb.com/durham/tickets/pnc-triangle-club
The Bulls' 2022 Schedule: Courtesy of Capitol Broadcasting Co.
https://www.milb.com/durham/schedule/2022-07
DBAP Seating Map: Courtesy of Capitol Broadcasting Co.
https://www.milb.com/durham/ballpark/seating-map

2. A Walk to the Ballpark

My Walk to the Ballpark: Courtesy of E. D. Cooper
Signs Outside and Inside the Chesterfield Building, Downtown Durham: Courtesy of E. D. Cooper and the author
McCoy's Chair: Courtesy of E. D. Cooper
A Commemorative Plaque on Parrish Street: Courtesy of E. D. Cooper
A Symbols of a City, Then and Now
Then: Public Domain
Now: Licensed from Estlin Haiss
The Snorting Bull: By Paxton Rembis, Courtesy of Capitol Broadcasting Co.
Welcome to the DBAP: Courtesy of Capitol Broadcasting Co.
https://der-weltreisender.com/wp-content/uploads/2022/04/Durham-Bulls-Athletic-Park-2.jpg
Durham Bulls Athletic Park: By Brian Fleming, Courtesy of Capitol Broadcasting Co.
Crash Davis Doll: Courtesy of Capitol Broadcasting Co.

3. Home Series 1: Opening Week

Baseball's Anthem, first published in 1908: Public Domain
https://www.loc.gov/exhibits/baseballs-greatest-hits/take-me-out-the-ball-game.html
The Real "Crash" Davis: Courtesy of Capitol Broadcasting Co.
War Heroes: Public Domain
https://medium.com/@riley.poole/baseball-heroes-of-world-war-ii-9d07e0093b3f
Dreaming of a Future in Baseball: By the author

An Outside World Intrudes: Courtesy of Capitol Broadcasting Co.
Billy Martin Kicks Dirt on an Umpire: Licensed from Getty Images
A League of Their Own poster: by IMDb, Fair use https://en.wikipedia.org/w/index.php?curid=1896760

4. Home Series 2: Kids and the K-Wall
Tyler Zombro: By Paxton Rembis, Courtesy of Capitol Broadcasting Co.
Hanging Ks: Licensed from Getty Images
The Author Works the K Wall: Courtesy of E. D. Cooper
Not a Bad Place to Watch a Ballgame: By the Author
Cervazas de Durham: Courtesy of Capitol Broadcasting Co.
https://milbstore.com/collections/cervezas-de-durham
The Best Fans of All: By the author
Bad News Bears poster: Fair use
https://en.wikipedia.org/w/index.php?curid=5819102

5. Home Series 3: Happy Birthday Wool E. Bull
The Author and His Nifty Cleaning Mitt: By the Author
Robert D. Manfred, Jr., MLB Commissioner: Licensed from Getty Images
No More Game Action for These Two: Courtesy of E. D. Cooper
The Scouts Produce the Bulls' Telecasts: By Paxton Rembis, Courtesy of Capitol Broadcasting Co.
https://www.milb.com/durham/ballpark/explorer-post
The Protective Netting Prevents an Injury: Courtesy of E.D. Cooper
Turn Back the Clock Night at DBAP, April 13, 2019: By Patrick Norwood, Courtesy of Capitol Broadcasting Co.
Political Affiliations of Sports Fans: Courtesy of National Media Research, Planning and Placement
https://web.archive.org/web/20100402234855/http://hotlineoncall.nationaljournal.com
    /archives/2010/03/sports_viewers.php
Wool E. Bull Plays the Drums: By Paxton Rembis, Courtesy of Capitol Broadcasting Co.
Wool E. Bull's Birthday Party: By Paxton Rembis, Courtesy of Capitol Broadcasting Co.
The Sandlot poster: http://www.impawards.com/1993/sandlot.html, Fair use https://en.wikipedia.org/w/index.
    php?curid=22520404

6. Home Series 4: Things Are Looking Up
Plenty of Help: Courtesy of E. D. Cooper
George Carlin: Public Domain
https://upload.wikimedia.org/wikipedia/commons/8/8e/George_Carlin_1975_%28Little_David
    _Records%29_Publicity.jpg
Catch on the Field Day: Courtesy of E. D. Cooper
The Perfect Game poster: Fair use
https://en.wikipedia.org/w/index.php?curid=18097864

IMAGE CREDITS 191

7. A Brief History of the Not-So-Minor Leagues

Cincinnati Red Stockings 1868: Public Domain
https://commons.wikimedia.org/wiki/File:1868_Reds.jpg
The New York Knickerbockers Baseball Club, circa 1847: Public Domain
https://en.wikipedia.org/wiki/Alexander_Cartwright
A Plaque Commemorating Jackie Mitchell's Feat Hangs at DBAP: By the author
Jackie Robinson and Branch Rickey: Licensed from Getty Images
Stay Team Stay!: Public Domain
https://www.mlb.com/cut4/why-did-the-dodgers-and-giants-move-to-california-c303090362
Minor League Team Affiliations: By the author
https://www.baseball-reference.com/register/affiliate.cgi?year=2022
Minor League Baseball Map: Courtesy of Paul Trap
https://www.baseballamerica.com/media/gx2h2vff/120_trapmap.jpg

8. Home Series 5: Memorial Day

Game Information Sheet for Fans (and Hosts): Courtesy6 of Capitol Broadcasting Company
Ariel, Elsa, Anna, Cinderella, and Belle Take Batting Practice: Courtesy of E. D. Cooper
Bingo Long poster: Fair use
https://en.wikipedia.org/w/index.php?curid=58838910

9. Home Series 6: Mid-Season Break

Renderings of the Durham Bulls Miracle League Field: Courtesy of Capitol Broadcasting Co.
https://www.mltriangle.com/2021/02/12/construction-has-begun/
https://www.mltriangle.com/durham-construction-blog/
Five County Stadium, Zebulon, NC: Courtesy of E. D. Cooper
Elbow Anatomy: Licensed from Getty Images

10. Home Series 7: Happy Birthday, USA

The Fourth of July Employees' Dinner at the Ballpark: By the author
Pregame Warm Up (Everyone Loves Wool E.): Courtesy of E. D. Cooper
Taking Away the Tarp: Courtesy of E. D. Cooper
How Pitches Move: Courtesy of Lokesh Dhakar
https://lokeshdhakar.com/baseball-pitches-illustrated/
Running the Bases: Courtesy of E. D. Cooper
Sugar poster: by Impawards.com, Fair use
https://en.wikipedia.org/w/index.php?curid=21544864

11. Home Series 8: Bull Durham Movie Night

Bull Durham Movie Night: Courtesy of E. D. Cooper
Friday Night Fireworks: Courtesy of E. D. Cooper

Bull Durham poster: by Impawards.com, Fair use
https://en.wikipedia.org/w/index.php?curid=22349503

12. Seasons Past: Club History
Mr. Peabody and His Boy Sherman Enter the WABAC Machine: Fair Use
https://en.wikipedia.org/wiki/Wayback_Machine_(Peabody's_Improbable_History)#/media/
    File:Waybackmachine3.png
William G. Bramham Center: Public Domain
https://en.wikipedia.org/wiki/William_G._Bramham#/media/File:William_G._Bramham_1946_(cropped).jpg
The Durham Bulls of 1913 at Doherty (East Durham) Ballpark: Public Domain
From "Baseball's Hometown Teams: The Story of the Minor Leagues" by Bruce Chadwick
https://www.opendurham.org/buildings/east-durham-baseball-park
Jonny Vander Meer Plaque: By E. D. Cooper
Kenesaw Mountain Landis Plays Himself in a Movie: Public Domain
https://en.wikipedia.org/wiki/Kenesaw_Mountain_Landis#/media/File:Judge_Landis_and_Warren_Cook_in
    _The_Immigrant.png
Batboy Roger Craig's Inset Outside DBAP: By the author
DAP Today, site of the movie *Bull Durham*: Courtesy of Ildar Sagdejev
https://en.wikipedia.org/wiki/Durham_Athletic_Park#/media/File:2008-07-26_Durham_Athletic_Park.jpg

13. Home Series 9: The Stakes Get Higher
A Defender of the Diamond: Courtesy of Capitol Broadcasting Co.
https://www.milb.com/durham/
Wool E. World T-Ball: By the author
The REAL Show: By the author
Camp Out Night: Courtesy of Capitol Broadcasting Co.
https://www.milb.com/durham/tickets/camp-out-nights
Police Mobile Command Unit: By the author
Million Dollar Arm poster: Fair Use
The poster art copyright is believed to belong to the distributor of the film, Walt Disney Studios Motion
    Pictures, the publisher, Walt Disney Pictures, or the graphic artist. - IMP Awards
https://en.wikipedia.org/w/index.php?curid=41442620

14. Home Series 10: Surf and Turf Week
The Way You Stand Communicates Much: Licensed from Getty Images, iStock
A Bit of Greenery: By the author
The Hounds Are Out: By the author
The Cause of My Misspent (?) Youth: Courtesy of Eric Furman
https://spookyshobbyshop.com/CADACO_all_star_baseball.html
Trouble with the Curve poster: Fair use https://en.wikipedia.org/w/index.php?curid=36674742

15. Home Series 11: A Playoff Preview?

The Ukraine Flag, Bulls Style: By the author
Ripken the Bat Dog's Baseball Card: Courtesy of Capitol Broadcasting Co.
The Phenom poster: Fair Use RLJ Entertainment
https://en.wikipedia.org/w/index.php?curid=51505012

16. Who's on First? The Ballplayers

All ballplayer pictures courtesy of Capitol Broadcasting Co. All pictures by Paxton Rembis except Phoenix Sanders by Brian Fleming.

17. Home Series 12: Yankees Invade North Carolina

Don't Let Your Face Get Stuck Like This!: Licensed from Getty Images, iStock.
A Walk-Off Wins Leads to An On-Field Celebration: Courtesy of Capitol Broadcasting Co.
https://www.milb.com/durham/news/bulls-walk-off-with-4-3-10th-inning-win
Fear Strikes Out poster: Fair use
http://www.impawards.com/1957/fear_strikes_out.html
https://en.wikipedia.org/w/index.php?curid=31836352

18. Home Series 13: The Season Comes to an End

Have You Seen This Man?: Courtesy of E. D. Cooper
Is That Eddie Munson?: Courtesy of E. D. Cooper
Beth Scores Her Funnel Cake: By the author
Level-AAA Champs: Courtesy of Capitol Broadcasting Co.
https://www.milb.com/durham/history/bulls-history
Field of Dreams poster: Fair use
The poster art can or could be obtained from Universal Studios
https://en.wikipedia.org/w/index.php?curid=2187831

19. Post-Season Wrap Up

Baseball Movie Tournament (but NOT the Major Leagues): Courtesy of E. D. Cooper
The Cooper Family Sneakers Emerge From the Corn at the Field of Dreams: Courtesy of E. D. Cooper

Images of film posters constitute fair use with the presence of film criticisms.

Additional photos courtesy of:
page v: Getty Images (ThePalmer)
page 26: Getty Images (Chuyn)
page 38: Getty Images (Patrick Clark)
page 50: Getty Images (Flavia Stan)
page 60: Getty Images (Raymond Boyd)

page 74: Getty Images (Azri Suratmin)
page 84: Getty Images (fredrocko)
page 92: Getty Images (Bruce Leighty)
page 104: Getty Images (Patrick Clark)
page 112: Getty Images (Tetra Images)
page 140: Getty Images (GoranQmin)
page 158: Getty Images (Thomas Barwick)

Index

A
Aaron, Hank, 22
Aaron, Henry, 68
Alaska Goldpanners, 61n1
All-American Girls Professional Baseball League, 68
Allston, Walter, 56
American Association, 63–64
American League, 21, 64–65
Amsterdam Rugmakers, 68
Anderson, Louie, 39
Aranda, Jonathon, 143, 151, 152, 156
Arbitration Committee, 64
Arizona Diamondbacks, 72
Arlington, Lizzie, 67
Atlanta Braves, 13, 72, 120

B
Bad News Bears, The (film), 37, 180, 182
Baltimore Browns, 69
Baltimore Orioles, 64, 72, 89, 125, 154, 168
Banks, Ernie, 68
Bard, Luke, 153
Barnes, Clint, 150
Barrow, Edward, 67
Barzun, Jacques, 9
Battered Bastards of Baseball, The (documentary), 180
Baz, Shane, 76
Bell, Cool Papa, 67
Berra, Yogi, 27, 113
Bingo Long Traveling All-Stars & Motor Kings, The (film), 81, 182
Birling, Mike, 5
Blair, Seth, 153
Blue Monster, 15
Boldt, Ryan, 151
Bonds, Barry, 61n1
Boone, Bob, 118
Boston Americans, 64
Boston Beaneaters, 65
Boston Braves, 69
Boston Red Sox, 72, 89
Boswell, Thomas, 121
Bouton, Jim, 17, 149
Bowden, Ben, 153
Bradley, Taj, 127
Bradley, Will, 157
Bragg, Braxton, 164

Bramham, William, 66, 114–115
Bronx Bombers, 2
Brooklyn Athletics, 63
Brooklyn Dodgers, 21, 69
Brooklyn Superbas, 65
Bruce, Lenny, 56
Brujan, Vidal, 151, 155
Buffalo Bisons, 67, 71, 89
Bull Durham (film), 1–2, 12, 20, 35, 36, 105, 107, 111, 182

C
Camden Yards, 14
Campanella, Roy, 68
Campbell, Kat, 18
Candlestick Park, 31
Canzone, Dominic, 174
Cardenas, Ruben, 151
Carlin, George, 17, 55–56
Carolina League, 117–119
Carolina Mudcats, 87–88
Carson, Ken, 41
Cartwright, Alexander, 65
Chadwick, Henry, 30
Charlotte Hornets, 114
Charlotte Knights, 51, 71, 174
Chicago American Giants, 66
Chicago Cubs, 68, 72
Chicago Giants, 66
Chicago Orphans, 65
Chicago White Sox, 72, 109
Chicago White Stockings, 64
Chomsky, Noam, 94
Cincinnati Reds, 44, 65, 72
Cincinnati Red Stockings, 63
Clark, Al, 121
Clemens, Cody, 155
Clemens, Roger, 155
Clemente, Roberto, 146
Cleveland Blues, 64
Cleveland Guardians, 72
Coastal Plain League, 28
Cobb (film), 81
college athletics, 79–80
Colorado Rockies, 72
Columbus Clippers, 71, 89
Competitive Balance Tax, 40

Cooper, Harold, 69
Coors Field, 14
Costner, Kevin, 6, 20
COVID-19 pandemic, 69, 70
Craig, Roger, 118–119
Cuban Stars, 66
Cummings, Candy, 63
curve ball, 63

D

Dare You To (McGarry), 39
Davis, Lawrence, 20, 20, 20–21, 116, 120
Dayton Marcos, 66
De Horta, Adrian, 90
Democratic Party, 45–46
Deshields, Delino, Jr., 44
Detroit Stars, 66
Detroit Tigers, 22, 44, 64, 72
Doby, Larry, 68
Donnelly, Rich, 61
Doubleday, Abner, 65
Duke, J. B., 12
Durham, North Carolina, 1–2, 9–10, 11, 12
Durham Athletic Park, 117
Durham Baseball Athletic Park, 4–16, 86–88, 90–91
Durham Black Sox, 13
Durham Bulls, 2, 3, 5, 7, 8, 16, 18, 22, 28, 29, 71, 88, 90, 115–116, 141, 151, 153, 159, 167, 175
Durham Tobacconists, 45, 114–115

E

Edwards, Xavier, 151, 152, 154
El Paso Chihuahuas, 174
El Toro Park, 116, 117
errors, 101
Erwin, Zack, 153
Explorer Post 50, 42–43

F

Faucher, Calvin, 153, 174
Fear Strikes Out (film), 81, 108, 166
Fenway Park, 15, 142
fielder's choice, 100, 100n6
Field of Dreams (film), 176, 182
50 Summers (documentary), 180–181
Five County Stadium, 87–88
Fleming, Josh, 43
Fort Bragg, 163–164

G

Gant, Ron, 118
Garciaparra, Nomar, 35
Garza, Ralph, 153
Gehrig, Lou, 67
Gibson, Bob, 21

Gibson, Josh, 67
Goodmon, Jim, 42, 119
Graves, Abner, 65
Gray, Tristan, 151, 152, 155, 174
Green, John, 12
Green Monster, 15
Guerra, Javy, 153
Gwinnett Stripers, 39, 43, 46, 71

H

Halberstam, David, 105
Haley, Jim, 151, 152, 156, 169
Hardball (film), 180
Harper, Bryce, 122
Harris, Franco, 57
Harwell, Ernie, 105
Hawaiian Islanders, 61n1
Hayes, Woody, 56
Henderson, Rickey, 113
Hickok, Wild Bill, 63
High Point Furniture Makers, 116
Hilchen, James, 15
Holmes, Oliver Wendell, Jr., 66
Hot Stove League, 13
Houston Astros, 72

I

Indianapolis ABCs, 66
Indianapolis Indians, 71
infield fly rule, 100–101
information sheet, 77
International League (IL), 16, 28, 41, 63, 67, 69, 89, 119–120, 141
International League East, 72
International League West, 72
Iowa Cubs, 71
Irvin, Monte, 68

J

Jackson, Reggie, 75
Jacksonville Jumbo Shrimp, 17, 19, 71, 128, 131, 132, 159, 167, 169
Johnson, Bancroft, 64, 66
Jones, Chipper, 18, 118
Jones, Tommy Lee, 81
Judge, Aaron, 21

K

Kansas City Antelopes, 63
Kansas City Athletics, 69
Kansas City Monarchs, 66
Kansas City Pomeroys, 63
Kansas City Royals, 72
Knight, Blaine, 173
Knight, Dusten, 153, 154
Komminsk, Brad, 118
K-Wall, 30–31, 78, 162

INDEX

L

Labosky, Jack, 90
Laloosh, Ebby Calvin "Nuke," 20
Landis, Kennesaw Mountain, 24, 117
Lange, Peter, 40
Lasorda, Tommy, 68, 149
Law, Keith, 180
Lazzeri, Tony, 67
League of Their Own, A (film), 25
Lee, Hao-Yu, 122
Lehigh Valley IronPigs, 71, 89, 121, 122, 131, 159
Leonard, Buck, 21
little league, 102
Los Angeles Angels, 72
Los Angeles Dodgers, 72
Los Dragones de Ciudad Trujillo, 67
Louisville Bats, 71, 85, 89
Lowe, Josh, 151, 154, 155
Lucky Strikes, 13

M

Major League Baseball, 3, 15, 40
Manfred, Robert D., Jr., 40–41
Manning, James S., 2
Mantle, Mickey, 131
Maris, Roger, 35
Martin, Billy, 24
mascot, 47–48
Mastrobuoni, Miles, 151, 152, 161, 169
Mays, Willie, 68
McBride, Arthur, 150
McCarver, Tim, 141
McCoy, Pierce, 10–11
McDuffie, Jatovi, 100, 132, 146–147
McGarry, Katie, 39
McGee, Chris, 153
McGee, Easton, 54, 153
Memphis Redbirds, 27, 71, 93, 131
Miami Marlins, 17, 72
Middleton, Mark-Anthony, 95
Million Dollar Arm (film), 130
Mills, Jim, 118
Mills, Joe, 118
Mills Commission, 65, 66
Milwaukee Braves, 69
Milwaukee Brewers, 64, 72
Minnesota Twins, 72
Minoso, Minnie, 68
Miracle League of the Triangle, 86–87
Mitchell, Jackie, 67
Moats, Dalton, 153
Modley, Randy, 41
Montgomery Biscuits, 23, 155
Montoya, Charlie, 120
Montreal Royals, 68

Morgan, Joe, 118
Morton, Wycliffe Nathaniel "Bubba," 21, 22
Mount, Thom, 75
Muller, Chris, 153
Murray, James Patrick, 51

N

Nashville Sounds, 18, 71, 75, 81, 141, 142, 174
National Agreement of Professional Base Ball Clubs, 63–64, 65
National League, 63–64
NCAA, 79
Negro League, 13, 21, 66, 67, 68, 81
Negro Minor Leagues, 13
New Bern Truckers, 114, 115
Newcome, Don, 68
New England League, 68
New York Giants, 65, 69
New York Knickerbockers, 62, 65
New York Mets, 72
New York Nine, 62
New York Volunteer Infantry, 62–63
New York Yankees, 67, 72, 89–90
Norby, Connor, 168–169
Norfolk Tide, 8, 30, 71, 106, 154, 167
North Carolina League, 114
North Carolina State League, 115–116
Northwestern League, 63–64
Norwood, Patrick, 142

O

Oakland Athletics, 72
O'Brien, Colin, 9
Ogando, Cristofer, 153
Omaha Storm Chasers, 71

P

Pacific Coast League, 69, 72
Paige, Satchel, 67, 68
Palau, 169
pandemic, 69, 70
Paredes, Isaac, 46
Paterson Silk Weavers, 67
Pawtucket Paw Sox, 69, 89, 159
Peguero, Joel, 153
percentages, 28
Perez, Delvin, 95
Perfect Game, The (film), 59, 182
Perkins, Anthony, 81
Phenom, The (film), 108, 148
Philadelphia Athletics, 64, 69
Philadelphia Phillies, 65, 72
Phillips, Brett, 172, 173
pick off moves, 70
Piedmont League, 116–117
Pinto, Rene, 151

pitch clock, 70
Pittsburgh Pirates, 65, 72, 155
Pittsburgh Steelers, 57
Poche, Colin, 90
politics, 45–46
Portland Mavericks, 180
Proctor, Ford, 151
Progressive Field, 14
Puerto Rican League, 146
Pujols, Albert, 126

R

Raleigh Pirates, 117
Raley, Luke, 151, 161, 173
Reith, Brian, 157
Rembis, Paxton, 142
Republican Party, 45–46
Rice, Jim, 118
Richardson, Ted, 21
Richter, Francis, 64
Rickey, Branch, 67–68
Riggsbee, Tony, 146
Rizzuto, Phil, 131
Robinson, Jackie, 21, 68, 109
Rochester Red Wings, 69, 71
Romero, Tommy, 153
rule changes, 70
Russell, Bing, 180
Russell, Kurt, 180
Ruth, Babe, 67

S

Sanders, Phoenix, 153–154
San Diego Padres, 72
Sandlot, The (film), 49, 182
San Francisco Giants, 72
Savannah Bananas, 94–95
Savoy, Annie, 1–2
Schenectady Blue Jays, 68
Scranton/Wilkes-Barre RailRiders, 21, 71, 159, 160, 167, 169
Seattle Mariners, 72
Seaver, Tom, 61n1
Selig, Bud, 40
Shaughnessy, Frank "Shag," 67
Shelton, Ron, 20, 125
Sherman Anti-Trust Act, 66
Shields, Benjamin Cowan, 80
Skinner, B. F., 18
Snow Hill Billies, 28
Southern League, 21
statistics, 28
Staub, Daniel Joseph "Rusty," 118
Stengel, Casey, 13, 159
Stevenson, Cal, 151
St. Louis Browns, 69

St. Louis Cardinals, 65, 67–68, 72
St. Louis Giants, 66
St. Paul Saints, 71
Strickland, Scott, 5, 6
Sugar (film), 103, 181–182
Sugar Land Skeeters, 155
Syracuse Mets, 71, 131

T

Tampa Bay Rays, 13, 23, 72, 78, 89, 90, 120, 154, 155
taxi squad, 150
Texas Rangers, 72
tobacco, 11–12
Toledo Blue Stockings, 64
Toledo Mud Hens, 71
Torchia, Tony, 61
Toronto Blue Jays, 72, 120, 180
Tripartite Agreement, 63–64
Trouble with the Curve (film), 139

U

Uecker, Bob, 159
umpires, 24

V

Vander Meer, John, 116
Van Dusen, Fred, 182
Veeck, Bill, 27

W

Walker, Moses Fleetwood, 64
Washington Nationals, 72
Washington Senators, 65
Wheaton, William R., 65, 66
Whitman, Walt, 1
Whitted, John, 12
Williams, Brady, 156
Williams, Ted, 28
Wilson, Earl, 51
Wilson, Reid, 45
Winfield, Dave, 61n1
Winston-Salem Dash, 109
Witherspoon, Grant, 107–108, 151
Wolff, Miles, 14, 119, 178
women, 64, 67, 68
Wool E. Bull, 47–48, 54
Worcester Red Sox, 71
World War I, 66
World War II, 68
Wright, John, 68
Wrigley, Philip k., 68

Z

Zettlein, George, 63
Zombro, Tyler, 29–30

About the Author

HARRIS COOPER is the Hugo L. Blomquist Distinguished Professor of Psychology and Neuroscience, Emeritus, at Duke University. At Duke, he served as chair of two departments and as the Dean of the Social Sciences for the College of Arts & Sciences, helping administer the departments of history, sociology, political science, and cultural anthropology, among others. He is the author of four textbooks, editor of three books on social science research methods, and four books on education policy. He is a Gold Chalk Award winner for Excellence in Graduate Education from the University of Missouri-Columbia. Dr. Cooper is also the author of *American History Through a Whiskey Glass: How Distilled Spirits, Domestic Cuisine, and Popular Music Helped Shape a Nation*. He has been an avid baseball fan since growing up in the shadow of Yankee Stadium. He lives in the Research Triangle of North Carolina with his wife, Beth.